CAPITALISM, SOCIALISM AND POST-KEYNESIANISM

ECONOMISTS OF THE TWENTIETH CENTURY

General Editors: Mark Perlman, *University Professor of Economics, Emeritus, University of Pittsburgh* and Mark Blaug, *Professor Emeritus, University of London, Professor Emeritus, University of Buckingham and Visiting Professor, University of Exeter*

This innovative series comprises specially invited collections of articles and papers by economists whose work has made an important contribution to economics in the late twentieth century.

The proliferation of new journals and the ever-increasing number of new articles make it difficult for even the most assiduous economist to keep track of all the important recent advances. By focusing on those economists whose work is generally recognized to be at the forefront of the discipline, the series will be an essential reference point for the different specialisms included.

A list of published and future titles in this series is printed at the end of this volume.

Capitalism, Socialism and Post-Keynesianism

Selected Essays of G.C. Harcourt

G.C. Harcourt

Reader in the History of Economic Theory, University of Cambridge, Fellow, Jesus College, Cambridge, UK and Professor Emeritus, University of Adelaide, South Australia

ECONOMISTS OF THE TWENTIETH CENTURY

Edward Elgar
Aldershot, UK • Brookfield, US

Published by
Edward Elgar Publishing Limited
Gower House
Croft Road
Aldershot
Hants GU11 3HR
UK

Edward Elgar Publishing Company
Old Post Road
Brookfield
Vermont 05036
US

British Library Cataloguing in Publication Data
Harcourt, G. C.
   Capitalism, Socialism and
   Post-Keynesianism: Selected Essays of
   G.C. Harcourt. – (Economists of the
   Twentieth Century Series)
   I. Title   II. Series
   330

Library of Congress Cataloguing in Publication Data
Harcourt, Geoffrey Colin.
   Capitalism, socialism, and post-Keynesianism : selected essays of
G.C. Harcourt / G.C. Harcourt.
      p.   cm. — (Economists of the twentieth century)
   Includes bibliographical references and index.
   1. Capitalism.   2. Socialism.   3. Keynesian economics.   I. Title.
II. Series.
   HB501.H3483   1995
   330.12'2—dc20   94–42154
                                                                           CIP

ISBN 1 85898 079 8

Printed and bound in Great Britain by
Hartnolls Limited, Bodmin, Cornwall

Contents

PART IV   GENERAL ESSAYS

Preface by Mark Perlman

Geoffrey Colin Harcourt is already a much-honoured man. Not only has his native Australia 'officially' noted his 'Service to economic theory and to the history of economic thought' (he was, explicitly for that reason, made an Officer of the General Division of the Order of Australia in 1994), but no less than four books of his selected essays have already been published (*The Social Science Imperialists*, 1982; *Controversies in Political Economy*, 1986; *On Political Economists and Modern Political Economy*, 1992; and *Post-Keynesian Essays in Biography: Portraits of Twentieth-Century Political Economists*, 1993). Each contains something of an autobiographical statement. In all he credits those who have taught him, either as his professors or as his colleagues, including many at Melbourne, Cambridge, Adelaide and Toronto. But in the Introduction to the 1992 collection he describes in detail the 'journey of his life', his seeking for a new political philosophy and religious creed. He goes on to analyse the evolution of his sense of priority problems and, in a significant way, the ordering of the disparate influences on his thinking. In his own words, what economics is about, he has come to believe, is:

> to make the world a better place for ordinary men and women, to produce a more just and equitable society. In order to do that, you have to understand how particular societies work and where the pockets of power are, and how you can either alter those or work within them and produce desirable results for ordinary people, not just for the people who have power. I see economics as very much a moral as well as a social science and very much a handmaiden to progressive thought. It is really the study of the processes whereby surpluses are created in economies, how they are extracted, who gets them and what they do with them. All economies have created surpluses in one way or another. Capitalism does it in a particular way and that is the process in which I am most interested because I live in capitalist economies. At the same time I would like to help to create a society where the surplus is extracted and used in a way quite different from a capitalist society.

If this credo is a melange of the personal impacts of Eric Russell's tutelage in Adelaide as well as of Marshall's, Pigou's, Maynard Keynes's and, particularly, Joan Robinson's and Michal Kalecki's Cambridges (and that is in my opinion, really what it is) it stands today to our students even more as 'pure Harcourt'. But how he has gone about espousing his view, his pedagogical style (if one may say so) is something else.

vii

The career of Geoffrey C. Harcourt has many facets not only because he is indefatigable, friendly and unusually courteous in a world where that virtue is rare, but because he has become of that rare breed, a teacher's teacher. Let me turn Shaw on his head and assert that, cleverness aside, among those who can teach there are only a few who really can teach others what and how to teach. And Harcourt is clearly one of those.

To some Harcourt may seem principally the Boswell to Joan Robinson's Cambridge. That too. But recent research shows that, whatever Boswell was to Dr Samuel Johnson (and where would Johnson be without Boswell?), not only was Boswell a strong character in his own right, but his very appreciation of Johnson was the product of his own brilliant insights into spirit and mores of the time. So it is with Harcourt; he is one of the most serious students of the economics of our time. Capable of appreciation of others, he has offered all of us an insightful standard for assessments.

Harcourt's writings can be classified generally into four groups:

a.   works analysing contemporary economic theoretical problems,
b.   works synthesizing states of debates in economic theory,
c.   works having a distinctly biographical flavour and pertaining to various contemporary economists, and
d.   works pertaining to economic and allied social policies.

Originally, his efforts were focused principally on the first of these rubrics. In retrospect the half-life of essays contributed in the quest for refinement of most contemporary economic problems is not long, and often the fairest way to evaluate contributions a third of a century later is simply to look at the formalism of the mode of presentation. Harcourt's 'A Critique of Mr. Kaldor's Model of Income Distribution and Economic Growth' (1963), his 'A Two-Sector Model of the Distribution of Income and the Level of Employment in the Short Run' (1965), 'The Accountant in the Golden Age' (1965) and 'Investment-decision Criteria, Investment Incentives and the Choice of Technique' (1968) were replete with the appropriate rigour, that is geometry and the calculus. True, they were not econometric in the testing sense (in fact, he reports that one referee as well as some readers of another paper of the same vintage, 'Biases in Empirical Estimates of the Elasticities of Substitution of C.E.S. Production Functions' thought it was 'amateur econometrics') but that era was not then truly upon us. A later effort under this same rubric was less abstract in presentation and strikes me as more mature. He 'took on' four of the leading figures of Anglo-American economics and, although Harry Johnson eschewed explicitly answering his criticisms, Maurice Dobb, John Hicks and Frank Hahn all did. Not unexpectedly, Dobb used a complaint of his generally being misunderstood (not by Harcourt but by many others) as an additional opportunity for restating succinctly the argument found in his *Theories of Value and Distribution Since Adam Smith* (1973), Hahn graded Harcourt's criticisms down (would Hahn do so now, now that he has softened the stridency of his earlier assessments?) but Hicks paid him the great compliment of creating a novel 'non-fiction', Uncle J.R. Hicks as contrasted with his nephew, (Sir) John Hicks, a *non*-neoclassic.

My belief is that Harcourt's *greatest* research contributions are the essays written under the second rubric, 'works synthesizing states of debates in economic theory'. Here he is something of a master because he not only gets each side's position 'straight' and sympathetically stated, but his judgements are original, pithy and sound. Originally, in 1968, Wilfred Prest had told me about Harcourt's unusual ability in this direction and, impressed with what Wilfred told me, I sought Harcourt out to explain to Americans the Cambridge-on-the-Cam side of the capital debate between Joan Robinson (and implicitly Wilfred Salter) and Solow/Samuelson. Afterwards, Machlup, no mean competitor on this score, also told me more than once of his personal admiration of Harcourt's balance and fluency (although he was not always in agreement with every detail of the product). Harcourt's work explaining the relative views of Sraffa, Joan Robinson and some of the later self-styled Keynesians, according to my taste, approaches the status of a canon.

His work in the area of biographical interpretations of the works of many recent economists will clearly stand the test of time. A great observer of the *de mortuis nil nisi bonum* rule, Harcourt nonetheless manages to cover comprehensively what future students should know about each person, and that includes the 'warts', too. The only problem that I see in this area is that Harcourt's chosen subjects are often people of whom he was a strong admirer. However, as the 'consulting editor on obituaries' for the *Economic Journal*, he commissions a great many biographical essays, and many of them are on people who did not share his judgements or preferences. These contributions to intellectual biography reflect the warmth of his personality, which may seem to be irrelevant to the 'scientific' quality of his research, but I believe that there is a place for rhetoric even in scientific discourse. In the case of the living, Harcourt is somewhat more candid. It is sufficient to refer to an essay on H.W. Arndt, with whom he disagrees far more than he agrees, in which his bite shows, yet he is humorous about their differences (Harcourt, 1993, pp. xii, 159–62).

For the most part I am unable to comment on his economic policy essays because they were written for particular times and particular audiences – times and places I was not at.

Finally, I have sensed that Harcourt's lack of personal reserve (perhaps it is a lack of academic snobbery) tends to make those who deal with him on a day-to-day basis often fail to realize how much he contributes positively to the academic bases of creative research. It is my understanding that, prior to the horrors of the First World War, Pigou gave Cambridge's economics tradition a creative warmth, that Maynard Keynes (for all of the put-downs of his colleagues) was unusually generous and warm to students, that Dennis Robertson, Maurice Dobb and many of their contemporaries (as stories were related to me by Alan Prest and even Harry Johnson) made Cambridge 'user-friendly' for its young. Many have contributed to this atmosphere, but I would rank Phyllis Deane and Harcourt among the best – unlike others, they did not limit their smiles to their disciples.

I venture the guess that history will judge Harcourt's mission and his style (properly his rhetoric) generously; if it does otherwise I would wonder about any history of academia which fails to appreciate the role of teachers' teachers.

References

Harcourt, G.C. (1982), *The Social Science Imperialists*, edited by Prue Kerr, London/Boston: Routledge & Kegan Paul.

Harcourt, G.C. (1986), *Controversies in Political Economy*, edited by O.F. Hamouda, New York: New York University Press.

Harcourt, G.C. (1992), *On Political Economists and Modern Political Economy*, edited by Claudio Sardoni, London/New York: Routledge.

Harcourt, G.C. (1993), *Post-Keynesian Essays in Biography: Portraits of Twentieth-Century Political Economists*, Basingstoke: Macmillan.

Acknowledgements

The author and publisher wish to acknowledge with thanks the following for permission to reproduce copyright material.

The National Centre for Australian Studies, Monash University and the editors of the *Australian Quarterly* for permission to reprint 'Markets, Madness and a Middle Way' (The Second Donald Horne Address, 17 February 1992) from *Australian Quarterly*, **64**, Autumn 1992, 1–17; the editors of the *Economic and Labour Relations Review* for permission to reprint 'Macroeconomic Policy for Australia in the 1990s', from *Economic and Labour Relations Review*, **4**, (2), December 1993, 167–75; the editor of the *Economic and Political Weekly* for permission to reprint 'Taming Speculators and Putting the World on Course to Prosperity: A "Modest Proposal"' from *Economic and Political Weekly*, **XXIX**, (28), 17 September 1994, 2490–92; Edward Elgar Publishing Ltd, Aldershot, Hants, for permission to reprint '[The] Capital Theory Controversies', from Philip Arestis and Malcolm Sawyer (eds), *The Elgar Companion to Radical Political Economy*, 1994, pp. 29–34; the editors of the *Cambridge Journal of Economics* for permission to reprint 'Kahn and Keynes and the Making of *The General Theory*', from *Cambridge Journal of Economics*, **18**, 1994, 11–23; the editors of *History of Political Economy* for permission to reprint 'Joan Robinson's Early Views on Method', from *History of Political Economy*, **22**, (3), 1990, 411–27; the editor of the *Journal of the History of Economic Thought* and J.A.T.R. Araujo for permission to reprint a revised version of 'Maurice Dobb, Joan Robinson and Gerald Shove on Accumulation and the Rate of Profits' and 'An Addendum', from *Journal of the History of Economic Thought*, spring 1993, 1–24, 24–30; Routledge, London, for permission to reprint a revised version of 'Some Reflections on Joan Robinson's Changes of Mind and the Relationship of them to Post-Keynesianism and the Economics Profession', from *The Economics of Joan Robinson*, 1995; Routledge, London, and Claudio Sardoni for permission to reprint 'George Shackle and Post-Keynesianism', from *Economics as the Art of Thought: Essays in Memory of G.L.S. Shackle*, Routledge, 1995, edited by Stephan Boehm, Stephen F. Frowen and John Pheby; the Macmillan Press Ltd, for permission to reprint 'The Structure of Tom Asimakopolus's Later Writings', from *Income and Employment in Theory and Practice*, edited by Geoffrey Harcourt, Alessandro Roncaglia and Robin Rowley, 1994, 1–16; the editor of the *Journal of Post Keynesian Economics* for permission to reprint 'Krishna Bharadwaj, August 21, 1935–March 8,

xi

1992: A Memoir', from *Journal of Post Keynesian Economics*, winter 1993–4, **16**, (2), 299–311, and 'Josef Steindl, April 14, 1912–March 7, 1993: A Tribute', from *Journal of Post Keynesian Economics*, summer 1994, **16**, (4), 627–42; the editor of *The Independent* for permission to reprint 'Ruth Cohen', from *The Independent*, Wednesday 31 July 1991 and 'Sir Austin Robinson', from *The Independent*, Saturday 5 June 1993; the editor of the *Guardian* for permission to reprint 'Amiya Kumar Dasgupta: Economist and Modern Sage', from the *Guardian*, Tuesday 21 January 1992; the editors of *Social Alternatives* for permission to reprint 'The Irrelevance of Conventional Economics: A Review Article', from *Social Alternatives*, **3**, (2), March 1983, 61–2; John Cornwell, Jesus College, Cambridge, for permission to publish 'On Mathematics and Economics'; Cambridge University Press and R.V. Mason for permission to reprint 'John Maynard Keynes 1883–1946', from *Cambridge Minds*, edited by R.V. Mason, 1994, 72–85, and the editors of the *Economic Review* for permission to reprint 'What Adam Smith Really Said', from *Economic Review*, **12**, (2) November, 1994, 24–7.

Introduction

As I nearly died four times during the period September 1992 to September 1994, I thought it a good idea quickly to respond to Edward Elgar's longstanding request that I publish a volume with him. So I have brought together under the rubric, *Socialism, Capitalism and Post-Keynesianism*, a set of essays written in the 1980s and 1990s. (I apologise immediately to the late J.A.S. for amending his well-known title but I do think it covers well the contents of the essays.)

I am both honoured and delighted that Mark Perlman has contributed the Preface to the selection. As with the rest of the profession, I am much in his debt for his many years of courageous and liberal editing of the *Journal of Economic Literature* since its foundation in 1969. I am even more indebted to him personally, for he took the risk of asking me almost sight unseen, following a one-day visit to Adelaide in 1968 at the suggestion of Wilfred Prest, to write the survey article on capital theory for the second issue of the *JEL*. The request was to have profound consequences for my subsequent development and career – I say nothing about what it may have done for or to the journal. I have included in the present collection an up-date, 25 years on, of my views on the controversies in capital theory which I was asked to write for *The Elgar Companion to Radical Political Economy*: see Chapter 4. I hope Mark approves of it as he so kindly did of my initial effort for the *JEL* in 1969. I also hope that, with the benefit of hindsight, I have put the issues into perspective as a result of the developments which have occurred since I first wrote the survey. I am conscious of a certain intemperate as well as despairing tone to the essay, because the profession seems steadfastly determined to ignore many of the results, conclusions and implications that were reached then and subsequently. Again, with hindsight, I think I may have been unduly harsh on Paul Romer, who has been generous in his acknowledgements to the work of Nicky Kaldor. Nevertheless, I have left the essay as it was because it accurately reflects the mood I was in at the time that I wrote it in the early 1990s.

The essays are classified under four broad heads: policy; theory from an historical perspective; intellectual biographies; and general essays, what Frank Hahn calls 'blah blah' (even some of his own). The first essay, 'Markets, Madness and a Middle Way', was the second Donald Horne Address given in February 1992 in the splendid setting of the Great Hall of the National Gallery of Victoria in Melbourne. It was part of the 'Ideas for Australia'

Week inspired by Horne and organized by the National Centre for Australian Studies of Monash University in cooperation with the Commonwealth government. The idea is to ask an Australian living abroad to come home to give a wide-ranging address on issues of vital importance for Australian citizens. The conjuncture of events to which mine was addressed was the launching of the Republican movement in Australia and the U-turn on economic policy of the Federal Australian Labor Party government that occurred around this time. The background was the emerging reaction against the 'let the market rip' policies of the 1980s which characterized part of economic policy in Australia, as in many other advanced industrialized economies, and the crowing over, and then second thoughts about, the implications of the collapse of 'communism' in what used to be the USSR and the Eastern European so-called 'socialist' economies. While I never held any brief for the awful regimes of those countries I do point out that the 'achievements' of those Western industrialized capitalist economies that had gone overboard on Hayekian/Friedmanite policies from the 1970s on were not that much to write home about either. There was therefore a case to be made for middle ways – the Kaleckian approach to socialism, for example, for Eastern Europe, the Keynes/Kaleckian (with modern additions) Post-Keynesian blueprints for Australia and other similar countries.

So in the Address I set about sketching the outlines of middle ways. I preceded this with an account of what modern (and not so modern) theory has to say about the conditions which need to be satisfied for markets to be safely left to do their thing. I pointed out that these conditions are spectacularly *not* satisfied in the markets for labour, foreign exchange, financial assets and housing. I was careful to say that it was a *non sequitur* to jump to the proposition that some form of intervention and regulation would *necessarily* do better – the case for *this* had always to be made.

I followed the Horne Address with two related papers: one on macroeconomic policy for Australia in the 1990s; the other, modestly entitled 'The Harcourt Plan to "save" the World', grew into 'A "modest proposal" for taming speculators and putting the world on course to prosperity'. The common theme connecting the papers was the argument that many markets and indeed economic systems themselves are characterized by cumulative causation processes such as those which Allyn Young (1928) discerned in Adam Smith and presented in a Marshallian framework, an approach which influenced Young's pupil, Kaldor, all his life. Gunnar Myrdal independently developed the same idea and it was also increasingly to become the viewpoint of Joan Robinson. Such a viewpoint implies that very different policy proposals and institutions are needed than those associated with the more orthodox equilibrium framework. In addition, radically different attitudes would be taken towards, for example, speculators and speculation because their systemic effects would not be the benign ones identified, for example, by Milton Friedman in his well-known article on the case for flexible exchange rates (1953).

The first of these essays relates principally to the problems of small open economies. It also allowed me to ride some of my hobby horses, for example that government expenditure should not principally be used for pump-priming but rather should fit in with the longer-term needs of economies, taking into account the social and political philosophy of the government in power. I drew attention as well to the danger of forgetting some old-fashioned but profound lessons from the writings of Eric Russell and Wilfred Salter concerning the macroeconomic effects of wages policies, lessons which are in danger of being overlooked as the latest version of the Accord in Australia moves into its enterprise bargaining stage.

In the next two papers (I include here only the second version as it encompasses the first), I tried to set out the problems of the various broad regions of the world, show how they are interrelated and what particular combination of policies and institutions might serve to tackle them effectively and simultaneously. Of course there is a Utopian tinge to such exercises but, unless such interrelationships and schemes are explicitly set out, it is difficult to get people of good will to think about the causes and cures of the world's ills. Next step the universe, of course.

Part II contains essays on theory set in an historical context, starting with an essay on the capital theory controversies. Chapter 5 is an evaluation of the crucial influence of Richard Kahn on Maynard Keynes in the making of *The General Theory* and, more briefly, of Richard Kahn's role as a 'disciple of Keynes' after Keynes's death in 1946. It was originally published in February 1994 in the memorial issue of the *Cambridge Journal of Economics* for Richard Kahn. The main thrust of the argument is that Kahn's life-long scepticism concerning the Quantity Theory of Money as a *causal* theory of price determination and his youthful seminal work on the economics of the short period in the late 1920s had a profound effect on the processes by which Keynes liberated himself from the hold which the Quantity Theory and the Marshallian dichotomy had on his own thought and on the form which *The General Theory* subsequently took. In this chapter I retell how Kahn's scepticism arose from a holiday experience when he was a schoolboy. It is ironic that the implicit argument of his critique, which should *not* make a dint in the application of the Quantity Theory properly understood, should nevertheless have led to such profound consequences.

Then follow three essays on aspects of Joan Robinson's writings. The first one (Chapter 6) relates to her first ever major publication, *Economics is a Serious Subject* (1932) in which she sets out her understanding of the methodology followed by economists, only to ditch a considerable part of it by the time she published *The Economics of Imperfect Competition* one year later. (She still remained a tool-kit provider economist.) In the original version of this essay, I should have referred to the effect it had on Ronald Coase, who cites its mind-clearing arguments favourably in his famous 1937 article on the nature of the firm (1937): see p. 386, where he provides 'a definition of a firm which is ... realistic [and] tractable'. Joan Robinson's essay itself not only illustrates what a sharp mind Joan Robinson had in her twenties but also how ready she was, *if* convinced, to scrap her own as well as scupper others' intellectual capital.

The next essay, written jointly with Jorge Araujo, arose from a veritable treasure trove of letters between Maurice Dobb, Joan Robinson and Gerald Shove which Michael Lawlor found in the Keynes papers in the King's College archives and which allowed us to track down as well some of Shove's letters housed in Dobb's papers in the Wren Library at Trinity. The essay revolves around the debate initiated by one of Joan Robinson's brilliant (but, in this case, ultimately mistaken) asides: 'The equilibrium rate of profit is that rate which induces zero net investment. But ... since the industrial revolution began, net investment has always been going on. The actual rate of profit, therefore, good years with bad, has exceeded the equilibrium rate. Abnormal profits are the normal rule' (Joan Robinson, 1942, pp. 60–61). In the essay we describe the original to and fro between the three protagonists, setting out some of their detailed and subtle analysis. We then advance two solutions to the original conundrum, one of which is derived from Paul Davidson's adaptation of Keynes's investment theory, the other from Joan Robinson's own mature work in which she amalgamated insights from the classicals, Marx, Keynes and Kalecki.

The essay in Chapter 8 arose from a paper on Joan Robinson and Post-Keynesianism which I was asked to prepare for the conference in honour of Joan Robinson held in Turin in December 1993, organized by Cristina Marcuzzo, Luigi Pasinetti and Alessandro Roncaglia. For the volume of the conference, and the present volume, I have slightly refocused it in order to relate Joan's changes of mind over her lifetime to Post-Keynesianism and to the profession generally.

Next are two essays which were originally given at conferences to commemorate the lives of two great economists and wonderful human beings, George Shackle and Tom Asimakopulos. Chapter 9, written with Claudio Sardoni, attempts to show how Shackle's profound thoughts permeate virtually all strands of Post-Keynesian thought, inspiring and instructing them. The essay on Asimakopulos (Chapter 10) examines his views on method in his later work, views which date from his St Paul-like experience at MIT in 1966, when he attended Bob Solow's lectures – and realized what Joan Robinson was really on about.

Part III contains intellectual biographies written, in the main, since I put together the essays which became *Post-Keynesian Essays in Biography* (1993). The main exception is an essay on Richard Stone, which I wrote in 1983 and revised following his death in December 1991. There are two other article-length essays, one on my great friend Krishna Bharadwaj who died far too young at 56, and the other on our mutual friend and mentor, Josef Steindl, who died in his 81st year. There was a wonderful 80th birthday conference for Josef in May 1992 which I was fortunate enough to attend. He thoroughly enjoyed it, both in *and* out of conference hours, though for different reasons. I have also included a number of shorter essays, which I wrote for the obituary pages of *The Independent* and the *Guardian*. The economists included are Ruth Cohen, A.K. Dasgupta and Austin Robinson.

Part IV contains essays of, I hope, general interest. Chapter 17 is a review article of Thomas Balogh's *The Irrelevance of Conventional Economics* (1982). Tommy Balogh was the first great overseas economist I met – he gave a seminar in Melbourne in the early 1950s when I was an undergraduate. It was not until this, the last book he ever wrote, however, that I realized fully how sound and deep was his grasp on the conceptual basis and weaknesses of mainstream economic theory. Since it was written, conventional theory has rethought in part the notion and need for the concept of long-period equilibrium and radicals are rethinking the nature of planning. But I thought it a good idea to show how perceptive Balogh was in the late 1970s.[1] Chapter 18, on mathematics and economics, was prepared for a conference on the use of mathematics in various disciplines organized by my polymath colleague in Jesus, John Cornwell, in September 1993. It contains what I believe is a balanced view on the role of mathematics in our trade. Since I wrote it I have become excited about the prospects for economics of complexity theory, as a result of reading M. Mitchell Waldrop's book about the developments occurring at the Santa Fe Institute (Waldrop, 1992), but I do not think I want to change significantly any of the conclusions to the essay, certainly not the main one that mathematics is a good servant but a disastrous master. Chapter 19, on Keynes, is based on the lecture which I gave to start the series on 'Cambridge Minds' to a summer school held in Cambridge in July 1993. (I lost my opening bat position in the Cambridge University Press volume of the lectures edited by Richard Mason, now coming in at number six. I do not know whether this is a reflection on the place in the pecking order of J.M.K. himself or on me in the list of lecturers concerned.) The principal theme is that Keynes's own life may be regarded as providing a resounding 'yes' to G.E. Moore's question: Is it possible both to be good and to do good?

The last chapter is an article I wrote for the *Economic Review*, a journal which is read by A level students of economics, on what Adam Smith *really* said. The objective was to apply the Jesuit injunction to get 'em young, to try to offset the misleading propaganda of the vulgar Smithian free marketeers of recent years. So I hope I have gone out as I came into this selection, with a bang, not with a whimper.

Note
1. I am indebted to Rathin Roy for pointing this out to me.

References
Arestis, Philip and Malcolm Sawyer (eds) (1994), *The Elgar Companion to Radical Political Economy*, Aldershot, Hants: Edward Elgar.
Balogh, Thomas (1982), *The Irrelevance of Conventional Economics*, London: Weidenfeld & Nicolson.
Coase, R.H. (1937), 'The Nature of the Firm', *Economica* (New Series), **IV**, November, pp. 396–405.
Friedman, Milton (1953), *Essays in Positive Economics*, Chicago: University of Chicago Press.
Harcourt, G.C. (1969), 'Some Cambridge Controversies in the Theory of Capital', *Journal of Economic Literature*, **7**, June, pp. 369–405.
Harcourt, G.C. (1993), *Post-Keynesian Essays in Biography. Portraits of Twentieth-Century Political Economists*, Basingstoke: Macmillan.
Robinson, Joan (1932), *Economics is a Serious Subject: The Apologia of an Economist to the Mathematician, the Scientist and the Plain Man*, Cambridge: W. Heffer and Sons.
Robinson, Joan (1933), *The Economics of Imperfect Competition*, London: Macmillan.
Robinson, Joan (1942), *An Essay on Marxian Economics*, London: Macmillan.
Waldrop, M. Mitchell (1992), *Complexity: The Emerging Science at the Edge of Order and Chaos*, Harmondsworth: Penguin.
Young, Allyn (1928), 'Increasing Returns and Economic Progress', *Economic Journal*, **38**, December, pp. 527–42.

PART I

POLICY

1   Markets, madness and a middle way*

Introduction

I am most honoured to be asked to give the second Donald Horne Address, opening the innings but not taking strike – Anne Summers did that with a typically forceful, insightful and positive approach in 1991, with her splendid inaugural Address, 'The Curse of the Lucky Country'. I greatly enjoyed reading *The Lucky Country* and *God is an Englishman* (She isn't). I also admired Donald Horne's principled stand during those incredible days in November 1975 when Sir John Kerr dismissed the leader of a democratically elected Federal government with a comfortable majority in the Lower House. I thought then (and I still do) that the litmus paper test for being a democrat in Australia was whether you approved of Don Dunstan's dismissal of the South Australian police chief and disapproved of the Governor-General's dismissal of the Whitlam Government.

May I therefore, at the outset of the Address, throw in my lot with the founders of the Australian Republican Movement which is headed by Donald Horne, Tom Keneally and other Aussie stalwarts? By trying to make Australia a republic in 2001, they hope to ensure that such an event never occurs again. Until 1975, I had no strong feelings either way about the monarchy and its representative in Australia because I thought that the Governor-General was a figurehead who opened Parliament, gave garden parties and went to the Melbourne Cup. But as that evidently is not the case, we had better be sure than sorry – so go to it, I say. But please make certain that the President (or whatever we call our Boss Person) has no real power because the proposal is that Parliament and not the people, at least directly, are to elect him or her.

Title of the Address

I have called this Address 'Markets, Madness and a Middle Way'. I belong to the generation of Australians who generally did not join the Communist Party but who did join the Australian Labor Party (ALP) – and the Student Christian Movement! Some of my best friends, though, the people I most admire, who were/are ten or more years older than I am, and who were passionate idealists, did join the Communist Party, only eventually to be bitterly

* The second Donald Horne Address, 17 February 1992. National Centre for Australian Studies, Monash University, Clayton, Victoria, Australia. Also published in *Australian Quarterly*, **64**, autumn 1992, 1–17.

disillusioned by Hungary in 1956 and then Khrushchev's revelations concerning the Stalin era. So when the momentous events of the late 1980s occurred in Eastern Europe, I was sickened by the ridiculous euphoria, the nauseating complacency and self-satisfaction which emerged in conservative quarters in Western societies. For, while I had never been an admirer of the authoritarian, cruel, inefficient and often corrupt regimes that were toppled, by the same token, it could not be said that the performance of the economies of the democratic capitalist West over the last 20 years or so was (or is) anything to write home about either. To have destroyed full employment as a goal, let alone the norm it had become; to have greatly increased the inequality of the distribution of income and of wealth; to have created an underclass and destroyed the dignity, self-respect and hope of large numbers of citizens; to have substituted ridiculous rewards for paper shuffling for just rewards for making real and useful things: none of these are achievements of which any society could be proud. Peter Nolan reminds me, though, that the standards of living of many of those in work in most of these economies over this period did rise at a healthy rate – even if, I may add, it was partly due to unacceptable redistributions, to eating the seed corn of future generations and, in the UK's case, to squandering the benefits of North Sea oil.

I shall argue that much of this experience may be traced to an uncritical acceptance of the dominance and the alleged superiority of 'getting back to the magic of the market', as it used to say on bags of the fruit stalls of the Adelaide Central Market. However, the choice is not between purely command or centrally planned economies, on the one hand, and free market systems, on the other. Rather, there is a vital place for a middle way which may contribute to the ongoing discussion concerning the creation of just and equitable societies, the ultimate aim of those of us who remain democratic socialists. In doing this we shall need to be guided by people with warm hearts and cool heads, with fertile minds that are not hidebound by dogma or received theory, and who are very much aware of the importance of sociological attitudes and characteristics, of historical events and of inherited institutions in the creation of explanations and policies. Here I have in mind my Australian mentors, especially the late Eric Russell and Hugh Stretton, and overseas Noam Chomsky, John Kenneth Galbraith and, alas, all now dead, Maurice Dobb, Nicholas Kaldor, Michal Kalecki, Joan Robinson, Piero Sraffa and, of course, John Maynard Keynes. I shall argue that in some vital aspects Australia in the 1980s was a partial exception to the above indictment, and that this was a sterling performance, especially when we consider the huge difficulties, not all of our own making, which we faced.

Ten years ago, in 1982, I gave the John Curtin Memorial Lecture on 'Making Socialism in Your Own Country' – the prerequisite was that its author should leave immediately. In it, I tried to outline the ingredients of such a middle way. They involved a package deal of redistribution through the public sector as the *quid pro quo* to wage-earners for accepting policies directed at the rate of increase of money incomes, using the traditional Australian institutions of indexation and the Arbitration Commission. Fiscal and monetary measures were to be directed towards employment and growth. I put nationalization of key industries, including financial intermediaries, back on the agenda for discussion and sat on the fence concerning the tariff; that is, leave it as it is and concentrate on export promotion. I opted for a fixed exchange rate with the proviso that we may need to contemplate a change from time to time. I like to think that Bob Hawke toyed with the idea of implementing such a package for a good half-hour after the election of the ALP government in 1983. I shall try to add to and amend some of these suggestions in the course of this Address. But first let me briefly examine both the virtues and limitations of markets as institutions.

Virtues and limitations of markets

Adam Smith is frequently invoked as the patron saint of competitive markets, often by people who have never read *The Wealth of Nations* (*WN*) and have never heard of *The Theory of Moral Sentiments* (*TMS*). Yet Smith himself regarded the *TMS* as complementary to and the equal of the *WN*. He believed in a natural order of morality: that 'man was endowed with the moral senti- ments which [made] society possible'.[1] The thrust of the argument of the *TMS* is the need to design institutions which allow altruism, or 'sympathy', to prevail. Only then would it be desirable and effective to dismantle the over- grown, overblown bureaucratic regulations and monopolies of the mercantalist period and allow the instinct of self-interest, guided by the invisible hand, to operate in an environment of vigorous dynamic competition. Such an envi- ronment would provide growth and promise a distribution of the product between the main classes of society which would, in turn, be favourable to a continuation of this growth. Smith approved of the government providing comprehensive and efficient infrastructures for society and a just and effi- cient taxation system for society's citizens. Smith, a wise person, recognized that one of the essential conditions for competitive markets to function in a 'socially desirable' manner was that economic and political power should be widely diffused so that consumer and producer, employer and employee would meet as equals – and pretty powerless equals at that – when products and services were exchanged. This notion has been formalized in modern economic theory in the concept of price-taking as opposed to price-making behaviour. With the latter, people have some, and often a lot of, discretion about the prices they charge for their products and/or services. Smith also had no illusions about what anti-social practices citizens could get up to if they had power, nor about how destructive and alienating free rein competitive, industrial production of the sort immortalized by Charlie Chaplin in *Modern Times* would be for those unfortunate workers inescapably involved in it.[2]

Again, another great economist whose name is invoked as an exponent of the virtues of free markets, Leon Walras, in fact wanted land and key durable capital goods to be nationalized. He then tried to show that, by using competitive markets for all remaining economic activities, a socially desirable and sustainable general equilibrium of purchases, sales and distribution of income and property could be brought about. So at least two of the patron saints of the free marketeers turn out to be closet Bolshies!

Moreover, modern theory has gone on to lay down very stringent conditions which have to be satisfied before it can be claimed, even in theory, that the market outcome is socially desirable. Of course it must be said – and this is the core of the argument of the serious pro-marketeers – that it is a non sequitur to go from establishing that there may be, in the fashionable jargon, market failures, immediately to claiming that therefore government intervention will make things better. It may well be that, in an imperfect world, the market failure outcome is nevertheless the best we can hope for, especially if a huge weight is put on the absolute desirability of individual freedom – this is the philosophical position of that most profound proponent of modern liberal thought, the late Friedrich Hayek. With this proviso let us now look at the commonsense meaning of some of the conditions which have to be met in order for markets to do their thing.

The first is that actual prices of products should be a true measure both of social costs of the resources used to create them and of the satisfaction which their use is expected to bring to their purchasers. That is why price takers are needed. Producers can then match their costs to externally given standards which simultaneously signal to purchasers the terms on which they can expect to achieve satisfaction. This requires that prices, most of the time, should be such that what is voluntarily demanded is equal to what is voluntarily supplied. This in turn requires that flows of purchases and flows of supplies in markets should dominate the setting of prices. Inventories or stocks, though important for smooth production and sales, nevertheless need to play a subsidiary role in the determination of actual prices. Moreover, if current prices are not achieving this match, they must directly or indirectly give out signals which encourage measures to be taken which will quickly achieve such a match, often a very tall order indeed in many important markets.

In fact, this brings out the big difference between vigorous free marketeers and the sceptics. The former think of individual markets, or even whole economic systems, as wolf packs running along smoothly. If, perchance, one or more of the wolves get ahead or fall behind, forces come quickly into play which return them to the pack. The latter group argue that, if the breakaways get ahead, or fall behind, the forces which come into play are much more likely to allow them to get further and further ahead – or fall further and further behind, at least for long stretches of time. Belief in the efficacy and equity of markets as institutions is fundamentally affected by which scenario is believed to be true of the 'real world', as we economists lovingly like to call that which I am sure many of you feel we have never experienced. It also has to be supposed that prices act solely as rationing devices. That is to say, nothing else may be deduced from the price of a good or service about its qualities other than its relative scarcity or abundance. Modern work suggests that the demand and supply of labour services, and of credit, do not set up prices with this required characteristic.

If demands are dominated, not by expected satisfaction but by guesses about what prices may be in the future, so that a large element of speculation is present in the formation of prices, and if supplies are offered, not in response to perceived costs but in anticipation of future movement of prices, or of other people's expected anticipations of such movements, then the ensuing prices which are set may bear no systematic or reliable relationship to the real economic factors of the regular economic activity which, it is argued, prices ought to reflect. And all this is independent of whether power is diffused equally on both sides of the market, or whether it is concentrated in the hands of either buyers, or sellers, or both.

To sum up the argument so far: if we want markets to work well we must beware of situations where stocks dominate flows, speculation dominates enterprise or real economic factors, power is not evenly diffused, prices give out complex signals and processes are cumulative rather than quickly equilibrating.[3]

Virtues and limitations of plans

What then of plans, their virtues and limitations? By plans, I have in mind conscious directions – usually from the centre, often in great detail and sometimes dominated by quantities alone – of much of the economic life of a nation. Nevertheless, we must distinguish between the intensity and comprehensiveness of planning that may be suitable for developing countries, on the one hand, and more advanced countries with different histories, on the other. I include in the first category the alternative scenarios that could have been played out in Poland, Hungary and so on after the Second World War if genuinely democratic socialist governments had been in charge rather than the often externally imposed authoritarian Stalinist regimes. We may lay down some very general propositions which are relevant for both sets of societies before we discuss where, on a whole spectrum of choices, it may be best for a particular society to be.

The first proposition is that the overall workings of economies are not just the sum of their parts but may have independent lives of their own, and often unsatisfactory ones at that. It follows that, even if market solutions are best for some of the individual parts in isolation, there is still a case for conscious guidance and direction of the broad compositions and levels of overall activity. Thus, had Kalecki's ideas on planning been accepted in Poland when he returned there in the 1950s, we would have seen a society where overall consumption levels per person could have risen gently year by year, so that there would have been jam today rather than forever being put off for a tomorrow which never comes. In addition, much of the detailed components of consumption production would increasingly have been left to small private businesses with prices set by market forces; even so, a minimum standard of essential social consumption would have been provided through the state with controlled prices set up by turnover taxes on costs. Full employment would have been an overriding aim so that the portion of the workforce which was not engaged in the production of consumption goods and net exports would have been available for the production of capital goods. Here the state would have given overall guidance, as well as developing rational investment criteria which individual managers of enterprises would have been urged to follow. Another overriding constraint would have been foreign exchange reserves and earnings, so that the composition of output between net exports, consumption and investment would again have been a result of conscious decisions. The overall growth rate of the economy would have emerged as a consequence of these interrelated decisions and actions.

Within such a framework individual citizens would have had very considerable freedom of action with regard to both their consumption behaviour and what work they chose to do – the sticks and carrots of the overall plan could have been manipulated so as to secure the appropriate numbers within each relevant group. In this way, Big Brother would not have run people's lives, nor decided in detail what was good for them, yet the overall performance of the society would nevertheless have been subject to continuous conscious direction.

I do not wish to minimize the possibilities for corruption and the emergence of undue privilege, but with properly democratic decision procedures, checks and balances, and suitable taxes, it should have been possible in principle to produce a relatively egalitarian and equitable society. It certainly would have been worth trying – and still is – rather than creating huge levels of unemployment, great cuts in the living standards of ordinary citizens, and lands safe for spivs alone, as we now see emerging in these countries. Mrs Thatcher's government had ensured this last in the UK several years beforehand! Some variant on the above scenario would, I suggest, hold out far more hope for many of the Eastern European countries struggling to come to grips with the collapse of their former regimes than the rather mindless rush for 'free' markets (with prices allowed a free-for-all, little or no protection or direction, and little attempt systematically to build up infrastructures for both production and distribution) that we are in fact witnessing.

Australia's plight

Let us now turn to Australia's experience and prospects. As David Vines reminded me, if we Australians had to start *ab initio*, we might well not choose to be a small open economy exposed on the Pacific Rim. But as we do not have this choice, let us evaluate what we have achieved over the 1980s, often in adverse and difficult circumstances, and sketch in the problems and constraints we face in the light of some of the general principles I set out earlier in this address.

At the very beginning of the period we put two separate bits of lead in our saddle bags, as it were, by deciding to have a freely floating currency and, following the Campbell Report, a deregulated financial system. Whether these were self-inflicted wounds, or were inevitably forced upon us by external pressures, I leave others to decide.[4] What is certainly true is that, together, they made our resulting problems much harder to tackle. Australia needed and needs a very considerable amount of restructuring of its industries. Its traditional export products have not only faced secularly declining demands over the last decade or so, but, for much of the period, demand has been pushed below trend by shorter-term cyclical demand deficiencies. This is one of the reasons for the horrendous state of our current account at the moment. Unlike the United Kingdom over the same period, we have not had anything like the cushion of North Sea oil to give us time and breathing space. Not that the Brits took advantage of their cushion; much of it was dissipated in a consumption expenditure, import spree by those made richer by Mrs T's income tax cuts.

To meet the adverse change in our economic position we needed to get our domestic cost levels under control, both in our tradeables section and, as equity and efficiency combined demanded, in the non-tradeables as well. One aspect of this was the implementation of the Accord, a splendid example of conscious and cooperative planning which drew on tried and tested institutions created by our past history and by an appeal to cooperation from the main classes in society, not only among themselves, but with the government as well. For this endeavour I think the wage-earning groups of Australia deserve great praise. Also, for my money, Laurie Carmichael should be voted Australian of the last decade. He played a major role in initiating the acceptance of the Accord, and used his strength of character, persuasiveness and fighting qualities to see it through – along with Ralph Willis, Bob Hawke and Paul Keating (in their earlier period as chums) in government, and Simon Crean, Bill Kelty and the impressive team which makes up the Australian Council of Trade Unions (ACTU). Certainly the Accord served to get inflationary pressures very considerably reduced and allowed employment to grow and unemployment to fall from the unacceptable levels of the early 1980s. Moreover, the employment that was created contained a greater proportion of full-time jobs for males than virtually any other OECD (Organization for Economic Cooperation and Development) country over the same period. In principle, part-time employment must be approved of for its ability to offer variety and expand choice for all citizens; but to raise employment by such opportunities alone is neither balanced nor socially healthy. For such jobs are likely to be both badly paid and associated with poor working conditions. The Accord also helped to create the potential surplus for the business classes and the governments combined to do their part with private investment and the provision of public infrastructure. That, by and large, this did not occur is not the fault of the Australian wage-earners.[5]

There are a number of reasons why, which we need briefly to consider. A freely floating exchange rate system and a deregulated financial system mean that neither the exchange rate nor the pattern of rates of interest and prices of financial and other assets that prevail reflect underlying economic realities or socially desirable levels. First, interest rates as a dominant tool of policy – in the UK, John Major's and Norman Lamont's single golf club. It was once said, apropos the bank rate in the UK, that though it had been called a beautiful and delicate instrument it was in fact a coarse and blunt one, that its effects could be both unpredictable and often undesirable. I argued earlier that markets only work well when flows dominate and speculative activity is relatively absent. Neither of these conditions is satisfied in these two particular sets of markets. Financial markets *par excellence* are characterized by huge stocks of existing assets relative to the new flows, so that the former dominate the prices which are set daily in order to persuade domestic and overseas people voluntarily to hold the existing supplies. This would not really matter if the bulk of the holders were looking to underlying economic realities when deciding what to hold. But if we have a position where, as Keynes once put it, 'enterprise becomes the bubble on a whirlpool of speculation [so that] the capital development of a country becomes a by-product of the activities of a casino, the job is likely to be ill done'.[6] For the patterns of interest rates and prices of financial assets, and the exchange rates which keep overseas holders in particular happy, may well not be the levels which are consistent with the rate of domestic investment spending – both public and private – that may be needed to bring about the desired restructuring and provide the proper level of activity and employment overall, and with which is associated a suitable supply of exports and demand for imports. In fact, as Barry Hughes has pointed out to me, hard-nosed financial analysts in the United States have recently rediscovered Keynes's liquidity preference theory of the rate of interest and his conjecture concerning a 'liquidity trap' level of the rate of interest. They claim to have discovered such a level in the United States – and they have praised Keynes for it. Keynes argued that the pattern of interest rates is fundamentally a conventional one, determined by what people, for all sorts of reasons, think are appropriate or at least sustainable patterns and levels. Yet for the economy to be able to function satisfactorily such levels may, in fact, be quite 'wrong'.

Again, implicit in the case for a floating exchange rate was not only a relatively minor and beneficial role for speculative activity but also an inference that there was a stable sustainable long-term exchange rate out there waiting to be found. This supposed that countries in their international relationships with each other were akin to the wolf pack which moved steadily along in unison, with any laggards or accelerators quickly induced to return to the group. But if the other analogy is the correct one, a floating exchange rate system combined with a deregulated financial market provides a speculator's delight and a policy maker's and a serious industrialist's nightmare.[7] This is exactly one of the arguments which Tom Fitzgerald made so eloquently and passionately in his splendid 1990 Boyer lectures.

There is another rather neglected aspect of the 'freeing' of financial markets in the 1980s, not only in Australia but worldwide. In earlier decades, and in the last century, the spending by capitalists was ultimately limited by their access to finance and the spending of wage- and salary-earners, by their incomes. The observed fluctuations in output and employment over the cycle thus originated in spending by capitalists on investment goods because ease of finance and optimism of long-term expectations, and tightness of finance and pessimism of expectations, tended to move in tandem. By contrast, because the spending of the other groups was limited by income and because changes in income affected saving as well as consumption, consumption spending tended to be a much more stable and predictable component of total national spending. This traditional feature of capitalism has now been all but swept away by the deregulation of financial markets and the consequent huge expansion of credit facilities for all. The greatly increased amplitude of fluctuations in spending, and the increased length of slumps, are its consequence. So, ironically, a by-product of the attempt to enhance the freedom of action of all citizens by allowing, through credit facilities, a closer match of lifetime needs and lifetime resources than the pattern of income receipts alone makes possible has been to accentuate the inherent cyclical fluctuations of capitalist economies which formerly were due to the spending behaviour of the capitalist class alone. For now the economic activities of our citizens, our enterprises and our country are vitally affected by their respective debt to income ratios, and changes in them, as well as by the incomes themselves.

Associated with this emphasis on the effects of wealth to income ratios and their changes is the distortion of the uses to which fundamental commodities may be put. Australians have long been rightly proud of their homes and of the very good chance of becoming a home-owner. In addition, we have had a number of splendid selfless Australians who have contributed notably to the provision of imaginative housing services for rental: for example, the late Alec Ramsay in South Australia, and the thoughtful and original ideas of Hugh Stretton. What has guided both these attitudes is the desire for shelter with security, so that the purchase of these services was a long-term, serious matter for both the householders and the providers of them. One of the by-products of deregulated financial services and the huge flows of short-term funds in and out of Australia has been that land and houses have often come to be regarded as commodities suitable for speculation, with hunches backed up by borrowing, and dependence on rising markets lasting long enough to allow the shrewd speculator to get in and out. Prices have come no longer to reflect the provision of shelter services but rather the feverish activity of speculators trying to anticipate what the average person thinks will happen – and beat them to it.[8] The same phenomenon may be seen in the overprovision of office blocks in our major cities in which resources that would have been more usefully allocated to other investment activity have gone instead into oversupply of office space. This is a financial disaster for lender and bor-rower alike; it is also a disaster for the medium-term future of our inner cities which face the prospect of becoming the commercial deserts so familiar in many United States cities and towns. Similar phenomena may be witnessed in the spate of takeover raids and mergers for quick gains (and huge losses) which has characterized much of the so-called 'entrepreneurial activity' of the 1980s.

Industrial and finance capital

In the old days, when we were allowed to talk about Marx and even admit that, however utopian the old buffer may have been about what a socialist society would and should be like, he certainly understood capitalism very well indeed, we used also to talk about how finance and industrial capital needed to advance in tandem in order for the system to work tolerably well. If one came to dominate the other, and especially if finance capital were to get on top, the seeds of crisis were readily sown.[9] It is this phenomenon that we have been witnessing not only in Australia but in much of the rest of the world, including the conditions which the International Monetary Fund and the World Bank have been laying down in developing countries. I often think that banks and other financial intermediaries, in their eagerness to respond to the vigorous winds of competition, forget a number of simple but profound truths that came to us from Alfred Marshall in particular. It was he who emphasized in economic theory the important distinction between the short period and the long period. Those whose job it is to advance or withdraw credit especially need to have this distinction at the forefront of their minds. It should have a sobering effect on the tendency, otherwise, for them to be swept away too often by bouts of cumulative optimism and even recklessness in their lending at particular times and, perhaps even more disastrous, to suffer bouts of cumulative and increasing pessimism and depression at others, so that they needlessly dry up the flow of lending just when it may be most needed.

The Marshallian distinction which is relevant here is that the appraiser of a potential borrower should give much more stress to long-term viability than to very immediate positions, especially with regard to current cash flow. If medium-to-long-term prospects are encouraging then any immediate difficulties should be taken on board and seen through by creditors. Now, obviously, this has to be an overall principle as no one creditor can be expected or be able to flow against the tide, but if it were to be articulated by both the Reserve Bank and the government loudly, clearly and frequently, the financial sector would be given a very lucid and sensible lead. No doubt I shall be told that this is already well known and is acted upon. All I can say is that the evidence from Australia and other economies does not completely persuade me that it is not worthwhile stating the principle again.

Another consequence of an undue concentration on the provision of services of financial capital is that reward structures and returns tend to get seriously out of line with their counterparts in industry and the public services, a classic case of perfectly reasonable private self-interest and response not leading to desirable social outcomes. Part of the reason for the failure to restructure adequately through sustained investment expenditure must surely be the irresistible signals which led many of the most energetic and best workers to work, and risk takers to operate, in the financial sector.

Universal use of markets

I am sure many of my listeners will regard what I have said so far as one-sided and unbalanced, that I have overly ignored the positive virtues of markets and competitive forces and have played down the rigidities and dangers of centralized power in bureaucracies of governments. I am certainly aware of both of these, of the advantages and achievements of the first and the dangers and the limitations of the second. I have often referred in my writings to the difficulty of designing hierarchies in bureaucracies which ensure that persons with more attributes than just high intelligence and great ambition emerge in key decision-making positions. And I am well aware of the need to think through how to provide effective safeguards against corruption and crime in key parts of both the private and public sectors as a result of the extraordinary damaging episodes that have been revealed in Australian public life in recent years.

But as there have been many other voices willing and able to expound these themes, I wanted instead to sound a few warnings. There are some activities and aspects of life where markets, accounting and business procedures are most appropriate and others where they are not. A universal application of them can have disastrous consequences. I always remember Doug Hocking, one of my earliest teachers, saying that sometimes a lack of efficiency, in a business sense, may be the necessary price to pay for a selfless and uncorrupt public service. And I often think that the zeal with which means have been designed to bring accountability and efficiency into higher education, for example, to flush out the inevitable minority of those who, when left to their own self-discipline, do not properly fulfil their obligations, may be in great danger of destroying the very environment that is necessary for excellent creative teaching and research to occur in the first place. This is a particular example of a general tendency which could be applied equally to the attitude shown, both in Australia and the UK, to recipients of unemployment and other social service payments in periods, moreover, when contractionary unemployment-producing policies have been deliberately used to 'tackle' inflation.

As a counterweight, may I in passing applaud the imaginative idea of a graduate tax to help finance tertiary education? The scheme reflects a sympathetic awareness of different social attitudes to borrowing. It removes, at one stroke, what otherwise would have been 'barriers to entry' to those we would most like to have access to tertiary education. Of course, as Ian DuQuesnay has pointed out to me, it does have some odd consequences. For example, if a graduate tax were operative in the United Kingdom, Mr Major would now be paying less tax than either Mrs Thatcher did or Mr Kinnock will, if he becomes Prime Minister, for doing the same job. But then, as Mrs T also reminded us, 'It's a funny old world'.

May I also add that an undue dependence on markets for organizing all activities may have unexpected consequences which are not necessarily desirable? The gist of this has recently been put very well by the American economist Samuel Bowles. He quotes James Buchanan's description of a purchase of fruit at 'a roadside stand outside Blacksburg'. Neither of the people concerned had any particular interest in the well-being of the other but they 'were able to...transact exchanges efficiently because both parties agree on the property rights relevant to them'. This creates, says Bowles, 'a psychological environment of anonymity, indifference to others, mobility, lack of commitment, autonomy'. He concludes: 'We learn to function in these environments, and in so doing become someone we might not have become in a different setting'.[10] I found this described succinctly my impressions of the profound changes which have occurred in the United Kingdom, the United States and, alas, also in Australia over the past 15 years or so.

Australia's future

So what is my plea to fellow Australians as we face an extremely uncertain and troubled future, while experiencing levels of unemployment undreamt of in postwar Australia, together with our unsustainable current account position?

First, it is that we continue to remember the strengths of our society with which our history has provided us and which has bequeathed to us certain distinct institutions. I fear that, with our economic exposure and the huge swings in demand for many of our products which will be outside our control, we will not be able to guarantee the average levels of unemployment of the years immediately after the Second World War and into the early 1970s. All the more reason, therefore, for more fortunate citizens to support positively proper unemployment allowances, comprehensive retraining and, if necessary, relocating schemes – many of which are already in place. And also for them to refrain from attitudes which imply that unemployment is the particular individual's fault – I always blush to remember that the term 'dole bludger' was in fact coined by a prominent ALP politician. We should also, at this moment, be aiming gently but steadily to raise employment and reduce unemployment. I understand that the Accord is now entering a new phase in which enterprise bargaining is to be tried. This has the blessing of all three groups which are directly involved – employees, employers and the government – and at least the acquiescence of the Commission itself. May I sound a caution? The new procedures may be necessary to get more flexibility into our *relative* wage structures, but let us never forget that the market for labour services is not at all the same as the market for peanuts. Moreover, the *overall* wage bill plays a different role in the operation of the economy from that of relative wages. The overall average wage cost is a major determinant of the level and rate of change of the general price level. Are we sure, especially if employment picks up, that we can have as effective control over our inflation rate under the new regime as we did under the earlier phases of the Accord? Finally, we should always remember that measures directed at moderating the rate of increase of overall money wages do not necessarily moderate the rate of increase of real wages. Indeed, in a small open economy, moderating the former may be necessary to achieve satisfactory advances in the latter.

Secondly, it does behove the Commonwealth and state governments, in conjunction with industry and labour, to have well worked out views on the broad composition of the major items of our national expenditure and product, and to be prepared to use investment incentives, for example, to induce private decision-makers to bring the desired compositions about. Commentators throughout the capitalist world are belatedly rediscovering the virtues of fiscal policy, both for its effects on longer-term developments, including equitable distributions of income and wealth, and its impact on short-term activity and employment.[11] Barry Hughes tells me that a package deal of measures, totalling about a half of 1 per cent of GDP, is being put together. The ingredients are measures designed to bring forward investment spending together with public spending on infrastructure and further retraining schemes. Peter Groenewegen tells me that there are little-used powers and means whereby the Loan Council could coordinate the provision of required infrastructure at state level. Writing in, of all places, *The New Republic* in 1991,[12] Paul Krugman has made similar suggestions for the United States. He cites the appalling deficiencies in education, housing, medical care and transport facilities: deficiencies that could be removed by the still richest country in the world if only its leaders and citizens had the public and private will to do so.

One of the crucial lessons that the monetarists taught us is that the economy should not be viewed as a mechanical tap which can be turned on and off at will. Rather, we must always have in mind the need to create a relatively stable and dependable environment in which those 'animal spirits' of our business people (which cannot be bottled, as the late Trevor Swan once put it) may be nurtured and enhanced, and the longer-term persistent and dominant forces at work in healthy, competitive societies may be given a chance to work themselves out effectively. This is what I think Keynes meant in his posthumously published paper in the *Economic Journal* in 1946. In it he quoted from his last speech to the House of Lords: 'Here is an attempt to use what we have learnt from modern experience and modern analysis, not to defeat, but to implement the wisdom of Adam Smith'.[13] (Keynes literally killed himself in his efforts to get the United Kingdom through the war and create appropriate international institutions for the postwar world.)

Thirdly, one awful consequence of the policies of the late 1970s and 1980s has been to create not only haves and have-nots but also a third category of have-lots, though, as we have recently seen, this may not be a permanent feature of the position of any one member of this group. It does not constitute the politics and economics of envy, nor a desire inevitably to cut down tall poppies, to be scandalized by the ostentatious display of great wealth and the ruthless use of power by a Robert Maxwell or by some of our own home-grown versions of him. Not that 'pinching the pension fund' for your own use is confined to Maxwell and the United Kingdom, though his performance is the most spectacular example of it. I understand that we have also had several examples, large and small, in Australia of this quite unacceptable aspect of the greedy, 'me alone, yet me too' attitudes of the 1980s. I suggest as an urgent measure a complete ban on such practices. I do not think the traditional Australian sense of fair play would be affronted by policies such as this which are designed to restrict the extremes of this phenomenon.

I must also say something about immigration and attitudes to immigrants. The most horrible potential scenarios are currently threatening to emerge in Europe, for example, as a result of the sustained and intolerably high levels of unemployment in Western Europe, and the collapse of the Communist regimes in what used to be the USSR and in Eastern Europe. The views expressed by Jean-Marie le Pen and his National Front are only strikingly awful examples of very widespread attitudes. It would be a tragedy if any spokespersons of our main political parties were to succumb, as their counterparts in France have, to this vile spew or its local equivalent here. Obviously, every country has a right to decide, from time to time, the upper limits to its annual intake of new citizens. Within these limits, and treating playing a decent humane role in the worldwide provision of emergency havens for the genuinely oppressed as a separate issue, it seems to me not only morally correct but also advantageous to continue to apply the broad principles of the Immigration Reform Group of the 1960s. These were set out with admirable clarity and decency in a splendid book, *Immigration: Control or Colour Bar?*, edited by my old teacher, Ken Rivett.[14] Basically, they require ensuring that no one ethnic group dominates any particular occupation, and that representatives of all groups are spread through the social structure, with regard both to occupations and to suburbs. When I contrast, say, the limited fare of my Melbourne childhood in the 1930s (much as I still adore meat and two veg plus pud) with the extraordinary range of dishes and wine that are so widely available today, I can only offer up a prayer – first for Arthur Calwell and then for Ken and his fellow reformers. For they have given us the blueprints whereby, coming from different starting places, we may nevertheless combine in a wonderfully varied community of 'dinky di' Aussies all.

Finally, I hope we will not let the horrendous economic problems facing us at the moment make us completely forget to continue, or to take up again, some of the more enlightened reforms begun especially in the Whitlam era. I have been reading Susan Mitchell's *Tall Poppies Too*.[15] It has reminded me how much Whitlam and his government tried to enlarge and enrich the opportunities available to women and to the original Australians. It would be a lasting tragedy if these ideals, no matter how imperfectly they may have been put into practice, were to be submerged under the false idea of leaving market forces to solve everything. It is good therefore that the Hawke–Keating governments have tried to continue in a more muted fashion these reforms. I understand that considerable strides have been made in the provision of child-care and that Australia is way ahead of the United Kingdom in this respect – not that the performance of Mrs T's and John 'Classless Society' Major's governments constitute an especially challenging *numéraire*. The same must be said about Australia's contribution to solving environmental problems. Let us not minimize these and ignore the huge social costs entailed for this, and even more so for future generations, in our understandably urgent desire to overcome our immediate problems.

My generation of economists, like the one before it, was rightly inspired to try to create sustained full employment. But it should never have become an end in itself. Now we must try to make it possible for us all to have purposive lives and that requires asking ourselves what employment possibilities are socially admirable and consistent with being good citizens, not only of our own country but of the world, too. In pursuing these aims I am sure cooperative pragmatism and 'give and take' have much more to offer than any simple fix emanating from either the market or overall decree.

Notes

1. Joan Robinson, *Collected Economic Papers*, V, Oxford: Basil Blackwell, 1979, pp. 46–7.
2. See Chapter 20 for an enlargement on this theme.
3. This theme is taken up again in Chapter 3.
4. I was really taken to task for this piece of fence-sitting. I should have said that they were inevitable and therefore that it was more useful to discuss the consequences of them for the system as a whole.
5. See below, p. 21, and Chapter 2 for some misgivings as the original Accord gives way to its enterprise bargaining stage.
6. John Maynard Keynes, *The General Theory of Employment, Interest and Money*, London: Macmillan, 1936, p. 159.
7. See Chapter 3 for further analysis of this issue and for some suggested policies with which to tackle its effects.
8. See Chapter 3 for a discussion of how to tackle these problems.
9. Ha-Joon Chang reminds me that in some successful developing countries, for example South Korea and Taiwan, industrial capital led and finance capital was often owned and always heavily controlled by the state.
10. *Challenge*, July/August 1991, p. 13.
11. See Chapter 2 for further discussion of this point.
12. *The New Republic*, 23–30 December 1991, pp. 20–21.
13. *Collected Writings*, XXVII, London: Macmillan, 1980, p. 445.
14. Ken Rivett (ed.), *Immigration: Control or Colour Bar?*, Melbourne: Melbourne University Press, 1962.
15. Susan Mitchell, *Tall Poppies Too*, Melbourne: Penguin, 1991.

2 Macroeconomic policy for Australia in the 1990s*

As I was called a squib for not setting out systematically the detailed ingredients of a middle way in the Donald Horne Address in February 1992,[1] I must try to do better this time. One reason why I 'squibbed' was because I believed (I still do) that a necessary prerequisite was to analyse the implications of important markets – those for labour, property, foreign exchange, financial assets – *not* behaving in a socially optimum manner as the textbooks would have it. Only then would it be possible to think about policies which were designed to deal with the many by-products of their individual and collective impacts on the working of the Australian economy. Moreover, as I had been away from Australia for nearly ten years, I thought it would have been a bit of a cheek to arrive home giving *detailed* advice as I stepped off the plane, as opposed to raising key issues and identifying real problems in a more general way. I did make *some* specific suggestions in my Horne Address whenever I felt I was competent to do so.

What is appropriate macroeconomic policy for a small open economy on the Pacific Rim which has an enduring and indeed horrendous balance of payments problem, reflecting the need to restructure its industries, an extremely serious unemployment problem, including a frightening level of long-term unemployment,[2] and major pockets of unacceptable levels of poverty in what basically is still an affluent and relatively harmonious society?

Over the last 20 years or so, we have had a bellyful of 'deficit size' fetishism, as though the economic health of a nation could be measured entirely (or even at all) by the *difference* between government expenditure (G) and government revenue (T), regardless of the *sizes* of G and T themselves, or of the state of the economy when it is measured. So let us get away from this obsession once and for all and reinstate our common sense. I would argue that, by and large, what G should be, at Commonwealth, state and local levels, should be determined by *longer-term* aspirations reflecting both the overall philosophies of the democratically elected government in power and, as a corollary of this, well thought out and integrated plans for the provision of social and industrial infrastructure, as well as inducements to and help for, the private sector.

* First published in *Economic and Labour Relations Review*, **4**, (2), December 1993, pp. 167–75.

However, as government expenditure impinges on the *immediate* overall activity of the economy too, the implication is that *most* of the adjustment from the government sector needed to fit in with the activity that the private sector is providing must be through T, complemented by appropriate monetary policy. The latter will have to be associated mostly with selective credit rationing – for if Australia continues to have a floating exchange rate, the structure of interest rates will primarily be determined by the overseas trading, and lending and borrowing positions. (Incidentally, as I am writing about appropriate monetary policy, may I refer readers to the passages in the Horne Address where I urged the Reserve Bank of Australia to give a lead in encouraging the trading banks to make longer-term assessments of their customers' viability and, if these are favourable, enable them to see through any short-term difficulties?[3] I would now say that the Reserve Bank should insist and *ensure* that they are able to do this.)

This way of looking at G and T brings to the fore some elementary and old-fashioned lessons which nevertheless are often forgotten: to remember that G itself may be divided into (at least) three categories – current expenditure, capital expenditure, and transfer payments. The first two have immediate and direct impacts on employment creation. Their longer-term effects differ markedly and so they should be sharply differentiated from one another. The third category only has indirect effects on activity here and now, and in the future. As it entails transfer between citizens, it is only the *net* effect on spending of such transfers that is relevant for activity and employment. (The equity aspects are, of course, most relevant but are outside the rubric of the essay. I also abstract here from the effects of transfer payments between us and overseas where the effects are much more substantial and direct, both immediately and in the future.)

Making a sharp distinction between current and capital expenditure should lead to a rethink about the nature and significance of government deficits and surpluses. Much of government capital expenditure consists of the provision of needed social and industrial infrastructure, the returns to which only come in the medium to distant future and the immediate impacts of which on employment are markedly different (housing, health, education and transport are obvious examples). It really is foolish economics therefore, to expect total G always to be covered by total T, regardless of where the economy is in the various stages of the trade cycle, or where it is at in its planned development over the medium to longer term. In an ordinary business which is both viable and growing, we would never expect its *entire* outlays, current and capital, always or, indeed, ever to be covered by its *current* receipts. Periodic profits are in fact struck before interest payments on long-term borrowed funds are taken into account and certainly after periodic amortization reckonings. (Measuring profits gross of interest payments reflects the fact that viability is in some respects independent of the pattern of finance of – at least – capital expenditures.) Why cannot we use this procedure as an analogy for the government sector and examine how *current* revenues measure up against *current* outlays? We should include in the latter imputed interest on the capital associated with the provision of infrastructure (here we depart from private practice) and estimates of the social rate of amortization of the capital projects.

It still may be that in some circumstances we would wish T greatly to exceed this associated estimate of G, depending on how the private sector was faring (and on how the government wished it to fare); but at least we would get away from the foolishness of a crude total G, total T comparison and from crying 'disaster' if there is a shortfall, even when T is adjusted to its 'full employment' level. There is, of course, nothing novel or original in these suggestions. They were made, for example, by Keynes in the 1930s and 1940s[4] and recently reiterated in 1992 in a United States context by Robert Heilbroner.[5]

The Australian scene is complicated by our Federal set-up, with the possibility that state governments may be of a different political complexion from that of the Federal government. As in any democracy, compromise and give and take will be needed. At least minimum agreement could be obtained on, first, accounting procedures and, secondly, implementation of those expenditures for which the Commonwealth government is responsible but which in practice are implemented at state levels through state institutions.

If budgets are not balanced over the cycle, that is, if total G on average is greater than T, it will be necessary to keep a close eye on the debt to income ratio implied. For if a deficit (on average) were also to imply a *rising* debt to income ratio, we would be building an eventual source of instability into the structure of our economy. If, however, the ratio were to remain constant over time, not least because increasing the debt in the first place indirectly helped to raise income over time at a satisfactory pace, then there does not seem to be any overwhelming reason to worry about G exceeding T. In general public debt is not a problem in Australia. By OECD standards, the ratio of public debt to GDP is low.

The vast amount of restructuring required almost certainly requires a brake on *total* consumption expenditure. While there is considerable room for redistribution within this total towards the less well-off, nevertheless the bulk of extra production in Australia at the moment ought to go into capital accumulation. This may require a rise in total T, even though, at the moment, there is heavy unemployment which needs steadily to be reduced. As in the United Kingdom, the long-term needs of the economy and the state of the balance of payments imply that we need a 'High Street'-led recovery (as the Brits say) like we need a hole in the head. I realize that constraints on consumption require a further period of real sacrifice by the bulk of the workforce for, unlike the Brits, Australia does not have the equivalent of a cushion of North Sea oil to allow eight to ten years of a fool's paradise to reign. Enterprise bargaining is going to complicate this task even more, for it will tend to make more unequal the pre-tax distribution of income. We will therefore need some carefully crafted revisions of rates of taxation in order to bear down on total consumption expenditure. Moreover, the instability built into the Australian consumption function by the vast extension of credit facilities for all will make the task even harder. But, as our erstwhile millionaire prime minister was prone to say, 'life was not meant to be easy' and it should not be beyond the wit of the Treasury to provide its ministers with a number of ingenious schemes from which the latter may choose, in order to attain the government's desired ends.

Nor would I suggest brakes on consumption for ever. In a mixed economy the ultimate stimulus to accumulation in large measure must be an expectation of a healthy rate of growth of the consumption demands of its citizens. Only then may we be sure that the 'animal spirits' of the decision makers in the private sector remain vigorous and dynamic.

I have mentioned our horrendous unemployment problem and the overseas balance constraint. I deplore the departure from a commitment to full employment – a departure, moreover, that had the blessing of a number of prominent Australian economists who, in retrospect, ought to be thoroughly ashamed of themselves.[6] However, I do think it is worthwhile remembering that Keynes and his closest colleagues thought that the statistical orders of magnitude of unemployment which would be associated with the *disappearance* of *involuntary* unemployment due to deficiency of aggregate demand were around 6–8 per cent of the workforce. (By the 1960s, though, there had been a sea-change in attitudes on orders of magnitude by Keynes's disciples. Richard Kahn, for example, thought that Frank Paish was a semi-Fascist for wanting unemployment in the United Kingdom to be over 2.5 per cent when it was currently at 1.75 per cent of the workforce.) There is a moral here: not that we should rest content with these higher orders of magnitude but that, when they do exist, in order to reduce unemployment to more socially acceptable levels, we should rely more on microeconomic policies (which should be occurring anyway) rather than continuing generally to increase *G* or encourage private spending. The policies would include retraining, relocation (of both capital and labour), and rehousing. Coupled with this understanding is the need to rethink the new moves in the Accord. For one of the essential aims of the Accord was to influence the overall increase of money-wages and therefore the overall cost level, an essential prerequisite for Australia to reach and *then sustain* levels of unemployment which we could reasonably regard as consistent with full employment and continuing growth.

In the move to enterprise bargaining and with the demand for more flexible labour markets, I fear we are in danger of losing sight of the benefits of some long-established Australian institutions for the overall working of the economy, and also of forgetting the fundamental lessons bequeathed to us by two of our greatest Australian political economists, the late Eric Russell and the late Wilfred Salter. The economic analysis underlying the demand for more flexible and competitive labour markets does tend to treat the demand for and supply of labour as though they were akin to the demand for and supply of peanuts. In particular, it assumes that the demand and the supply curves of particular sorts of labour, and even of labour in general, may be regarded as independent of one another. But modern theory and applied research alike suggest that this is a very dubious assumption indeed. For the productivity of labour may often depend upon the wage (and other conditions of work) of the labour force concerned. Therefore, in so far as the demand for labour depends upon its anticipated productivity, there is a whole family of demand curves, each member of which corresponds to a specific wage level. Moreover, the concept of a supply curve of labour is undermined, for the *quality* of the supply of labour services will vary with the wage postulated to be paid; so that what is measured on the horizontal axis can no longer be regarded as different quantities of a *homogeneous* flow. At best, therefore, we are faced with the possibilities of multiple equilibria and it is not obvious which of them in fact will be established – or, even more daunting, which ought to be. Indeed, the analysis, strictly speaking, becomes incoherent and so is certainly not a satisfactory guide for policy.

Nor is this all. Let me rehearse the main policy conclusions of Salter's 1960 classic, *Productivity and Technical Change*:[7]

Salter draws three important and topical policy implications .... The first is that government economic policy should be directed towards creating a flexible economy which enables an easy transference of resources from declining, high cost and price industries to expanding, low cost and price ones. The second is that wages policy should be national in scope rather than related to the circumstances of particular industries. Relating earnings to the 'capacity to pay' of particular industries tends to bolster declining industries and hamper expanding, progressive ones. It delays the introduction of new techniques and has a harmful effect on overall economic growth. Third, a high rate of gross investment is necessary to allow the structure of production to change quickly and, given the structure of demand, to increase the output and productivity of those industries where technical advances are most rapid. (*The Social Science Imperialists*, p. 136)

Russell (allied with Salter until the latter's tragically early death in 1964) fought a lonely but ultimately successful battle to have established the principle that money-wage levels should be adjusted through the Arbitration Commission so as to reflect changes in prices *and* effective productivity. Not only is this consistent with equity, with the traditional Australian sense of fair play, it is also the appropriate macroeconomic policy to follow. Most importantly, it allows, *ceteris paribus*, the accumulation processes, which Salter analysed so incisively, to have their maximum impact on the growth in productivity, both in individual industries and overall. The early years of the Accord enshrined this excellent principle. As I said in the Horne Address (Chapter 1, p. 16), it was not the wage-earners but the Australian capitalists who failed to play their part, to wit, to 'Accumulate, accumulate, that is Moses and the prophets' (and also, so as to keep John Hewson and his constituency happy, the profits as well).

Another aspect of restructuring associated more with microeconomic policy and the role of government should be the provision of government help via information services and back-up generally to exporters (and entrepreneurs involved in import replacement) to help them find and then secure niche markets. This is an obvious lesson which Australia could learn from those newly industrialized countries (NICs) which gave business people their heads but backed them up in the national interest as well. A by-product of being successful in this regard may be a reversal of the trend whereby the 'brightest and the best' were attracted to services and finance sectors by the grossly distorted signals which were given out in the 1980s.[8] Another lesson from the NICs is that we should leave tariff levels where they are, at least in the medium term.

We need also to think of measures which will eliminate harmful speculation in finance and property markets so that prices and rewards there may more fully and fruitfully reflect useful economic activity. In this way present and past savings will be gathered together in a more socially useful way.[9] On the side of real investment the government should take the lead in designing investment incentives which persuade business people to invest in those areas which, overall, the government has decided most need to be developed. Provided these areas are defined broadly enough, the chances of corruption will be lessened, yet neither the government nor its public servants will be able to dodge the responsibility for giving leadership in what should be a partnership between the public and private sectors.

Australia must not accept unemployment close to 10 per cent as an appropriate 'natural' rate of unemployment (a non-existent concept anyway, if ever there was one, within the analytical approach taken in this chapter). A greater rate of capital accumulation and appropriate macroeconomic policies, as spelled out in this chapter, can enable a substantial reduction in unemployment over the next five years without a blow-out in the foreign debt or a rapid resurgence of inflation.

I thank but in no way implicate Jonathan Michie, John Nevile, Peter Nolan, Claudio Sardoni, Rod Tyers, John Wells and an anonymous referee, for comments on a draft of this chapter.

Notes

1. Chapter 1.
2. In May 1993, 366 000 had been unemployed for more than one year.
3. Chapter 1, p. 19.
4. Donald Moggridge tells me that Keynes was the author of Chapter XXIX, 'The Reform of the National Accounts', in the Report of the Liberal Industrial Inquiry, *Britain's Industrial Future* (The 'Yellow Book'), Ernest Benn Limited, 1928, where this matter is discussed in detail. The most clear-cut argument by Keynes on this matter is in his Memorandum, 'National Debt Inquiry: The Concept of a Capital Budget', *CW*, XXVII, 1980, pp. 406–13. I am indebted to Bradley Bateman for this reference. Robert Skidelsky has drawn my attention to note 2 on p. 348 of *CW*, IX, 1933 [1972], 'The Means to Prosperity'. There, Keynes wrote: 'I strongly support ... the suggestion ... that the next budget should be divided into two parts, one of which shall include those items of expenditure which it would be proper to treat as loan expenditure in present circumstances.'
5. Robert Heilbroner, 'The Deficit: A Way Out', *New York Review of Books*, **XXXIX**, (19), 19 November 1992, pp. 11–12.
6. I vaguely remember being summoned by a well-known professor of economics some time in the 1970s to a highly secret meeting of about ten or so Australian professors of economics at the University of Melbourne. There we were urged to 'educate' the public to accept higher levels of unemployment than had been the feature of the postwar world. I remember that only I and one other person present were scandalized by the request; in retrospect I bitterly regret not 'spilling the beans' about it all at the time. Now that I am, I cannot remember exactly when it occurred or who was there!
7. Immodestly, this is taken from the review article I wrote of Salter's book, which was published in the *Economic Record* of September 1962 and reprinted in *The Social Science Imperialists* (Routledge & Kegan Paul) in 1982.
8. Chapter 1, p. 19.
9. See Chapter 3 for an elaboration of this theme.

3 A 'modest proposal' for taming speculators and putting the world on course to prosperity*[1]

Following the Horne Address and its sequel on macroeconomic policy for Australia in the 1990s (Chapters 1 and 2), I wrote a jokey paper with a serious intent for the undergraduate Marshall Society journal at Cambridge, my plan to 'save' the world. In this chapter I go over some of the arguments in these three papers, and expand them into a discussion of possible policies for the United Kingdom and Europe in particular, though I continue to argue for the need to take a world perspective and to call for international institutions and cooperation.

Initially, I divided the world and its problems into three broad groups: (1) the developed industrial nations; (2) the former, so-called 'socialist' countries of Eastern Europe and what was USSR; and (3) the developing countries. I said I realized that this was far too crude a classification but that it would do for the purposes I then had in mind. Now I want to add a fourth and fifth group: (4) the rapidly growing NICs on the Pacific Rim – Singapore, Malaysia, Taiwan, South Korea, Thailand, Hong Kong and Indonesia (to a lesser extent); and (5) China, which *is* following a middle way, freeing up some markets and industries to capitalist influences and creating some capitalist institutions, for example stock exchanges, while attempting to maintain a tight authoritarian grip on social and political life. As a broad generalization and relative to the first three groups, the internal problems of groups 4 and 5 are under control and their impact on the first three groups is broadly that of an expansionary injection. So I shall continue to concentrate on the first three, for they have, again relatively, the most pressing problems.

The principal economic problem of the first group is sustained mass unemployment with which is associated the need for many of them to restructure in order to solve persistent balance of payments problems; of the second, the need to get through transitions to more market-oriented economies without complete social, political and economic disintegration; of the third, the need to provide necessary infrastructure for development, capital goods for their industries and to find outlets for their exports at steady prices in order to create jobs and raise living standards.

* First published in *Economic and Political Weekly*, **XXIX**, (28), 17 September 1994, pp. 2490–92.

Before setting out what should be done, let me briefly remind readers of the 'vision' of the nature of economic processes that forms the backdrop to the policy proposals that follow. As we argued in Chapter 1, pp. 12–13, there are two alternative 'visions' in economics: one likens markets, or even whole economic systems, to a wolf pack running along smoothly. If, perchance, one or more wolves get ahead or fall behind, forces immediately come into play which quickly return them to the pack. In the other 'vision', the forces which come into play when the breakaways get ahead or fall behind are much more likely to allow them to get even further ahead (or fall further and further behind), at least for long stretches of time. The latter 'vision' underlies the following analysis.

Let me also recapitulate what I wrote in Chapter 1 about the nature of markets, their workings and the conditions necessary for them to be beneficial rather than socially harmful. Modern theory has laid down very stringent conditions which have to be satisfied before it can be claimed, even in theory, that the market outcome is socially desirable. (I repeat that it is a non sequitur to go from establishing that there may be, in the fashionable jargon, market failures, immediately to claiming that therefore government intervention will make things better.) The first condition is that actual prices of products should be a true measure both of the social costs of the resources used to create them and of the satisfaction which their use is expected to bring to their purchasers. That is why price-takers are needed. Producers can then match their costs to externally given standards which simultaneously signal to purchasers the terms on which they can expect to achieve satisfaction. This requires that prices, most of the time, should be such that what is voluntarily demanded is equal to what is voluntarily supplied. This in turn requires that flows of purchases and flows of supplies in markets should dominate the setting of prices. Inventories or stocks, though important for smooth production and sales, nevertheless need to play a subsidiary role in the determination of actual prices. Moreover, if current prices are not achieving this match, they must directly or indirectly give out signals which encourage measures to be taken which will quickly achieve such a match, often a very tall order indeed in many important markets. It also has to be supposed that prices act solely as rationing devices. That is to say, nothing else may be deduced from the price of a good or service about its qualities other than its relative scarcity or abundance. Modern work suggests – perhaps I should have written 'has rediscovered' – that the demand and supply of labour services, and of credit, do not set up prices with this required characteristic.

If demands are dominated, not by expected satisfaction but by guesses about what prices may be in the future, so that a large element of speculation is present in the formation of prices, and if supplies are offered, not in response to perceived costs but in anticipation of future movements of prices, or of other people's expected anticipations of such movements, then the ensuing prices which are set may bear no systematic or reliable relationship to the real economic factors of the regular economic activity which, it is argued, prices ought to reflect. And all this is independent of whether power is diffused equally on both sides of the market, or whether it is concentrated in the hands of either buyers, or sellers, or both.

Let me now add a little more on speculation and its effects. The traditional case for speculation was that it reduced the amplitude of fluctuations in prices and helped markets to reach their equilibrium levels more quickly than otherwise would have been the case. But if, as we mentioned, markets behave like the second wolf pack analogy, we have to deal with cumulative movements, either virtuous or vile, rather than supposing there to be an equilibrium 'out there' to be found. We have already mentioned that a number of important markets are dominated by speculative forces: for example, the market for foreign exchange and the stock market, in both of which recent technical progress has reduced the short *period* to a length of historical time which is probably even shorter than the corresponding length of Marshall's market *day*. The housing market, too, has tended to be dominated by people who are speculators rather than genuine purchasers of long-term housing services; or, at least, the two often conflicting purposes may be combined in the one purchaser, egged on by estate agents and the suppliers of finance.

Now all these phenomena are spread, if not worldwide, at least over most of the developed world, so we need to think about international agreements with which to tackle their effects. Rather than attempting to reintroduce controls, for example, on international capital flows, which both the ideological climate and recent technological advances make unrealistic, there is a lot to be said for getting agreements on some 'Pigovian' carrot and stick measures: that is to say, while not directly stopping anyone from doing anything, yet indirectly giving them incentives radically to change their behaviour.

Let us take the foreign exchange markets as an example. If we want exchange rates to reflect real economic forces – trading prospects, real investment opportunities – we need greatly to reduce speculation and thereby its effects on the determination of exchange rates in both the short and longer terms. For neither in the short term nor on average over longer periods do exchange rates at the moment reflect these economic activities. This is especially so if we accept that there is no underlying set of long-term equilibrium exchange rates, reflecting a long-term equilibrium of an interrelated system, but, rather, changing structures which reflect the appreciation and depreciation of individual rates because of the underlying differences in the growth rates of productivity and national products. As I shall argue later, these processes should be tackled by having a fixed exchange rate system with which are associated agreed rules for periodic changes if other measures for attaining internal and external balance in individual countries are not working.

A simple way of tackling speculation and its effects is through the taxation systems of the various countries. The taxation authorities would require that the turnovers of the foreign exchange dealers who pay tax in their countries be classified into three broad categories: foreign exchange bought and sold for purposes of trade (and consumption, for example, tourism[2]) and for long-term investment either in securities or directly. (In so far as the traders were concerned with the sale or purchase of commodities, spot or future, a case would have to be made by the taxpayers that these were to help production, or that they were legitimate sales, rather than for speculation.) This would leave a residual third category which would be mainly accounted for by speculative activities. Then the proportions of each category in total turnovers would be used to assess the total taxation paid on the profits of the dealers. There would be a much higher rate for the third category than for the first two, so that the larger was the amount of speculation which was financed by foreign exchange purchases or sales, the greater would be the taxation on the profits of the dealers.

Similarly, the purchasers or sellers for whom the dealers were acting would have their business or private incomes taxed at different rates according to the categories into which their transactions fitted. For companies, a higher rate of taxation would be levied in relation to their speculative purchases or sales. For individuals, a surtax on their income tax would be levied, according to the extent of their speculative activities.

Exactly the same sorts of schemes could be used to curb speculation on the stock exchange and in the housing market. The taxation authorities would tax dividends at lower and lower rates, the longer shares were held. The rates of capital gains tax, similarly, would be lower, the greater was the length of time between purchase and sale. The taxes placed on stockbrokers would vary according to the proportions in their turnovers which were accounted for by quick sales and purchases of the same shares – the other side of the coin of the measures outlined above. For the housing market, purchase taxes would be varied according to the number of times the taxpayer had bought and sold a house. Exemptions from higher rates would be granted if it could be shown that the sales and purchases were for legitimate economic and social reasons: labour mobility (that is, persons changing jobs and localities), a larger house for an expanding family or for elderly 'reles' to come to live/die in, and so on. Similarly, the transactions of real estate agents or solicitors would be monitored and they would pay higher taxes according to the proportions of *their* turnovers which were associated with speculative transactions, as opposed to the economically and socially acceptable ones identified above. All these schemes need to be implemented in individual countries to stop nationals going 'off shore' and so escaping taxes.

Let me conclude by setting out briefly some broad measures with which to tackle the problems we identified for the first three groups. For the first group, we need a set of coordinated measures, both fiscal and monetary, macro and micro, which together will bring about gentle but sustained expansion. These should emanate from the EC countries in cooperation with the United States and Japan and, to a lesser extent perhaps, the Antipodes. Included in the set of measures would be not only the more short-term measures of lower rates of interest, investment subsidies,[3] possibly tax cuts (much more debatable for those countries with restructuring problems), but also longer-term institutional changes as well. For example, as we argued in Chapter 1, it would be most desirable for central banks to encourage trading banks to take medium- to long-term views on the viability of their customers' business and/or projects and, if these are favourable, to back up the banks in seeing through any short-term problems of their customers.

At the same time, the advanced countries should give a lead in creating institutions which have aims which are similar to those of Bretton Woods, especially the set of proposals that Keynes argued for. Especially do we need measures which make both deficit and surplus countries react to their situations in such a way as to allow employment to be sustained and growth to continue, individually and collectively. That is to say, we need to have re-established a regime of reasonably stable exchange rates, but with the well understood and accepted proviso that coordinated changes may need to occur from time to time, that nothing needs to be carved in stone for ever (except the well-known relationships between marginals and averages). If the taxation measures in regard to speculation were instituted internationally, establishing 'Bretton Woods in spirit' would be more feasible.[4]

The second group – the former so-called 'socialist' countries – eventually will hope to make all manner of goods and services that will be able to compete successfully in the markets of the developed and developing countries. At the moment, though, they have idle people and idle capacity even in the activities they are able to handle, mostly in the heavy industries which are a legacy of their 'Stalinist' pasts. Many parts of the developing world, by contrast, lack basic capital goods for both needed infrastructure and industry and agriculture, as well as the wherewithal with which to pay for them. The World Bank needs to be revamped, and its activities vastly extended, so that it can be one of the main channels whereby purchasing power is provided for these countries to buy this equipment, principally, in the first instance anyway, from the former 'socialist' countries that have the people and the capacity to provide it. This will help to give the latter economies the required breathing space to develop their needed, longer-term, restructuring.

The role of economists at the World Bank (whose comparative advantage is surely in microeconomics) should be to vet individual schemes put forward by governments and industries in the developing countries. A prerequisite for these processes to be able to start up through World Bank grants is first to wipe out, preferably completely, the current huge indebtedness of many developing countries which is now a dead-weight drag on their activities. Such a cancelling of debt will require coordination between the advanced and developing countries in order to make sure that the banking systems of the former are not destabilized – again a role for coordinated central bank actions in these countries.

If the first group are successful in getting their act together, the sustained expansion in their production and incomes will spill over into world markets so as to put a floor under the prices of, and increase the demand for, the export products of the developing countries. This, in turn, will do much to help them to help themselves with their own development. However, it will also be necessary to guard against overshooting – prices spiralling upwards, for example; so we need to turn attention again to some form of buffer stock scheme, perhaps like those proposed by Keynes and, in the postwar years, by Richard Kahn; see, for example, Gabriel Palma, 'Kahn on Buffer Stocks', *Cambridge Journal of Economics*, **18**, February 1994, 117–27.

Finally, to guard against the re-emergence of inflationary pressures in the developed world, alongside the proposed coordination of fiscal and monetary policies and microeconomic reforms should be developed incomes policies which are allied with trade-offs through their public sectors. These should be package deals which are suited to the institutions, history and sociological characteristics of the countries concerned. It is to be hoped that these may reverse the trend towards the euphemistically named 'flexible labour markets', which, quite apart from the social harm they cause, are also economically inefficient. As we saw above, pp. 28–30, money-wage movements which broadly reflect changes in effective productivity *plus* the general price level are beneficial to overall growth, as Wilfred Salter argued many years ago. For such a policy favours technologically advanced, growing industries and discourages those whose time has not only come but has gone.

I hope it may be seen that all this hangs together and that it is underlaid implicitly by theoretical structures which emanate from Keynes, Kalecki, Kaldor, Myrdal and Joan Robinson.[5] Were it to come to pass, the economies of the world could enter a virtuous upward spiral of sustained expansion and development.

Notes

1. While many of the specific policy prospects discussed here have been suggested by others such as Ruth Kelly and James Tobin, perhaps I may claim some novelty for the entire

package deal of interrelated measures which follows. I thank without implication Philip Arestis, Ha-Joon Chang, Ruth Kelly, Peter Nolan, Nevile Norman, Ajit Singh, Beth Webster, the participants of the Queens' Seminar, Lent Term 1994 and of the Post-Keynesian graduate students workshop in the Lent Term 1994 for their interest and comments.

2. Ha-Joon Chang reminds me that, if this is not to become a loophole, some upper limit on purchases will be needed.

3. On the side of real investment, governments should take the lead in designing investment incentives which persuade business people to invest in those areas which, overall, governments have decided most need to be developed. Provided these areas are defined broadly enough, the chances of corruption would be lessened, yet neither governments nor their civil servants would be able to dodge the responsibility for giving leadership in what should be partnerships between public and private sectors.

4. Paul Davidson has developed some imaginative scenarios which give detailed content to the policies outlined above: see, for example, '*The General Theory* in an open economy context', a chapter in the book on a 'second edition' of *The General Theory* which Peter Riach and I are editing for Routledge.

5. Though urged to do so by Nevile Norman, I have deliberately not gone into much detail on any one proposal. I thought it better to set out an overview which could be easily absorbed and so let others, if persuaded, provide detailed recommendations for each part. For the same reason, I have also not included orders of magnitude of, for example, the huge rise in the turnover of business on the foreign exchanges in recent decades which reflects the increasing dominance of speculative movements.

PART II

THEORY FROM AN HISTORICAL PERSPECTIVE

4 The capital theory controversies*

Looking back with hindsight from the early 1990s, we may say that the capital theory controversies of the 1950s to 1970s related not so much to the *measurement* of capital as to its *meaning* (Harcourt, 1976). Related to this perspective is the following question: what is the appropriate method with which to analyse processes occurring in capitalist economies (especially those related to production, distribution and accumulation)? In addition there are queries about the meaning of price and the source of value in two opposing traditions: price as an index of scarcity and utility as the source of value in the subjective theory of value; or price as an index of the difficulty of reproduction and labour as the source of value in the labour theory of value. (The last is a portmanteau term which encompasses an explanation of the origin and size of profits in the capitalist mode of production.)

The bulk of the controversies took place within the confines of the theory of value and distribution. In the 1970s, the application of the results was extended to a critique of the foundations of mainstream international trade theory; see Metcalfe and Steedman (1973a, 1973b). Very recently, the results have been applied, principally by Colin Rogers (1989), to a critique of the foundations of mainstream monetary theory. This *should* lead to a revival of interest in the results of the debate themselves, but it would be optimistic to expect this actually to come about. With the deaths in the 1980s of Joan Robinson, Piero Sraffa, Nicholas Kaldor and Richard Kahn, the bulk of the profession has started to behave as if they and their work never existed. Aggregate production function models and accompanying marginal productivity results, together with the long-period method, are being applied in the work which reflects the new interest in growth theory of the late 1980s and early 1990s, associated, for example, with the contributions of Lucas and Romer. The intellectual dishonesty – or, at best, ignorance – which characterizes these developments is breathtaking in its audacity and arrogance, reflecting the ruthless use of power by mainstream economists in dominant positions in the profession.

The first question posed historically in the modern debates was: can we find a unit with which to measure capital which is independent of value and distribution? Why should anyone want such a measure? If we are to use a demand and supply approach in an explanation of distributive variables –

*First published in *The Elgar Companion to Radical Political Economy*, edited by Philip Arestis and Malcolm Sawyer, Aldershot: Edward Elgar, 1994, pp. 29–34.

the rate of profits (r), the wage rate (w) – and distributive shares; if we are to make explicit the intuition of this approach, that price is an index of scarcity; and if we are to accept that in a competitive situation there is a tendency to uniformity of r in all activities, so that we need a theory to explain the origin and size of the overall economy-wide rate of profits, *then* we need an answer to the question: what do we mean by a quantity of capital? For if the intuition is to be confirmed, *one* of the reasons why r is high or low must have to do with whether we have a little or a lot of 'capital' (relative to labour). (Incidentally, with labour there is not a similar problem. We may for simplicity assume homogeneous labour measured in terms of hours and so have only one competitive wage rate to be explained. But if we wish to consider different types of labour, we may easily adjust our theory to include a different wage rate for each class, measuring each in terms of hours of work by each class.) The measure of 'capital' must exist *before* the analysis starts; that is, it must be exogenous or a given, a determinant measured in its own technical unit, not endogenous, something to be determined by the analysis itself. So the criticism that people such as Joan Robinson or Piero Sraffa did not understand the nature of mutual determination is beside the point. They did, but they also understood the difference between what is in the list of determinants and what is in the list of what is to be determined.

If it is not possible to find a unit with which to measure 'capital', then it is not possible to say that r takes the value it does partly because we have so much 'capital' and also because 'its' marginal product has a particular value. The marginal product of 'capital' becomes an incoherent concept if it is not possible to say what a quantity of 'capital' is and feed the answer into the production function format to help determine the values of w and r and the respective shares of labour and 'capital' in the national product. So far, the problem has not been solved by the demand and supply theorists. Joan Robinson's 'solution' – measure 'capital' as real capital in terms of labour time – was an attempt to answer a neoclassical question in a neoclassical setting: what limited meaning may be given to 'capital' as a factor of production? She showed that real capital could not be defined until we knew the value of either r or w and that the limited meaning that we could give with this construction to the marginal product of 'capital' produced results which have no simple obvious relationship to the accompanying return to 'capital'. Champernowne's (1953–4) chain index measure of 'capital' *seemed* to restore the 'good old theory'. However, when his analysis is examined closely, it is seen that the measure is *not* independent of distribution and prices and that the marginal product of 'capital' which is related in a simple manner to r (as is the corresponding marginal product of labour to w) is in fact subtly different from the traditional concepts.

Piero Sraffa's 1960 book (which was over 30 years in the making) is subtitled *Prelude to a Critique of Economic Theory*. The particular criticism which forms the core of his critique is made abundantly clear in his reply (1962) to Roy Harrod's review of the book: 'what is the good of a quantity of capital ... which, since it depends on the rate of interest, cannot be used for its traditional purpose ... to determine the rate of interest[?]' (Sraffa, 1962, p. 479). While the problem of induction means that the door will always be left open for such a measure to be found, at this moment it seems it is still a search for a will-o'-the-wisp, or even for the grin of a black cat in a dark room who is not there anyway.

Two further avenues of discussion arose from this aspect of the debate. The first relates to the distinction between differences and changes – the results of the debate are mostly drawn from comparisons of long-period positions and reflect differences in the initial conditions. They are unable to tell us anything about processes, in particular the process of accumulation. This led on to the methodological critique which Joan Robinson made of the neoclassicals and neo-Ricardians alike, summed up in the phrase, 'history versus equilibrium' (see Joan Robinson, 1974).

A favourite analogy was the pendulum. Its ultimate resting place is independent of whether it is given a slight nudge or is arbitrarily lifted high and let go – not so for analogous disturbances in a market or an economy. Thus, many years ago, Joan Robinson (and Kaldor (1934) even earlier) put back on the agenda what we now call path-dependent equilibria. (Ultimately, she went even further, arguing that equilibria may not even be 'out there' to be found, thus denying the legitimacy of distinguishing the factors which determine existence from those which determine stability, and of separating of those responsible for the trend from those responsible for the cycle.)

The second avenue relates to the *nature* of the accumulation process itself. Here we may identify two different visions. The first is the Fisherian, whereby the dominant force is the consumption/saving behaviour of individuals over their lifetimes and all other entities and institutions – firms, stock exchanges and so on – are subservient to the primary purpose of achieving maximum utility over the lifetimes of consumers. Rates of time preference, rates of return over cost and the money rate of interest which clears the market for money loans are crucial here. In the other scenario, which is more associated with Marx, Keynes, Veblen, Kalecki, Robinson and Kaldor (and the later Hicks), accumulation and profit making are ends in themselves. The ruthless swashbuckling entrepreneurs call the tune and all else must dance to it. Profits and the rate of profits arise from social relationships in production, together with the forces of effective demand associated with the different saving and spending behaviour of the main classes and the animal spirits of business people.

The reaction to the criticism of the aggregate production function approach to distribution associated with the exchanges between Joan Robinson, Swan, Champernowne and Solow was to revert to the Fisherian model, trying to explain r without ever mentioning 'capital' or 'its' marginal product – not always successfully, it has to be said. This was the rationale of Solow's 1963 de Vries lectures: to use the social rate of return on investment as the key concept in capital theory, a concept which provides on the productivity side of the story what the rate of time preference does on the psychological side. Again price as an index of scarcity is the conceptual background.

Parallel with this movement was the attempt by Samuelson (1962) to rationalize the use by Solow of J.B. Clark–J.R. Hicks models in growth theory and econometric work by showing that the rigorously derived results of the simple model were robust, that they were illuminating of the behaviour of the more complex n commodity general equilibrium systems with which the high theorists at MIT were more prone and happy to work. Lying behind this was the same conceptual understanding that 'capital' and r were related in such a way that the demand curve for capital was well-behaved, that is downward-sloping. It was this result in particular, as well as the other neoclassical parables – a negative association between r and the capital–output ratio, and sustainable levels of consumption per person – together with the marginal productivity theory itself, which were put at risk by the capital-reversing and reswitching results. The capital-reversing result (or Ruth Cohen Curiosum) was that a less productive, less capital-intensive technique could be associated with a lower value of r; the reswitching result has it that the same technique, which is the most profitable for a particular range of values of r or w, could also be the most profitable for another range, even though a different technique is more profitable at the range of values of r and w in between. Both of these results are counter-intuitive in the supply and demand framework and both contradict the rigorous results of the simple model, so destroying its robustness. Luigi Pasinetti (1966) was the first to understand and emphasize the significance of these phenomena for the critique of the supply and demand theories. The methodological debate also becomes relevant, in that it is not always clear in the discussion whether it is the existence, or the stability of an equilibrium, or both, that is being queried.

The outcome of the surrogate production function debate of the 1960s was to show that Samuelson's simplifying assumption of the same capital–labour ratio in each sector for a given technique in effect took seemingly heterogeneous models back into the simple one-commodity world where it was known that the intuitively satisfying neoclassical parables and the marginal productivity theory 'ruled OK'. This, together with the Robinsonian critique that short-period equilibria cannot in general be regarded as stations on the way to the long-period equilibrium cross, put paid to the application of the aggregate production function (Lucas and Romer please note) but what was the implication for Fisherian theory as revived and extended by Solow?

In 1969, Pasinetti argued that price as an index of scarcity in Solow's work only survived if an 'unobstructive postulate' – no capital-reversing allowed – was slipped into the analysis. Otherwise a well-behaved demand curve for 'capital' could not be guaranteed and the rate of return over cost did not lead to an intuitively satisfying explanation of *r* within the supply and demand marginal framework. This was disputed by Solow (1970), while Fisher was defended by Dougherty (1972). Yet those who claimed that proper general equilibrium theory was immune to these criticisms also conceded that general equilibrium theory itself, properly understood, was not descriptive theory anyway. Moreover, its own equilibrium solutions were not necessarily either unique or stable, an admission that supply and demand curves are not necessarily monotonic. So the simple theory did not provide coherent results and the logically immune theory was not applicable. Here the matter rested: Cambridge (UK) won, but who cares, let us assume that they never existed – a good economist's ploy.

In the 1980s, the implications of the application of the results in another area came to the fore. Rogers (1989) identified two major traditions leading to the foundations of modern monetary theory, the neo-Wicksellian and the neo-Walrasian. The central concept of the former was the natural rate of interest, a *real* concept that dominated the money rate of interest which ultimately had to conform to it. The capital theory results suggested that the natural rate was not a coherent concept or, at least, only a concept within an analysis where neither existence nor stability could necessarily be proved – an argument which goes back to the exchange between Garegnani and Bliss in 1970. As for the neo-Walrasian tradition, it was argued that it was unaffected by the capital theory results (a view not unanimously accepted; dissenters include Garegnani, Eatwell, Milgate and Panico); but, in any case, the neo-Walrasian foundations support an approach in which, as Hahn in particular has pointed out, it is impossible to introduce money in any meaningful sense. Again it has to be said that the critique is more successful than the alternatives proposed. This, essentially, is because they lack both the coherence – there are internal disagreements within the Post-Keynesian camp concerning both method and theory: see Hamouda and Harcourt (1988) – and the generality of the system that has been attacked.

Thus the current position is an uneasy state of rest, under the foundations of which a time bomb is ticking away, planted by a small, powerless group of economists who are either ageing or dead.

References

Bliss, C.J. (1970), 'Comment on Garegnani', *Review of Economic Studies*, **37**, pp. 437–8.

Champernowne, D.G. (1953–4), 'The Production Function and the Theory of Capital: a Comment', *Review of Economic Studies*, **21**, pp. 112–35.

Dougherty, C.R.S. (1972), 'On the Rate of Return and the Rate of Profit', *Economic Journal*, **82**, pp. 1324–50.

Garegnani, P. (1970a), 'Heterogeneous Capital, the Production Function and the Theory of Distribution', *Review of Economic Studies*, **37**, pp. 407–36.

Garegnani, P. (1970b), 'A Reply', *Review of Economic Studies*, **37**, p. 439.

Hamouda, O.F. and G.C. Harcourt (1988), 'Post-Keynesianism: From Criticism to Coherence?', *Bulletin of Economic Research*, **40**, pp. 1–33.

Harcourt, G.C. (1976), 'The Cambridge Controversies: Old Ways and New Horizons – or Dead End?', *Oxford Economic Papers*, **28**, pp. 25–65.

Kaldor, N. (1934), 'A Classificatory Note on the Determinateness of Equilibrium', *Review of Economic Studies*, **1**, pp. 122–36.

Metcalfe, J.S. and Ian Steedman (1973a), 'Heterogeneous Capital and the Heckscher–Ohlin–Samuelson Theory of Trade', in Michael Parkin (ed.), *Essays in Modern Economics*, London: Longman, pp. 50–60.

Metcalfe, J.S. and Ian Steedman (1973b), 'The Non-Substitution Theorem and International Trade Theory', *Australian Economic Papers*, **12**, pp. 267–9.

Pasinetti, L.L. (1966), 'Changes in the Rate of Profit and Switches of Techniques', *Quarterly Journal of Economics*, **80**, pp. 503–17.

Pasinetti, L.L. (1969), 'Switches of Technique and the "Rate of Return" in Capital Theory', *Economic Journal*, **79**, pp. 508–31.

Robinson, Joan (1953–4), 'The Production Function and the Theory of Capital', *Review of Economic Studies*, **21**, pp. 81–106.

Robinson, Joan (1974), 'History versus Equilibrium', *Thames Papers in Political Economy*, London: Thames.

Rogers, Colin (1989), *Money, Interest and Capital. A Study in the Foundations of Monetary Theory*, Cambridge: Cambridge University Press.

Samuelson, P.A. (1962), 'Parable and Realism in Capital Theory: The Surrogate Production Function', *Review of Economic Studies*, **29**, pp. 193–206.

Solow, R.M. (1963), *Capital Theory and the Rate of Return*, Amsterdam: North-Holland.

Solow, R.M. (1970), 'On the Rate of Return: Reply to Pasinetti', *Economic Journal*, **80**, pp. 423–8.

Sraffa, P. (1960), *Production of Commodities by Means of Commodities. Prelude to a Critique of Economic Theory*, Cambridge: Cambridge University Press.

Sraffa, P. (1962), 'Production of Commodities: a Comment', *Economic Journal*, **72**, pp. 477–9.

5 Kahn and Keynes and the making of *The General Theory**

> I am going through a stiff week's supervision from RFK ... a marvellous critic
> and suggester and improver – there never was anyone in the history of the world
> to whom it was so helpful to submit one's stuff. (Maynard Keynes to Joan
> Robinson, 29 March 1934; Keynes, *CW*, Vol. XIII, 1973, p. 422)

I

Richard Kahn always pooh-poohed the suggestion that he should have been
regarded as the co-author of *The General Theory*. For example, he described
as 'clearly absurd' Schumpeter's suggestion (1954, p. 1172) that Kahn's
'share in the historic achievement cannot have fallen very far short of co-
authorship'. And he rebuked Luigi Pasinetti for questioning this rejection,
asking him why he regarded 'it as extraordinary that Keynes preferred not to
work in a vacuum?' (Kahn, 1984, p. 240). Nevertheless, it is fair to say that,
without the crucial influence of Kahn, Keynes would not have reached his
new position as quickly, nor with the particular insights that he did.

The object of this chapter is to substantiate this evaluation. The occasion for
it is threefold: the first, a sad one, is the death of Richard Kahn in Cambridge
on 6 June 1989. The second is the publication for the first time in English[1] of
Richard Kahn's Fellowship Dissertation for King's College, Cambridge, *The
Economics of the Short Period* (Kahn, 1929, 1989).[2] It was submitted in
December 1929 and Kahn was elected to a Fellowship in March 1930. The
third is the publication of Edward Amadeo's account of the transition from the
Treatise on Money to *The General Theory* (Amadeo, 1989), which several
scholars believe may well become the definitive account in the literature.
Additional objects are to document the mutual benefits of the association of
these two colleagues and friends, in order to argue that some of the major
themes of Kahn's own work after Keynes's death in 1946 may be traced back
to what Kahn took to *and* from his close intellectual collaboration with Keynes.

*'First published in *Cambridge Journal of Economics*, 1994, **18**, pp. 11–23. I thank without
implicating Edward Amadeo, Peter Clarke, Ken Coutts, Bill Gerrard, Jan Kregel, Mike Lawlor,
David MacDonald, Cristina Marcuzzo, Luigi Pasinetti, Austin Robinson, Bob Rowthorn, Jo
Runde, Tom Rymes, Paul Samuelson, Ajit Singh and Bob Solow for their comments on a draft
of this paper. Long after this article was accepted for publication in May 1992, there was
published in the May 1993 *Economic Journal* an article by Don Patinkin (Patinkin, 1993) on
the same general issues, together with James Meade's recollections of his 'Relation' (Meade,
1993). Rather than weave an item-by-item account of agreement and disagreement through the
present text, readers are urged, instead, to read both accounts.

II

Richard Kahn came up to King's as a scholar in October 1924. He read mathematics for one year, obtaining a first, and then physics for two years, obtaining a second in Part II. His scholarship allowed him a fourth year. He read economics, obtaining a first in Part II in June 1928. His supervisor was Gerald Shove and he also went fortnightly, with some other gifted undergraduates, to Keynes. He was encouraged by Keynes, Gerald Shove and Piero Sraffa (who had come to Cambridge in 1927 and who was then associated with King's) to write a fellowship dissertation. Keynes wanted him to work on a monetary topic and tried to get him access to the statistics of the Midland Bank. Kahn could not 'conceive what use he could have made of [them]'; but he was 'unwilling to resist Keynes's influence', even though he had always been sceptical of the quantity theory of money as 'an expression of causation', a position which he felt Keynes and Dennis Robertson still held at that time. In the event, partly as a result of Keynes's rejection of an article submitted to the *Economic Journal* in April 1928 by A.W. Crick, the head of the Intelligence Unit of the Midland Bank, Kahn was bluntly told by Crick that 'if anybody was going to make use of their statistics, it was he and his staff'. 'It was,' Kahn wrote, 'a miraculous escape from disaster' (Kahn, 1989, pp. x–xi). So Keynes left Kahn to choose his own subject. 'Under Marshall's influence', it was 'The Economics of the Short Period'. The empirical sections of the dissertation (Chapter 9) were based on 'a mass of statistics' on the UK cotton industry which dated from 1926 and which Keynes had accumulated as a result of his advisory role to the industry. Kahn (1989, p. xi) commented that neither Keynes nor he 'had the slightest idea that [his] work on the short period was later on going to influence the development of Keynes's own thought' and that there were 'no traces of Keynesian thought in the dissertation itself'. Nevertheless, his decision to work on this topic was important for at least two reasons.

First, as we mentioned above, Kahn was sceptical of the quantity theory as a causal explanation of the general price level. This prejudice dates from August 1923 when he was 'just eighteen years old' and was holidaying with his family at a resort on the Baltic Sea. The German bank note printers went on strike and Kahn, at his father's request, spent three hours each morning queuing up for a sum of notes which was 'entirely inadequate for the family's needs. But the strike did not put any curb on the regular doubling of prices every 24 hours' (Kahn, 1984, p. 52).

Looking back in the early 1970s, Kahn (1975, 1978) describes the hold which the quantity theory had on Keynes, how the *Tract* 'on the analytical side ... was quite remarkably traditional', and how Keynes thought that the quantity theory was 'fundamental. Its correspondence with fact ... not open to question' (Keynes, *CW*, Vol. IV, p. 61). Yet Keynes, the pupil of Marshall, was also already the rebel, for this 'correspondence with fact' was only true of *'the long run* [in which] we are all dead' (Keynes, *CW*, Vol. IV, p. 65) emphasis in original). In the short term, 'a change in the quantity of money ... is itself the cause of a change in the ratio of the quantity of money to the price-level' (Kahn, 1975, p. 4), so that 'economists set themselves too easy, too useless a task if in tempestuous seasons they can only tell us that when the storm is long past the ocean is flat again' (Keynes, *CW*, Vol. IV, p. 65).

Nevertheless, Kahn maintained that Keynes *was* dominated by the quantity theory right up to the publication of the *Treatise on Money*, so much so that there is a glaring internal inconsistency in the theoretical parts of the *Treatise on Money*.[3] Thus Keynes claimed that in *long-period* equilibrium, the value of the general price level as determined by the traditional statement of the quantity theory and the value of the general price level as determined by the fundamental equations of the *Treatise on Money* are one and the same thing. '"Equilibrium conditions" prevail *"when the price-level is in equilibrium with the cost of production"*' (quoted by Kahn, 1975, p. 7, emphasis in original). Yet, as Kahn points out, when Keynes first discussed his fundamental equations, 'the quantity of money [did] not figure in them in any sense' (Kahn, 1975, p. 6). Moreover, one of the struggles for Keynes in the writing of the *Treatise on Money* was associated with the attempt to 'escape from the stranglehold of the Quantity Theory ... in its crude form' (Kahn, 1975, p. 6) because it obscured 'the causal process by which the price-level is determined' (Keynes, *CW*, Vol. V, p. 120). Keynes himself in the *Treatise on Money* thought that he only allowed the conventional determination of the price-level *not* to be operative when investment failed to equal saving (on the *Treatise on Money* definitions). Certainly Keynes was to say with hindsight that the significant liberating force which, in effect, released the creative and intuitive energies which allowed him to write *The General Theory* was that which freed his system of thought from the stranglehold Say's Law and, as a corollary, the quantity theory of money, had on it. This led him to the realization, which is set out explicitly in *The General Theory*, that the Marshallian dichotomy between Volume I and Volume II of an ideal *Principles* was no longer admissible. Thus, in the opening pages of Chapter 21 on 'The Theory of Prices' he wrote:

> The division of economics between the theory of value and distribution on the one hand and the theory of money on the other hand is ... a false division. The right dichotomy is ... between the theory of the individual industry or firm and of the rewards and the distribution between different uses of a *given* quantity of resources on the one hand, and the theory of output and employment *as a whole* on the other hand ... [As] soon as we pass to the problem of what determines output and employment as a whole, we require the complete theory of a monetary economy.[4] (Emphasis in original)

In this process of liberation Kahn's influence played a vital role.

Secondly, Kahn's decision to work on the 'short period' was fundamental. In the 'Introduction' which he wrote to the version of the dissertation published in English in 1989,[5] Kahn spells out again the significance of the meaning of the short period, especially in a prolonged slump. In the dissertation itself he quoted with approval Dennis Robertson's remark, 'the short period is not the same length at both ends and never has been' (p. 2). As Kahn points out, in Marshall's thought the short period always played a subordinate role to the long period – 'the real business of the *Principles*' (p. xxiii) – mere stations on the way to the long-period cross. The conditions of the nineteenth century which Marshall had in mind may have justified such a procedure. But in the new situation of the staple industries of the United Kingdom in the 1920s, the short period came into its own as a legitimate separate issue of study, as an analytical concept in which sustained and persistent forces responsible for employment, output and price determination could be identified *and* analysed in a systematic manner. Kahn, as careful then as he ever was, does say that 'the closer we approach a static state, as opposed to a state of progress, the more important does the study of the short period become' (p. xxiv). And he continues: 'To some extent I shall have in mind an industry that is depressed. *But much of the treatment is of more general application*' (p. xxv, emphasis added).

Kahn also gives a lucid account in the new 'Introduction' of why it is the facts of life rather than logical necessity which give rise to the possibility of a distinction between the short period and the long period, and between 'fixed' and 'working' capital. Thus the concept of the short period arises, not from a logical classification, but from the technical fact that there is only a sparse population of commodities between those which take a short time to make and subsequently to use, and those that not only take a long time to make but also may be used for several, often many, periods. This observation was crucial for Kahn's own work and for the structure of Keynes's thought in *The General Theory*, as well as for the transition in Keynes's thinking between the *Treatise on Money* and *The General Theory*,[6] in the sense that it provided the rationale for making an analysis of the short period in the context of the economy as a whole, a study in its own right.

While Keynes was to use simple Marshallian short-period competitive pricing as his microfoundations in *The General Theory*, there are various asides which make it clear that he knew of Kahn's contributions in his dissertation in which non-perfectly competitive models prevailed (as well of course as Joan Robinson's synthesis of these and other ideas in her 1933 book).[7] Nevertheless, it also seems clear that Keynes felt that, *for his purposes* in *The General Theory*, the modifications and complications introduced when imperfect competition was explicitly taken account of were *not* significant. Thus, in stating the 'two fundamental postulates' of 'the classical theory of employment', he adds to the statement of the first, the phrase: 'subject ... to the qualification that the equality [of the wage with the marginal product of labour] may be disturbed, in accordance with certain principles, if competition and markets are imperfect'; and to the second, the phrase: 'subject to the qualification that the equality [of the utility of the wage with the marginal disutility of that amount of employment] may be disturbed by combinations between employable units analogous to the imperfections of competition which qualify the first postulate' (Keynes, 1936; *CW*, Vol., VII, 1973, pp. 5–6). It is also significant, I believe, that, when Kalecki reviewed *The General Theory* in early 1936, he obtained the principal propositions of *The General Theory* by use of a model which was general enough to include both perfect *and* imperfect competition without making any relevant qualitative differences to the results obtained (see Targetti and Kinda-Hass, 1982).

What was important was that in *The General Theory* Keynes had been converted to Kahn's scepticism about the quantity theory as a theory of the general price level. So he used instead the received theory of value with which each of them was comfortable and in which changes in the values of those 'homely but intelligible concepts [of marginal cost and elasticity of short-period supply play] a prominent part' (Keynes, 1936; *CW*, Vol. VII, p. 292). This was the basis of the theory of prices in Chapter 21 of *The General Theory* and of Kahn's 1931 analysis of the multiplier. In both, the *short-period* elasticities of supply curves play central roles, first, in suggesting that in a deep slump they are likely to be large (but *not* infinite), but also, second, that when activity is higher, their values will be much less, so that an expansion in demand has to be analysed in terms of its impact on both quantity (and employment) *and* on prices. Included in the latter is the effect of the possibility of a rise in the wage-unit itself – this became and remained a central emphasis of Kahn, who found in the fundamental equations of the *Treatise on Money* a clear statement of the wage-units's pivotal role in determining the general price level. (The shrinking and stretching of profit margins in response to excess supply and excess demand, respectively, was the other major ingredient of a *non*-quantity theory of prices that he saw in the fundamental equations.) These themes were to be stressed and developed by Kahn and Joan Robinson in the postwar years, and were eventually to be united with Kalecki's independent development of the same themes. In Kalecki's treatment, the distribution of income loomed as large as the level of employment, and the setting of prices by price-making entrepreneurs was to become an integral part, indeed, the microfoundations, for Post-Keynesian macro theories of employment and distribution.

III

We have mentioned the hold which the quantity theory had over Keynes from the *Tract* to the *Treatise on Money* and that Kahn (1975, p. 4) quotes Keynes's own comment in the *Tract* 'as a loyal follower of Marshall and Pigou' that it was 'fundamental' (*CW*, Vol. IV, p. 61). In 1923, Keynes shared 'Goschen's contempt for [the] Philistines … who cannot bear the relation of the level of prices to the volume of currency confirmed without a feeling akin to irritation' (ibid.). Kahn also stressed, as we have seen, the inconsistency in the *Treatise on Money* itself. Between the *Tract* and the *Treatise on Money* economists in Cambridge (and elsewhere of course) were becoming more and more interested in short-period problems but the core of their *theory* was still the theory of long-period value, the account in Book V of the *Principles* of the determination of long-period normal equilibrium prices and quantities by the interplay of the forces of supply and demand. Even in the *Tract* Keynes had strayed into the short period most of the time – hence his famous dictum about death and the long run needed to be placed in its appropriate context of the contrast between the storm and the flat ocean (*CW*, Vol. IV, p. 65). Nevertheless, it was the inflation and deflation of prices which principally concerned him analytically in the *Tract* and, even though he succumbed at times to temptation in the *Treatise on Money* and discussed the intricate problems of fluctuations in short-period output and employment, he felt distinctly uneasy at having done so. As Kahn (1984, p. 68) tells us, 'Keynes expressed reluctance to be led "too far into the intricate theory of the economics of the short period"' (*CW*, Vol. V, p. 145).[8]

Moreover, as Austin Robinson pointed out and Robert Bigg's (1990) study of Cambridge monetary theory up to 1929 confirms, economists in Cambridge (and, of course, elsewhere) were becoming increasingly aware of the *analytical* implications of the fact that acts of saving are done by different groups and for different reasons than acts of investment. One of the offshoots of these strands of thought was that in the *Treatise on Money* there were sections in which sequence analysis dominated the exposition. In each sequence output and employment were given and the fundamental equations determined the price level of available (consumption) and unavailable (investment) goods and, *as a consequence*, whether investment and saving (on the *Treatise on Money* definitions) were equal or not. As is well known, income and saving but not investment were defined in a Marshallian long-period sense, so that windfall gains or losses corresponded to the differences between saving and investment. The responses of business people to these windfalls also affected the levels of output and employment in the next sequence in which the fundamental equations again determined the new price levels. It was *only* in long-period equilibrium where these windfalls were nil by definition that the level and composition of the stock of capital goods and of the employed workforce were such that long-period normal rates of remuneration were received. Only here did the quantity theory and the fundamental equations give the same answer, so that the former was, in Kahn's view, redundant, a third wheel on a chariot. If the results of short-period positions were such as to provide a convergent sequence, we have a typically Marshallian analysis of short-period equilibrium positions on the way to the long-period equilibrium position.

IV

Another section of the *Treatise on Money* which is significant for later developments is the parable of the banana economy. In the parable there is no *endogenous* mechanism by which a fall in income initiated by a change in saving behaviour, or in investment spending, may be brought to an end (other than by mass starvation or an *ad hoc* change in the attitudes to thrift or to accumulation – there is no evidence that Keynes was *then* aware of the Pigou effect; see *CW*, Vol. V, pp. 158–60). This is because, on the *Treatise on Money* analysis, the creation of profits is a widow's cruse.[9]

Elsewhere, there are sections in which the vital roles of changes in money-wages in allowing the economy to find the new equilibrium price level, and of the impact of differences between the money and the real (or natural) rate of interest on divergences between saving and investment, are emphasized. (The latter process is recognized as akin to the similar process analysed by Wicksell).[10] All these strands were jumbled rather untidily together in the process of writing that failed masterpiece, *A Treatise on Money*. This led Keynes to write to his mother when the book was done that: 'Artistically it is a failure [because he had] changed [his] mind too much during the course of it for it to be a proper unit' (*CW*, Vol. XIII, p. 176), a forerunner of the 'Author's melancholy [which] set in at the end' of writing *The General Theory* (Kahn, 1975, p. 11).

We know, though, that his thoughts were running ahead of his book. (Peter Clarke (1988) reports in a fascinating manner the interactions between his appearances at the Macmillan Committee and the drafting of the *Treatise on Money* and after.) Moreover, Keynes was later to respond to the strictures of the 'Circus' discussions and others which followed, that he *had* considered changes in production and employment as well as in prices. Thus he wrote to Joan Robinson (*CW*, Vol. XIII, p. 270): 'I think you are a little hard on me as regards the assumption of constant output ... in my *Treatise* ... I have long discussions with [of?] the effects of changes in output ... it is only at a particular point in the preliminary theoretical argument that I assume constant output ... one must be allowed at a particular stage of one's argument to make simplifying assumptions of this kind.'

Yet Keynes himself had not been able to use the apparatus of the *Treatise on Money* to provide clinching (as opposed to merely plausible) arguments with which to overthrow the notorious Treasury View in its most stark form.[11] Thus, in *Can Lloyd George do it?*, written with Hubert Henderson in 1929 (*CW*, Vol. IX, pp. 86–125), the authors could not put figures on what the secondary rise in employment and the total change in employment would be if public works expenditure were to be increased. Nor could they answer satisfactorily the charge that there was only a given volume of saving available, so that to use more for public works could mean less for private investment. Indeed, Keynes was still writing about saving going to waste *because* of lack of investment, instead of there not being enough saving created because of deficient investment in the he first place.

It was at this point that Kahn with his detailed knowledge of the workings of the 'long' end of the short period and his mastery of the apparatus of the *Treatise on Money* made a crucial contribution with his 1931 *Economic Journal* article on 'The relation of home investment to unemployment', (Kahn, 1931, 1972). There he gave a precise account of what, under carefully specified conditions, the ultimate change would be (and of the dynamic process by which it would be approached).[12] Moreover, through 'Mr Meade's relation', there is as well a precise account of the creation of the extra saving and of why a cumulative process such as the one Keynes had described in the banana economy parable could be brought to an end by an endogenous process, the leakage associated with the newly created saving (in a closed economy, of course. In fact, the Meade–Kahn analysis was much richer, for it took into account both the government and the overseas sectors). Moreover, this new saving was not only due to the rise in output but also, if the elasticities of short-period supply curves were less than infinite, to rising prices and any changes in the distribution of income in favour of profit receivers which accompanied them. Kahn was, as ever, overly modest about his achievement: 'Nobody can suppose that there is anything new in the idea of the multiplier. When I was aged about 8, my father explained to me the cumulative effect of providing one extra man with employment. What he did not explain to me – and what I was too young to ask – is why the multiplier is not "infinite"' (Kahn, 1984, p. 101).

Thus in these particular ways did Kahn help to clear the way for Keynes to liberate himself from Say's Law and the quantity theory, to reintroduce aggregate demand and the concept of effective demand into economic analysis (together with an old friend in a new guise, aggregate supply), to create the consumption function and relate it to the multiplier, to formulate a new monetary theory of the determination of the *money* rate of interest which was to rule the roost, to transform the real rate of interest into the marginal efficiency of capital, and to provide a simple short-period Marshallian account of the general price level in which the money-wage played a central role – in short, to write *The General Theory*. By doing so, he established the distinct possibility of sustained underemployment short-period equilibria or rest states in capitalist economics.[14] In the process he overthrew the Marshallian dichotomy between a *Principles* Volume I (real things) and Volume II (monetary things) with his account of the workings of a monetary production economy.[15] Something of a mystery remains, though, as to why Kahn himself, after having made such remarkable advances in the analysis of actual pricing behaviour in his 1929 dissertation,[16] reverted to short-period Marshallian theory in his 1931 article and allowed Keynes to do the same in Chapter 21 of *The General Theory*.

V

In the *Treatise on Money* and also, to a lesser extent, in *The General Theory*, there is a confusion in Keynes's thought concerning the mode of determination of the prices of capital goods. (Perhaps it would be better to say that the confusion came from the exposition of his thoughts which, Jan Kregel assures me, were always clear *and* consistent on this issue, as between the *Treatise on Money* and *The General Theory*. It was, he argues, Kahn, Joan Robinson and Sraffa who were confused about what Keynes was trying to say; see Kregel (1984, 1985) for an elaboration of these points.) Kahn tried to counter this, both at the time and later on in his work in the postwar period. The confusion arose from two sources. First, he did not always distinguish clearly between the determination of the demand prices and supply prices of capital goods, the two being equated, of course, at equilibrium. In *The General Theory*, at least on the supply side, he did reinstate short-period marginal cost pricing in both the consumption goods *and* the capital goods trades. In the latter, as we know, marginal cost pricing and rising short-period supply curves for capital goods played key roles in Keynes's account of the determination of short-period investment flows – an account, which, because of its difficulties, was ultimately abandoned in the theory of the determination of investment in the postwar period (see, for example, Kalecki, in Targetti and Kinda-Hass, 1982; Joan Robinson, 1965, pp. 96–7; Asimakopulos, 1971).[17]

Second, it was not always clear whether Keynes was discussing the determination of the prices of capital goods as such or the prices of their financial counterparts on the stock exchange. Sometimes he attempted to write as if the two were interchangeable. Moreover, he was not always careful to distinguish clearly between, on the one hand, the prices of those assets, real and financial, which already were components of existing stocks and, on the other hand, the prices associated with the corresponding flows of newly issued financial assets and newly created capital goods. It was not until the postwar discussions on the valuation ratio by Robin Marris, Nicholas Kaldor and Kahn in the United Kingdom, of Tobin's q in the United States (Tobin, 1969) and the financial markets aspect of the determination of the prices of capital goods in Minsky's work (1975), that the issues involved were even on the way to being coherently sorted out.

Kahn also regretted a simplification that Keynes made in the discussion of the determination of the money rate of interest in *The General Theory* so that the rich fare in the relevant sections of the *Treatise on Money* was taken as read by Keynes (but unhappily not by the post-*General Theory* generations). Kahn himself, and Joan Robinson, tried to restore a proper perspective in Kahn's *Manchester School* paper (Kahn, 1954, 1972), his evidence to the Radcliffe Commission (1958, 1972) and in Joan Robinson's paper on the rate of interest (Robinson, 1951).[18] One of the objectives of these papers was to defend liquidity preference theory, suitably expanded, against the criticisms of Robertson, J.R. Hicks and Kaldor. Kahn and Joan Robinson drew on their Keynesian heritage, pointing out that, in the analysis of the economy as a whole, it is not always possible to use the device of the representative individual. So often macroeconomic outcomes reflect the uneasy balancing of forces associated with the behaviour of different individuals or groups, often with different power and, most important, different expectations in uncertain situations. In this context, the differences in attitudes of 'bulls' and 'bears' immediately come to mind as being of the essence of the matter, and the role of prices (here the structure of rates of interest and the pattern of prices of financial assets) is to bring about a precarious balance between the bulls and bears (or even the bullishness and bearishness of particular individuals).

VI

It is still a matter of controversy whether Keynes's results in *The General Theory* were derived for a long-period or a short-period position; and if not derived by him for a long-period position, could they be and should they be in order to be able to argue that he had made a genuine revolution in theory? The most forthright proponents of the latter viewpoint are, of course, Garegnani, Eatwell and Milgate (see, for example, Eatwell and Milgate, 1983, where most of the key papers are gathered together). Their arguments are well-known, certainly to readers of the *Cambridge Journal of Economics*. As far as Kahn's role is concerned, though, his perception of what needed to be done and what *was* done by Keynes goes very much against their interpretation.[19] So, too, was Joan Robinson's perception. For example, she wrote to Keynes towards the very end of the gestation period of *The General Theory* that he had 'stopped [*sic*] rather suddenly in this section [Chapter 17] out of the short period with fixed equipment to which the rest of the book belongs'; that she herself had 'been working out this long-period stuff' and had found 'that to make a proper job of it [she needed] to bring in several considerations that are not really relevant to [his] main theme'. She added that 'this section is in a limbo between long and short period; [he] could make [his] point without bringing the long period in it at all. [If he did] a definition of "equilibrium" [would be] essential' (*CW*, Vol. XIII, pp. 647–8).[20] And both Kahn and Joan Robinson thought consciously of their postwar work on growth theory as generalizing *The General Theory* to the long period.

The most compelling evidence to my mind, though, is the change in the notion of equilibrium that occurs between the *Treatise on Money* and *The General Theory*. Amadeo (1988) has documented this most tellingly. Full equilibrium in the first book requires that normal rates of remuneration be received by both profit-receivers and wage-earners; in the second book, all that is required is that short-period expected profits be achieved and so maximized *at that point in time*. The construction of the aggregate supply curve and the definition of the point of effective demand imply this *and nothing more*. In particular, there is no further implication that the stocks of capital goods in existence are either at their 'right' levels or that their compositions are 'correct' in any *long-period* sense. And, of course, employment levels are only 'correct' from the point of view of employers (except in the unlikely event of a full-employment equilibrium being established unaided by outside intervention). The unemployed may dislike their situation but are unable to do anything about it.[21] After all, it was these possibilities, albeit at an industry level, that led to Kahn's own dissatisfaction with Marshallian orthodoxy in the first place and so to the writing of his 1929 dissertation and, partly, at least, his 1931 article.[22]

VII

The final theme which runs through Kahn's work and which arises from his close relationship with Keynes is the emphasis he was to put in the postwar period on the need for sustained full-employment policies to be allied with some form of continuing incomes policy. As we have mentioned, this came from his realization, which dates from his understanding of the fundamental equations, that the money-wage and its stability are the fulcrum on which the stability of the whole system turns with regard to *both* output and prices: hence his criticism of Keynes for departing from the fundamental equations where the possibility of an *income* inflation as well as a *profits* inflation is made so explicit. Indeed, Kahn was to say (1975, pp. 14–15), that Keynes had 'improved on Wicksell' who had argued that, once the money rate of interest was made consistent with the real rate of interest, inflation (or deflation) would stop, whereas Keynes's work showed that another, independent source of inflation was still present. It was to this theme that Kahn returned again and again.[23]

VIII

Richard Kahn wished to be known as a disciple of Keynes (see Marcuzzo, 1988). He made selfless inputs into Keynes's work as well as the work of many others at Cambridge. He was instinctively modest about his own achievements. Yet, had his dissertation been published closer to the time when it was first written, it and his 1931 multiplier article together would surely have meant the subsequent receipt of the Nobel Prize, for his major contributions to what Keynes, Kahn himself and other gifted members of the Cambridge Faculty felt the discipline of economics ought to be.

Notes

1. An Italian translation was published in 1983, through the offices of Professor Marco Dardi.
2. Richard Kahn corrected the proofs of the 1989 book version but, sadly, he was never to see a copy of the published version.
3. Edward Amadeo has pointed out to me that there was no inconsistency. The two expressions for the price level – the quantity theory equation and the fundamental equations – were, rather, complementary to one another, they both held for the short period and the long period provided that a distinction was made between the *short-period* and the *long-period* values of the variables in the quantity theory equation. This may well be true of the way in which Keynes saw the issue at the time and the logic is, in any event, impeccable. Kahn's point was, I think, a different one: that, perhaps inadvertently, Keynes had already hit upon a fundamentally different approach to modelling the working of the economy as a whole in which the quantity theory as traditionally understood had no role.
4. Keynes then added an alternative division within which we may discern (again with hindsight) the genesis of the postwar generalization of *The General Theory* to the long period, especially by Kahn and Joan Robinson. (In the process the *emphasis* on the role of money was unfortunately lost.)

   Or, perhaps, we might make our line of division between the theory of stationary equilibrium and the theory of shifting equilibrium – meaning by the latter the theory of a system in which changing views about the future are capable of influencing the present situation. *For the importance of money essentially flows from its being a link between the present and the future.* We can consider what distribution of resources between different uses will be consistent with equilibrium under the influence of normal economic motives in a world in which our views concerning the future are fixed and reliable in all respects; with a further division, perhaps, between an economy which is unchanging and one subject to change, but where all things are foreseen from the beginning. Or we can pass from this simplified propaedeutic to the problems of the real world in which our previous expectations are liable to disappointment and expectations concerning the future affect what we do to-day. It is when we have made this transition that the peculiar properties of money as a link between the present and the future must enter into our calculations. But, although the theory of shifting equilibrium must necessarily be pursued in terms of a monetary economy, it remains a theory of value and distribution and not a separate 'theory of money'. Money in its significant attributes is, above all, a subtle device for linking the present to the future; and we cannot even begin to discuss the effect of changing expectations on current activities except in monetary terms. (Emphasis in original)
5. As we mentioned, an Italian version was published in 1983. This was the first time Kahn had reread his dissertation since he submitted it. Indeed, a feature of Kahn's life was that he rarely reread things once he had done with them. Thus, when he gave the Fourth Keynes Lecture in Economics to the British Academy in 1974, appropriately entitled *On Re-reading Keynes*, he mentioned that it was the first time that he had reread both the

Treatise on Money and *The General Theory* since before they were published, when he read them in proof, in the case of *The General Theory*, over many drafts. When he drafted some papers for publication – they were on topics in the least important part of his dissertation, that in which perfect competition was assumed – he wrote them afresh rather than take the text of the dissertation as starting points. He followed the same procedure with his important *Economic Journal* paper on duopoly in 1937. This had the unfortunate effect that he forgot to thank Piero Sraffa for his substantial help (Kahn, 1989, p. xviii). For reasons of space – an editorial decision – his references to the literature were also severely reduced in the article, though not in the dissertation itself.

6. It also led Kahn, many years on, to wonder why Sraffa, who was always so careful to base his own theoretical work on empirical observations, had not explicitly taken the similar point about 'fixed' and 'working' capital into account in his later work on production interdependence and the theory of value and distribution (p. xiv). Bob Solow (20.2.91) made an astute comment on Kahn's distinction which makes me think now that it is not as illuminating as I initially thought it to be: 'How do you know that most commodities take a long (short) time to make and a long (short) time to use? Wheat takes a year to make and a minute to eat. Light bulb vice versa (rather not eat it, of course).'

7. Steven Kates has found further evidence in Keynes's unpublished correspondence with his wife. Thus, in a letter of 21 October 1929, we read: 'Pigou has now been reading Kahn's Essay and I am very happy to find that he agrees with me. He thinks it is the best he has read from a young man since mine more than twenty years ago, and perhaps the best he has ever read. So there ought to be a good chance of getting Kahn a fellowship this year.' And in a letter of 26 January 1930: 'I am reading Kahn's dissertation which is hard work but very interesting.' The date of the first letter raises a query as to whether Kahn's '*Essay*' *was* his dissertation. I possess Joan Robinson's copy of Kahn's dissertation and on the title page is typed 'Submitted to the Electors to Fellowships by R.F. Kahn, of King's College, on December 7th, 1929'. [Since this chapter was published in the *Cambridge Journal of Economics*, Kahn's papers have become available in the King's College Archives. The modern archivist, Ms. Jacqueline Cox, and Professor Yoshihiko Hakamata of Chuo university, Tokyo, have solved the puzzle. 'Kahn's Essay' refers to the version of his research work which was submitted for the Adam Smith Prize.]

8. This judgement is confirmed by Keynes's reply (28 November 1930) *after* the *Treatise on Money* had been published, to comments by Ralph Hawtrey on proofs of the book. For example, Keynes writes that: 'The question *how much* reduction in output is caused ... is important, but not strictly a monetary problem. [Keynes had] not attempted to deal with it in [his] book [because he was] primarily concerned with what governs prices' (*CW*, Vol. XIII, p. 145, emphasis in original). And again: 'I am not dealing with the complete set of causes which determine the volume of output ... this would have led me an endlessly long journey into the theory of short-period supply and a long way from monetary theory ... [He agreed] that it will probably be difficult in the future to prevent monetary theory and the theory of short-period supply from running together' (*CW*, Vol. XIII, pp. 145–6), prophetic words indeed! For a succinct and convincing interpretation of the development of Keynes's own thinking during the transition from the *Treatise on Money* to *The General Theory*, based on a detailed study of Keynes's own writings and the lecture notes taken by students at Keynes's lectures in the early to mid-1930s, see Rymes (1989, pp. 14–15).

9. I am indebted to John Coates for pointing out to me the crucial significance of the banana economy parable in the story and to Bob Rowthorn for reminding me of the significance (and neglect) of the Pigou effect in this context.

10. Paul Samuelson (1.3.91) suggested that what I have called the 'money' rate of interest would be better called the 'market' rate, in order to make clear that what Wicksell and Keynes were comparing was *not* 'quite what is involved in today's contrast between the "real" and "money (or nominal)" rates'. See also, on this, Rogers (1989, pp. 22–3, n. 1).

11. The reference is to Frank Hahn's dilemma, as set out in the Preface to his Mitsui Lectures at Birmingham (Hahn, 1982), that 'on occasions [he has] had to rest satisfied with arguments that are merely plausible rather than clinching' (p. ix).

12. For example, 'Towards the end of [Kahn's] article [he] was careful to state that it was based on the assumption that "the state of general confidence [was] not affected"' (p. 197). '[This] did not mean that this was at all probable – but merely that in the study of one type of causation it is necessary to abstract from others ... devoted only three concluding paragraphs to the subject ... not the subject of the article' (Kahn, 1984, p. 93).

13. See Rymes (1989, pp. 27–44) for a fascinating account of the relationship between Kahn's multiplier arguments and the exchanges with Keynes over the 'Manifesto' which Kahn, Joan and Austin Robinson wrote after Kahn, Joan Robinson and Piero Sraffa 'spied' on Keynes at his first lecture on 25 April 1932 and then came back for more at his second lecture in early May. See also Kregel (1984, 1985). Jan Kregel discusses the benefits and costs associated with their influence on Keynes's thinking of the fact that at the time Kahn, Austin and Joan Robinson and (to a lesser extent) Sraffa were not primarily monetary economists, as Keynes always was, but were rather more expert on the theory of the firm and the industry, and of value and distribution generally.

14. Bob Solow (20.2.91) would prefer me to say 'conjectured' rather than 'established' because he (Solow) does not think that Keynes 'had the tools'.

15. Bill Gerrard reminds me that Keynes's rejection of the Marshallian dichotomy is most clearly stated in the early drafts of *The General Theory* in the distinction Keynes made between the cooperative economy, the neutral economy and the entrepreneur (or monetary production) economy. There, Keynes argued that money must be introduced from the beginning of the analysis, not only because in the entrepreneur economy transactions of necessity occur in money – he especially emphasized the wage bargain – but also because he had begun to map out the sequence nature of production and the manner in which investment expenditure was the link between future and present happenings. From this he was led to consider the essential properties of liquidity and to formulate the theory of interest to go with his understanding of the essential properties and role of money. It was probably a mistake for Keynes to have omitted the discussion of these three sorts of economies from the final version of *The General Theory*. Much modern work has been concerned with these issues and it would have been a great help to have had Keynes's insights in the public domain, instead of having to wait until the contents of the laundry basket at Tilton made their way into Volume XXIX of Keynes's *Collected Writings*.

16. See Maneschi (1988) for a lucid account of what the advances were and Marcuzzo (1994) and Marris (1992) for their proposed solutions of the mystery.

17. David MacDonald (1991) has a splendid paper in which he points out that Abba Lerner's analysis in 1952 of 'The essential properties of interest and money' avoided the pitfalls into which Keynes fell here and so the criticisms of Kahn, Joan Robinson and Sraffa.

18. Joan Robinson's paper may also be seen as a forerunner to the recent debate about finance, saving and investment in the work of Keynes and Kalecki which started with Asimakopulos's 1983 paper in the *Cambridge Journal of Economics*.

19. That the analysis needed to be and could be expanded to the long period to be placed alongside the long-period theory of value and distribution associated with Sraffa's work is perhaps a separate question which we put to one side here.

20. One of the most perceptive articles on these and related points was written by Paola Potestio (1989). She points out that there are two explanations of unemployment equilibrium in *The General Theory*, one in Chapters 1–15, the other in Chapter 17. The first explanation deals with the short period, the second with the long period. She argues – this is still a controversial argument – that they are incompatible with one another and that they contain 'different implications of the conception of money' (p. 257). Jan Kregel (9.6.1991) reminds me that, in so far as there is a concept of long-period equilibrium in *The General Theory*, it depends upon a state of long-term expectations having been held, and confirmed, for a sufficiently long period of time, so that a steady level of employment is attained (see Keynes, 1936, p. 47). Such a definition rules out any disappointment of short-term expectations or, at least, any feedback from such a disappointment to the state of long-term expectations. Keynes argued that, in the actual world, such feedbacks generally occurred. It follows that the possibility of *attaining* the long-period position (which was itself akin to Marshall's long-period equilibrium position, but in an economy-wide

setting) disappears, though it was still correct, in Keynes's view, to argue that 'every state of expectation has its definite corresponding level of long-period employment' (Keynes, 1936, p. 47).

21. Bob Solow (26.2.91) argues that there has to be a rest point in the labour market too, that he thinks 'Keynes was right, but the argument wasn't tight'.

22. Further clinching evidence for a short-period interpretation is to be found in Keynes's correspondence with Joan Robinson concerning her 1942 *Essay on Marxian Economics*. As we know, Keynes attached central importance to the units of measurement 'for the purpose of a causal analysis, which ought to be exact; (Keynes, 1936, p. 39). In replying to Joan Robinson concerning whether he was or was not adopting the labour theory of value, Keynes wrote (27.8.42): 'For my units to work two conditions must be fulfilled, namely that labour in some sense is the only factor of production and that we are functioning in short-period conditions.' This was also a response to her comment (21.8.42), 'that your units work because capital equipment is given'. I am indebted to Mike Lawlor for bringing these exchanges in the Keynes papers in King's College Library (MM/18) to my notice.

23. His most succinct statement is perhaps to be found in his British Academy Keynes Lecture (1975), especially pp. 16–32.

References

Amadeo, E.J. (1989), *Keynes's Principle of Effective Demand*, Aldershot: Edward Elgar.

Asimakopulos, A. (1971), 'The determination of investment in Keynes's model', *Canadian Journal of Economics*, **4**, August.

Asimakopulos, A. (1983), 'Kalecki and Keynes on finance, investment and saving', *Cambridge Journal of Economics*, **7**, September.

Bigg, R.J. (1990), *Cambridge and the Monetary Theory of Production: The Collapse of Marshallian Macroeconomics*, London: Macmillan.

Clarke, P. (1988), *The Keynesian Revolution in the Making, 1924–1936*, Oxford: Oxford University Press.

Eatwell, J. and M. Milgate (eds) (1983), *Keynes's Economics and the Theory of Value and Distribution*, London: Duckworth.

Hahn, F.H. (1982), *Money and Inflation*, Oxford: Basil Blackwell.

Kahn, R.F. (1931), 'The relation of home investment to unemployment', *Economic Journal*, **41**, June (reprinted in Kahn, 1972).

Kahn, R.F. (1937), 'The problem of duopoly', *Economic Journal*, **47**, March.

Kahn, R.F. (1954), 'Some notes on liquidity preference', *Manchester School of Economic and Social Studies*, **22**, September (reprinted in Kahn, 1972).

Kahn, R.F. (1958), 'Memorandum of evidence submitted to the Radcliffe Committee', reprinted in Kahn, 1972.

Kahn, R.F. (1972), *Selected Essays on Employment and Growth*, Cambridge: Cambridge University Press.

Kahn, R.F. (1975), *On Re-reading Keynes* (Fourth Keynes Lecture in Economics, Oxford: Oxford University Press.

Kahn, R.F. (1978), 'Some aspects of the development of Keynes's thought', *Journal of Economic Literature*, **16**, June.

Kahn, R.F. (1984), '*The Making of Keynes' General Theory*, Cambridge: Cambridge University Press.

Kahn, R.F. (1929, 1989), *The Economics of the Short Period*, Basingstoke: Macmillan; Italian translation (1983), *L'Economia del Breva Periodo*, Turin: Boringheri.

Kaldor, N. (1966), 'Marginal productivity and the macro-economic theories of distribution: comment on Samuelson and Modigliani', *Review of Economic Studies*, **33**, October.

Keynes, J.M. (1923), *A Tract on Monetary Reform, Collected Writings* (CW), Vol. IV, 1971, London: Macmillan.

Keynes, J.M. (1930), *A Treatise on Money*, 2 vols, CW, Vols V, VI, 1971, London: Macmillan.

Keynes, J.M. (1931), *Essays in Persuasion, CW*, Vol. IX, 1972, London: Macmillan.

Keynes, J.M. (1936), *The General Theory of Employment, Interest and Money*, CW, Vol. VII, 1973, London: Macmillan.

Keynes, J.M. (1973), '*The General Theory and After: Part I Preparation*, CW, Vol. XIII, London: Macmillan.

Kregel, J.A. (1984), 'Review of R.F. Kahn, *The Making of Keynes' General Theory (1984)*', *De Economist*, **132**, (4).

Kregel, J.A. (1985), 'Hamlet without the Prince: Cambridge macroeconomics without money', *American Economic Review*, **75**, May.

Lerner, A.P. (1952), 'The essential properties of interest and money', *Quarterly Journal of Economics*, **66**, May.

MacDonald, D.D. (1991), 'Keynes' theory of investment and the price of investment goods', mimeo, Cambridge.

Maneschi, A. (1988), 'The place of Lord Kahn's *The Economics of the Short Period* in the theory of imperfect competition', *History of Political Economy*, **20**, summer.

Marcuzzo, M.C. (1988), 'Richard F. Kahn, A Disciple of Keynes', mimeo, Modena.

Marcuzzo, M.C. (1994), 'R.F. Kahn and imperfect competition', *Cambridge Journal of Economics*, **18**, (1).

Marris, R.L. (1964), *The Economic Theory of 'Managerial' Capitalism*, London: Macmillan.

Marris, R.L. (1992), 'R.F. Kahn's Fellowship Dissertation: a missing link in the history of thought', *Economic Journal*, **102**, pp. 1235–43.

Meade, J.E. (1993), 'The relation of Mr Meade's relation to Kahn's multiplier', *Economic Journal*, **103**, May.

Minsky, H.P. (1975), *John Maynard Keynes*, New York: Columbia University Press.

Patinkin, D. (1993), 'On the chronology of *The General Theory*', *Economic Journal*, **103**, May.

Potestio, P. (1989), 'Alternative aspects of monetary theory in *The General Theory*: Significance and implications', *Recherches Economiques de Louvain*, **55**.

Robinson, J. (1933), *The Economics of Imperfect Competition*, London: Macmillan.

Robinson, J. (1942), *An Essay on Marxian Economics*, London: Macmillan.

Robinson, J. (1951), 'The rate of interest', *Econometrica*, **19**, April; reprinted in *Collected Economic Papers*, Vol. II, (1960), Oxford: Basil Blackwell.

Robinson, J. (1965), 'Kalecki and Keynes', *Collected Economic Papers*, Vol. III, Oxford: Basil Blackwell.

Rogers, C. (1989), *Money, Interest and Capital. A Study in the Foundations of Monetary Theory*, Cambridge: Cambridge University Press.

Rymes, T.K. (1989), *Keynes's Lectures 1932–35. Notes of a Representative Student*, London: Macmillan.

Schumpeter, J.A. (1954), *History of Economic Analysis*, London: Allen & Unwin.

Targetti, F. and B. Kinda-Hass (1982), 'Kalecki's review of Keynes's *General Theory*', *Australian Economic Papers*, **21**, December.

Tobin, J. (1969), 'A general equilibrium approach to monetary theory', *Journal of Money, Credit and Banking*, **1**, pp. 15–29.

6   Joan Robinson's early views on method*

I

Joan Robinson's later views on method and its traps for orthodox economic theory are very well known. Not only did she write many times on these themes, lucidly and challengingly, but also Gram and Walsh in their 1983 evaluation of her writings over a span of 50 years put considerable emphasis on this aspect of her contributions. What may not be so well known is that her first ever major publication, the pamphlet *Economics is a Serious Subject* (Robinson, 1932a), was also on method.[1] By the end of her life – she died in August 1983 – she was almost nihilistic about economic theory, method and their potential development. She rejected the idea of providing a rival 'compleat theory' to replace the orthodox neoclassical one (as she saw it) which she had been attacking, as far as the content of the theory was concerned, from the late 1920s on and, as far as what she considered its method to be, from the mid-1930s on. She said that 'any other "complete theory" would be only another box of tricks. What we need is a different habit of mind – to eschew fudging, to respect facts and to admit ignorance of what we do not know' (Robinson, 1979, p. 119).

The two principal influences on her approach to these views were, first, Keynes of *The General Theory* (together with the work leading up to and away from it, especially in the 'circus' on the *Treatise on Money*) and, second, from the mid-1930s on, Marx, including under this rubric the overwhelming influence of Kalecki. How to tackle time, how to account for institutions, how to be properly historical in method and analysis, were her persistent emphases; how we may and ought to escape from the straitjacket of equilibrium analysis – of, first, finding existence and, maybe, uniqueness, *then* considering stability, both local and global – was her oft-repeated message. Though by the end of her life she herself was very pessimistic,[2] there are straws in the wind that suggest that others accepted the message (whether they were influenced by her or not), some long ago. Thus one of Kaldor's earliest papers (1934) was about the problem of path-determined equilibria, as we would say now, a subject to which Hahn has returned very recently (1987, 1988) and, of course, Kaldor's last book was called *Economics without Equilibrium* (1985). But whatever the ultimate outcome of these strands, it may be useful to go back to Robinson's early views, to see what they were and why, very quickly, she was to move away from them, so that by 1933, in

* First published in *History of Political Economy*, 1990, **22**, (3), pp. 411–27.

the Introduction to *The Economics of Imperfect Competition* (Robinson, 1933a) she had already discarded much of what she had written only the year before.[3]

II

Robinson published *Economics is a Serious Subject* when she was 28. She had graduated in 1925 and had spent nearly two years in India with Austin Robinson before returning to Cambridge in the late 1920s. There, in addition to the influence of Keynes, Shove and Pigou and the start of the influence of Kahn on both her own and Keynes's thought, Piero Sraffa was causing an uproar. This came about through his published papers – his 1926 *Economic Journal* article and his contribution to the 1930 *Economic Journal* symposium on increasing returns and the representative firm – and his lectures of the late 1920s. The manuscript of *Economic is a Serious Subject* is among Robinson's papers in the library of King's College, Cambridge.[4] It is dedicated 'To Piero Sraffa whose introduction of pessimism into Cambridge has made ECONOMICS a serious subject'. The dedication was taken out of the published version, and, indeed, in the manuscript it is crossed out and Robinson has written in 'The Fundamental Pessimist' in its place. In the published version the dedication page reads:

To

THE FUNDAMENTAL PESSIMIST

Evidently Sraffa was the inspiration for the writing of the paper.

The manuscript also has marginal comments in Robinson's handwriting, identifying specific examples of the economists she is either applauding or criticizing in the paper itself. In addition there are letters about the paper to Robinson from Mary Paley Marshall, Sraffa, Charles Gifford (a former pupil of Austin Robinson), Hubert Henderson, Gerald Shove, Keynes and a close friend, Max Newman (1897–1984), a pure mathematician who was a Fellow of St John's and whose views Robinson took very seriously indeed. Thus in the manuscript copy of the paper the list of dedications to various economists included as well the following one to Newman: 'And to the pure mathematician whose sympathy and well-deserved contempt have had a beneficial effect on the serious economist.'[5] No doubt partly because of these reactions, she soon abandoned many of the arguments in *Economics is a Serious Subject*.[6] Parts of it are reproduced in the early pages of the Introduction to *The Economics of Imperfect Competition* (Robinson, 1933a), which was published the next year but most of which must have been written when Robinson wrote the earlier piece. Thus, in a letter from Shove (King's College, 9 June 1932) he discusses overlaps between *The Econom-*

ics of Imperfect Competition and his own proposed work on value and distribution (which was never to see the light of day). Shove wants to cut down or out from his own work what will appear in Robinson's book. He refers to a talk they had 'last Christmas' about their different treatments of factor homogeneity within each industry, Shove saying that he assumes that Robinson had not altered her treatment 'so as to make it still more like mine'.[7]

III

The pamphlet itself was subtitled *The Apologia of an Economist to the Mathematician, the Scientist and the Plain Man*. Its primary object evidently was to make known our peculiar ways to these groups. The difficulties Robinson discussed included the problem that the words and terms we use mean different things to us than to the other three groups. At various points in the pamphlet she lists as examples: 'unemployment, real wages, famines, over-population and the maximum possible national income [which to] the practitioners of a subject [are] purely verbal definitions, [not] the concepts themselves, as they occur in the real world' (p. 3). The use of the word 'concept' is unfortunate, for a concept is the product of the intellectual activity of the observer/interpreter/theory-maker. Presumably what Robinson had in mind were the real-world counterparts of the concepts in the theory, real-world entities which moreover *had* an existence of their own that was independent both of the observer (the cow *was* still in the field when the Philosophy supervision was over) and of their theoretical counterparts in the theory of the observer.

Nevertheless, because of these differences, sentences and indeed arguments which make sense to economists, because they know what the words used mean in their contexts, often are incomprehensible to the other groups. This problem is related to the age-old problem of the gap between the world 'out there' that the techniques and theory of the discipline are meant to illuminate and the techniques themselves – the method and the resulting theory itself. The theory has in effect to pass two tests. The first is its own logical consistency and coherence; the second (which is probably even more important) is its ultimate applicability, either directly, or indirectly as a benchmark, a comparison.

At this point Robinson confronted a basic problem. It led her to distinguish between two types of economists: the English optimists and the Continental pessimists. Evidently the former settle for manageable assumptions which may be unrealistic, the latter for realistic assumptions which may be unmanageable with existing techniques. Hence, she argues, to be 'a serious subject', at least 'in the academic sense', is for the subject matter to be 'neither more nor less than its own technique' (p. 3).

There had been great advances in technique by 'the present generation of economists' (this is the early 1930s): 'The work of Professor Pigou on the Economics of Welfare ... the analysis of the output of particular commodities, and the recent work on the Theory of Money, or, as I prefer to call it, the analysis of output as a whole,[8] has built up a body of technique ... of which we need none of us be ashamed [albeit] imperfect, primitive, incomplete, only capable of giving unreal answers to unreal questions' (p. 5).

Early on in the pamphlet Robinson compares economics with the physical sciences and places economics somewhere past its alchemy stage but not yet at the equivalent stage where 'Doctor Cockroft transmutes the elements in his laboratory' (p. 4). As a result the plain man may think us 'heartless' in that we are supposed to be concerned with human welfare yet our concepts must be treated as 'mere definitions' and not as their real-world counterparts of the same name. Nevertheless, economics 'must resolutely turn its back on the pursuit of gold, however precious it may be to human welfare, and embark upon the path of an austere and disinterested search ... for a single self-consistent system of ideas'. This is a difficult if not impossible task for some people because it requires a 'strange temperament ... a strong interest in human welfare [combined with] the capacity for ... detachment which makes it possible ... to accept ... that the subject matter of economics is neither more nor less than its own technique' (p 4). Of course, as we mentioned above, Robinson was ultimately to think of the end result of the 'austere and disinterested search' as 'only another box of tricks'.

Robinson then discusses the nature of controversy in economics. The rarest kind is when someone has made a logical error and someone else has seen it. (In later years she was to wonder whether logical errors were *that* rare, though she continued to argue that, while others saw them, they could not always get the makers of them to accept this. 'He who is convinced against his will / Is of the same opinion still' was a couplet she often quoted.)[9] The more usual source of controversy was one akin to two knights fighting about whether a shield is black or white, only to find out later that one side was black and the other white. She adds that 'conducting an economic controversy is a delicate business' (p. 5). (She herself was to come to know only too well how true this was.) You must not be either too rude or too polite: 'The proper technique of controversy is to say: "That's interesting – what makes you say it is white?"' (p. 6). For then differences come down to differences in assumptions.

This view may be contrasted with that of Keynes, who, in *The General Theory* anyway, thought that he could not achieve his 'object of persuading economists to re-examine critically certain of their basic assumptions except by a highly abstract argument and also by much controversy'. While wishing that 'there could not have been less of the latter', he nevertheless thought 'it important, not only to explain [his] own point of view, but also to show in what respects it departs from the prevailing theory'. His 'controversial passages [were] aimed at providing some material for an answer [to overcome the doubts of those] who ... will fluctuate ... between a belief that [he is] quite wrong and a belief that [he is] saying nothing new' ([1936] 1973, p. xxi). Robinson's view may also be contrasted with Marshall's view. The latter arose, at least in part, Keynes has argued, because Marshall was 'too much afraid of being wrong, two thin-skinned towards criticism, too easily upset by controversy' ([1933] 1972, p. 199). This led him to overdo the application of 'the essential truth ... that those individuals who are endowed with a special genius for the subject and have a powerful economic intuition will often be more right in their conclusions and implicit presumptions than in their explanations and explicit statements' ([1933] 1972, p. 211 n.2). Hence 'passages imputing error to others [were] rare [and Marshall always] explained that earlier writers of repute must be held to have *meant* what is right and reasonable, whatever they may have said' (p. 211, italics in original) – a principle to which Keynes was to appeal more than once in his own defence. Robinson's attitudes were soon to become closer to those of Keynes than to those of Marshall.[10]

Two questions may be asked of assumptions: 'Are they tractable? and: Do they correspond to the real world? The first question can only be answered by the application of analytical technique to the assumptions' (Robinson, 1932a, p. 6). Usually, it will be found that one set is manageable and the other is realistic so that 'the choice between them is ... one of temperament ... not opinion'. Evidently, the optimistic, analytical, English economist will choose the former and the pessimistic, methodological, Continental economist will choose the latter. She adds: 'If we choose to draw a demand curve and a supply curve on a plane diagram we are assuming that the conditions of demand for the commodity in question are virtually independent of the amount of it produced.... To maintain that the assumption is illegitimate because actually demand and supply are often not independent is merely the naivity of the "plain man"' (p. 7) – and, presumably, of Piero Sraffa, for this had been one of the principal thrusts of his critique of Marshallian partial equilibrium analysis in his 1926 *Economic Journal* article. Was Robinson, then, at this point preparing her defence of the method of *The Economics of Imperfect Competition* against a possible Sraffian onslaught, even though she had taken the precaution in her book of adopting the more realistic assumption of the latter part of his article, that each competitive firm is nevertheless its own little monopolist?[11]

Or was she guarding herself against the arguments that were to be voiced by Wassily Leontief in his attack in 1937 (1966) on the Cambridge vice of implicit theorizing? Leontief cited examples from the writings of Robinson –

he praised her for recognizing her error (1966, p. 67) – Richard Kahn, and especially Keynes, who was such a sinner that it was 'the embarrassment of plenty ... which [made] the proper choice of an example particularly difficult' (p. 69). Basically, the 'vice' consists of dodging difficult theoretical problems (for example, aggregation conditions, mutual interdependence) by cutting the link between the basic postulates of an argument and its final conclusions by treating intermediate steps which introduce difficulties as if they too were basic postulates, and so not open to criticism or perusal *within* the construction of the theory itself. Thus Leontief criticized Keynes for interpreting the aggregate supply and demand functions *as if* they were Marshallian independent, partial equilibrium supply and demand functions, even though they were known to be traceable back to much the same set of factors. They were therefore fundamentally interdependent, so that one could not be changed without the other also changing at the same time as a consequence – an argument which seems to me remarkably close to Sraffa's criticism of Marshall's partial equilibrium analysis of competitive values![12]

There are only two kinds of objections possible: that an illegitimate assumption has been introduced, or that the assumption is unrealistic (in the latter case the distinction between the logical confines of the model and the real-world happenings that it is intended to illuminate becomes relevant). The optimist will admit the distinction but will add that when he or she understands how to work with a simple model a more complicated one will be constructed, and so the gap, it is hoped, will be narrowed and eventually closed. While Robinson continued to hold this view in *The Economics of Imperfect Competition*, she was later to agree with Kaldor[13] that this was akin to chasing a will-o'-the-wisp, at least within the neoclassical approach of which she was then an expositor, albeit already a critical one. She adds that the optimistic economist must not attack 'the pessimistic economist [who] prefers sitting at the apex of a pyramid of completely self-consistent, realistic but intractable assumptions to solving unrealistic problems' (pp. 7–8); they must just agree to differ.

She also refers to 'the bad habit of the English economists of never giving a proper account of their assumptions' (p. 8) – the Marshallian vice which had led Keynes always to search for the hidden assumptions in other people's work (while not always revealing the assumptions of his own).[14] She asserts that the fundamental assumption on which 'the present simple technique of analysis is based is that each individual person acts in a sensible manner from the point of view of his own economic interests' (p. 10). More than 40 years on, modern micro theory is still working out the implications of assuming a world of greedy people (to use Frank Hahn's phrase) doing the best they can for themselves in a competitive environment. Robinson in 1932 hoped that the optimistic economists would evolve 'a technique which would allow them to assume the existence of whatever other human motives have an influence in the economic sphere' (p. 10), a criticism that was neither novel nor new then and which is usually countered by the orthodox theorist with the argument that a sharp cutting edge is needed to obtain clear-cut, definite *analytical* results.

The job of the 'methodological pessimist' is to remove from the analysts' toolbox 'all tools which appear to involve conceptions that are not capable of measurement' (p. 11). (The toolbox became a favourite metaphor of Robinson's – its origin is to be found in the Sidney Ball Lecture at Oxford by Pigou in 1929.) This move from motives to measurement is, of course, a different criticism. Many years later, Robinson was in a sense hoist with her own petard when critics interpreted her strictures in the capital theory debates as relating solely to the measurement of 'capital'. She herself primarily had in mind its meaning and whether its meaning as a concept could be made coherent within the neoclassical framework. But it is no surprise that in 1932 'utility', 'a quantitative concept that there is no known way of measuring', was mentioned as one such concept that should be removed and that her marginal note at this point reads, 'Aside for DHR'. It is also no surprise that key chapters in *The General Theory* are concerned with measurement, preciseness and appropriate units of measurement in theory and that Sraffa was later (1961), in a well-known passage, to laud the necessity of absolute precision in theoretical work if it were to avoid incoherence.

I had thought that Robinson herself would have heartily approved these sentiments, both then and later. But would she? In the preface to *The Accumulation of Capital* (1956) , she writes that 'it is ... no use framing definitions [of the concepts and categories required for the analysis of accumulation] more precise than the subject-matter to which they apply'. She quotes with approval from Popper on appropriate measurement and meaning and adds: 'Economic concepts such as wealth, output, income and cost are no easier to define precisely than wind. Nevertheless these concepts are useful, and economic problems can be discussed' (pp. viii–ix). Was she then subject like the British economy (according to Nigel Lawson) to 'blips'? For if she was later to criticize the orthodox for not being clear about what *they* meant by 'profits' and 'capital', for example, why was she not open to the same criticism of her own work? Or was she adopting Keynes's message: 'To say that net output today is greater, but the price level lower, than ten years ago or one year ago, is a proposition of a similar character to the statement that Queen Victoria was a better queen but not a happier woman than Queen Elizabeth [I] – a proposition not without meaning and not without interest, but unsuitable as material for the differential calculus'? For he immediately added: 'Our precision will be a mock precision if we try to use such partly vague and non-quantitative concepts as the basis for quantitative analysis'

(1936, p. 40). Nevertheless, as Robert Dixon has reminded me, Robinson did write a follow-up essay (1962) to *The Accumulation of Capital*, partly in order to get the definitions and so on clearer.[15]

It seems, though, that the English may be pessimists after all and that the pure ones 'who like Nothing but Facts'[16] dampen the spirits of the optimists. However, the logical ones, 'of whom Mr. Shove is the prototype', have a beneficial effect: they propose new sets of assumptions which are too hard for existing techniques to handle, but at the same time they use their own methods to 'prospect for more complicated techniques adapted to realistic problems', thus ensuring the continuing development of the techniques themselves.[17]

Shove (19 October 1932) declared himself 'a little hurt' by the implications of Robinson's argument. She seemed to suggest (but could she *really* mean this?) that economists should concentrate for the time being on solving problems which the existing techniques could handle. Shove thought they could and should get to work immediately to develop a technique capable of dealing with assumptions not at present tractable but rather nearer to reality (and that this would not prevent them using now any existing techniques for suitable problems). This was what Shove himself had been trying to do for several years; hence he was 'a little hurt' by being publicly relegated to the duty of suggesting 'fresh problems for you to solve'.

IV

Finally, the argument of the pamphlet moves to the plain man, and here an analogy with physiology and medicine is used. Just as inadequate knowledge of physiology 'led in the past to a medicine that killed more patients than it cured', so in the past hundred years 'an economics, at once primitive and over-confident, [had] done more harm than good in the sphere of political life' (p. 13). Nevertheless, we should continue to give advice to governments but should 'explain frankly the limitations of [our] knowledge'. For governments have been alienated by our 'unjustified self-assurance', which 'has led them to prefer the advice of bankers, industrialists and other practical men' – has *anything* changed? Robinson closes on a prophetic note for today: it is better for a patient to ask a physiologist what is wrong with him than to ask the first person met – for the latter 'may be an undertaker who has his own view on the course that the disease ought to follow' (p. 14).

V

If we may judge from the letters that Robinson received, the arguments of *Economics is a Serious Subject* were not universally accepted by those for whom it was intended. The most charming response came from Mary Paley Marshall:

Balliol Croft,
6 Madingly Road,
Cambridge.

28.x.32

My Dear Joan,

I am so pleased to have your Apologia with its charming inscription. It is not easy reading to one whose economics are rather rusty and I can't be sure at present whether I am an optimist or a pessimist but I shall work away and find out and meanwhile call myself

Your affectionate friend
Mary P. Marshall

Piero Sraffa (Thursday, no month or year) thanked Robinson for the pamphlet and 'for the anonymous dedication'. He wanted to know who was 'the idiotic Continental economist', the one who was at the apex, and added that 'any how he had no right to disgrace a whole continent'. On 31 October 1932, Sraffa wrote that he agreed that they disagreed 'right at the bottom' and with that their agreement ended. He would regard as 'mystical bunk' a statement that there was no possibility of having a serious subject which dealt with the behaviour of human beings. He also had no doubts about the seriousness of economics, though he did think that economics had taken the place in modern times that theology had had in the Middle Ages ('and there was never anything as serious as that'). It was exactly because theology could not stand rational criticism that it was possible to have a scientific study of its objects. 'The fog is not outside, or in the air or in human society, but inside the heads of theologians (and economists).'

The mathematician, Newman, thought that Robinson had not quite made out her case, 'if you are *really* justifying your subject to the Three Persons on the cover, and not trying to cure your colleagues of a number of "beastly practices"'. He made a number of methodological criticisms. Unless economics was to be identical in method and content with pure mathematics, assumptions could not be 'quite arbitrary' but 'like physics must have some relation to a certain class of phenomena'. The ultimate aim must be to make some predictions about these phenomena. To be a serious subject, economics has to have some class of objects 'of tolerable complexity' for which theory 'gives approximately correct results', something analogous to Newton's first law which was confirmed by a study of the planets. From the start there must be some application possible to *real* phenomena. The pamphlet had not developed this but rather suggested the opposite and did not give examples.[18] He summed up his objection: Robinson had shown where economics would have to go to work to prove itself a serious subject – it had to show that it can find assumptions which though not too hard to handle nevertheless give results that are true for something or other. 'But to sketch this programme is not the same as actually carrying out the demonstration' – a criticism that was to be levelled against much of Robinson's work (not least by herself) in the years to come. Her ultimate response was different, as we saw above.

Charles Gifford (writing from Graduate College, Princeton, 26 November 1932) urged her to be 'more militant and less philosophically tolerant' of the pessimists, as he himself was, advice she certainly took in later years. He wondered in a postscript whether she was 'really a Shovian pessimist'. Hubert Henderson (31 October 1932) wrote that he disagreed fundamentally with her view that 'economists must state their faith in their technique and not search for the truth but a self-consistent system of ideas' – an uncanny prophecy to be delivered on her twenty-ninth birthday about her later ideas.

Richard Kahn (Monday 11.20 p.m., no date, King's College) sent her a glorious Sraffian anecdote, which may have originated at a three-way discussion between Kahn, Keynes and Sraffa about her pamphlet: JMK: 'Your assumption, Piero, is that there is no such subject as economics. Kahn is assuming that there is such a subject.'

VI

Evidently, some little time after Robinson wrote *Economics is a Serious Subject*, she also prepared a nine-page typed memorandum titled 'Teaching economics', which has never been published.[19] Joseph Schumpeter came to know of both through Richard Kahn, who used to look after him when he visited Cambridge, usually twice a year. Robinson's papers include four letters from Schumpeter, three to her, one to Kahn, for the year 1933, in which both the pamphlet and more especially the memorandum on teaching are discussed and very much approved.

Schumpeter's old-world charm, courtesy and subtle (perhaps!) flattery, of which he was well aware, are to be seen to very good effect in these letters. He mentions that 'our friend Kahn' had told him of the memorandum and that Robinson 'was perfectly ready to tell [him her] ideas about the subject beyond that memorandum. [While Schumpeter would not have] the impertinence to ask [her] to go to the trouble of lecturing [him] on the teaching of economics [he] should be very grateful indeed … if he could have a copy' (2 Scott Street, Cambridge, Mass., 20 March 1933). On 15 May, he wrote from Harvard that 'he had learnt a lot especially from the memo'. He approved of the physiologist–doctor analogy: 'In fundamentals we fully agree – in fact it is a stock phrase of mine that the economist should aim to be the physiologist rather than the doctor of the economic organism, and that his practical contribution should consist in sharing in the training of the "doctors" as it means teaching them tools and neither aims nor experience, which are both entirely out of place.'

Schumpeter liked her suggestions concerning the teaching of economics, feeling that they responded harmoniously to his views of an earlier letter (20 March 1933) in which he confessed that in his 'old age' (he was 50!) he was 'getting interested much more than [he] used to be in the problems of teaching our science'. This arose out of his 'interest in young people generally' and of the 'conviction which more and more impose[d] itself upon [him], that our teaching is hopelessly inefficient [so that] when we turn out a man we have a feeling ... that he really knows nothing and ought not to be let loose. [While we have] little reason to be satisfied with the state of our science [it is] undeniable that what we succeed in transmitting to the victims of our pedagogical efforts is still less than the science itself is able to give'.

The memorandum on teaching may be seen as a forerunner of *Exercises in Economic Analysis* (Robinson, 1960a). Both advocated a 'do-it-yourself' technique for students as the best way of mastering both the concepts and the techniques of economic analysis. Both works contain concrete examples of how pupil and teacher may respond to each other's efforts. Robinson concluded the memorandum with the hope that 'by such means the propositions at one time considered advanced can be brought within the grasp of beginners within a few weeks. The students can be saved from falling either into [the] sulky acquiescence of the unconvinced pessimist or the glib self-assurance of the unchecked optimist, and the subject can be freed from the miasma of mysticism and given a clear and definite outline in the light of common sense' (p. 9).

VII

In the event very little of the original pamphlet survived in the Introduction to Robinson's *Economics of Imperfect Competition*. The Pigovian tool-maker and -user analogy starts off the Introduction. This book was to provide some new tools for the tool-user. The gap between the real world and the application of theory is again stressed and traced to the nature of assumptions and to the conflict between realism and tractability. Robinson stresses the need always to make assumptions explicit, something she tried to do in her book. (She mentions the possibility that people may not always *know* what their assumptions are.) The analytical economist, she says, is conscious of 'an agonising sense of shame' in the presence of the plain man. This gives rise to a strong temptation either to include realistic assumptions, which, however, make the problem insoluble, 'or to confine the problem within the limits that make it soluble but to hide the assumptions ... in a dusty corner of the footnotes where he hopes no one will notice them' (p.2) – an obvious reference to Marshall and his desire that his *Principles* be read by businessmen.

So we should be quite open, as she has tried to be in her book, and approach the problem 'by the only route along which there is even a chance of finding the answer' (p. 3).

But, as she was later to tell us in 'Thinking about thinking' (1979, pp. 110–19), she 'soon ceased to believe in its main argument ... that to avoid unacceptable methods of argument is a necessary but not a sufficient condition for establishing a genuine discipline' (p. 110). Her 'old saying about technique was a half truth. The other half concerns the subject to which technique is applied ... the proper subject matter of economics is the examination of the manner of operation of various economic systems' (p. 119).[20] It was to *that* end that Joan Robinson was notably to contribute in the years that followed her first excursion into that heart-sinking subject, the scope and method of a serious subject.

Notes

I thank but in no way implicate Conrad Blyth, Robert Dixon, Richard Kahn, Jan Kregel, Tony Lawson, Donald Moggridge, Peter Nolan, Terry O'Shaughnessy, and Austin Robinson for their comments on a draft of this essay. I am especially indebted to Bob Coats for a wide-ranging set of comments and suggestions for extensions, of which I have tried, I fear inadequately, to take account in the final draft.

1. 'Beauty and the beast' was written jointly with her friend Dorothea Morison (later Mrs R.B. Braithwaite) while Robinson was still an undergraduate, but it was not published until 1951 in her first volume of collected papers. In the April 1930 issue of the *Fabian Quarterly* she published a review of *The Problem of Industrial Relations* by Henry Clay. (I am indebted to Cristina Marcuzzo for this information.)

2. A more optimistic note was sounded in the Preface to volume 5 of her collected papers (1979), where she writes of her theoretical works in the collection that they 'operate on two planes, an attempt to get the logic clear in a tightly specified model and an attempt to loosen it up in the form of approximations to make it useful for discussion of actual problems'. She adds: 'On the logical plane, I frequently had occasion to complain of the inability of neo-neoclassical writers to distinguish between a *difference* in the parameters of an equilibrium model and the effects of a *change* taking place at a moment of time' (p. vii).

3. We may note in passing, as Bob Coats (1 May 1989) has pointed out to me, that one of Robinson's pupils at this time was Terence Hutchison, who subsequently was to emerge as a major contributor to the literature in English on economic methodology. Coats's review of Hutchison's writings suggests that Robinson's pamphlet had a significant impact on him, 'either originating his interest in methodology ... or stimulating it further'.

4. I am greatly indebted to Michael Halls, the modern archivist of the library of King's College, Cambridge for allowing me access to Joan Robinson's papers, for his personal help, and for his *Hand List* of the papers. All my references to letters and manuscripts relate to this collection.

5. It may have been Keynes who persuaded Robinson to omit the dedications from the published version. He wrote (46 Gordon Square, 21 October 1932[?]) that 'the dedications at [the] end [were] too esoteric for publication ... no one would have the slightest idea who [they stood for]'. I report them in the appendix to this essay, both for their intrinsic interest and for the insight that they give into Robinson's assessments of the characteristics and characters of her contemporaries.

6. She gave her own account of why many years later in 'Thinking about thinking' (1979, pp. 110–19).

7. Shove and Robinson also had an exchange in the *Economic Journal* over her paper 'Imperfect competition and falling supply price' (1932b), to which Shove responded and she replied, both in the next quarterly issue (Robinson, 1933c; Shove, 1933). (It was remarkable how quickly papers could be published in those days.) In a letter to James Meade (21 February 1933) from 3 Trumpington Street, Cambridge, Robinson wrote: 'You will see in the *E.J.* some backchat between me & Gerald. When I talked to him I found a far more deep and subtle difference in our methods than could be put into print at the last moment ... I don't think there is any difference in results, but I am not sure till I have another go at him.' I am indebted to Warren Young for bringing this letter to my attention and to James Meade for allowing me to quote from the letter, which is in the Meade papers at the British Library.

8. In the manuscript *I* is underlined and a marginal comment reads: 'For JMK who thought he was the one to think of it.' This was the time when the deliberations of the 'circus' on the *Treatise on Money* were much in their minds and also when Robinson was writing, as we can now see, two progress reports (1933b, 1933d) on where the thinking in Cambridge had got to on the road from the *Treatise on Money* to the *General Theory*. For a precise dating, in the summer, and the winter and spring, respectively, of 1931, see *The Collected Writings of John Maynard Keynes*, Vol. XIII, pp. 268, 342.

9. Perhaps even more to the point, she wrote: 'I was delighted to find in a dictionary the word mumpsimus, which means stubborn persistence in an error after it has been exposed' (1978, p. xix). (The couplet is a slight paraphrase from Samuel Butler's *Hudibras*, canto 3.)

10. John Maloney (1985, pp. 51–2) has put his finger on the reason why there were these differences between Joan Robinson and Keynes, on the one hand, and Marshall, on the other. Marshall, he says, was 'a timid man' but not 'a particularly modest one', that his 'characteristic mixture of timidity, conscientiousness, anxiety to be liked, priggishness and vanity suggests a highly introverted man who would temperamentally be more interested in resolving his own contradictions than the disagreements of his colleagues'. Neither Keynes nor Robinson could be called timid; both were noted for their courage, as well, it must be said, as for their arrogance.

11. How thoroughly she subsequently took on board his criticism is well illustrated in, for example, her 1953 lecture by a Cambridge economist at Oxford (Robinson, 1953). Jan Kregel reminds me that Robinson always claimed that, while *The Economics of Imperfect Competition* was inspired by the hint from Sraffa, the main influence was Pigou, who 'seemed to have reduced Marshall's *Principles* to a logical and consistent scheme' in which nevertheless 'there was an obvious defect, [to wit, that] "price equals marginal cost"' (Robinson, 1978, p. xi).

12. Bob Coats remarks (16 February 1989) that in so far as Robinson did recognize the kind of objections that Leontief was later to express, was she not 'quite prescient ... already, in 1932, half-way out of her Marshallian heritage – though *Imperfect Competition* is very Marshallian?'

13. 'It is the hallmark of the neoclassical economist to believe that, however severe the abstractions from which he is forced to start, he will "win through" by the end of the day – bit by bit, if he only carries the analysis far enough, the scaffolding can be removed, leaving the basic structure intact. In fact, these props are never removed; the removal of any one of them ... is sufficient to cause the whole structure to collapse like a pack of cards' (Kaldor, 1966, p. 310).

14. Bob Coats (16 February 1989) has suggested to me that the device of concealing assumptions was not peculiarly British but more the characteristic of literary economists, wherever they may have come from. He added that 'in Marshallian economics...the assumptions were hidden not so much for the sake of concealment, but because everybody "who mattered" knew what they were anyway. They were ... taken for granted.... Also businessmen did not want to be given a list of assumptions.' Bob has always been charitable.

15. Bob Coats (16 February 1989) has remarked to me that her emphasis on measurement is curious and not particularly Marshallian, though perhaps more sympathetic to the views

expressed by Wesley Mitchell in his 1925 Presidential Address to the American Economic Association (Mitchell, 1925). There Mitchell took as his starting-point Marshall's claim in the early years of this century that 'qualitative analysis [had] done the greater part of its work' and that the 'higher and more difficult task' of quantitative analysis 'must wait for the slow growth of thorough realistic statistics' (p. 1). He argued by contrast that 'the increase in statistical data, the improvement of statistical technique, and the endowment of social research are enabling economists to make a larger use of quantitative analysis' (p. 9). This in turn had led the quantitative theorists to 'bring about radical changes in economic theory ... to make the treatment of behaviour more objective, to emphasise the importance of institutions, and to promote the development of an experimental technique' (pp. 9–10). His view was to be contrasted with the then prevailing view that quantitative analysis was but the handmaiden of qualitative analysis. Mitchell himself thought that we must put 'our ultimate trust in observation' (p. 11), a view which both Robinson and Kaldor were later strongly to endorse.

16. The marginal comment reads 'One for Rowe', a reference to J.W.F. Rowe, a Fellow of Pembroke whose main work was the study of commodities.

17. In the letter to James Meade referred to above, in note 7, Robinson wrote: 'I am very pleased to have got [Shove] into print. It illustrates my "optimists and pessimists" very nicely.'

18. Peter Nolan has suggested to me that this is the absolutely fundamental failure of economics, as much now as when Newman wrote this. I think I agree with him.

19. I added this section to the essay after reading Marjorie Turner's account (1989, pp. 21–22) of the reactions to *Economics is a Serious Subject* in the United States. It drew my attention to the relevance of the letters from Joseph Schumpeter to Robinson for the issues discussed in her pamphlet.

20. In another place and earlier, she said: 'The purpose of studying economics is not to acquire a set of ready-made answers to economic questions, but to learn how to avoid being deceived by economists' (1960b, p. 17).

References

Gram, Harvey and Vivian Walsh (1983), 'Joan Robinson's economics in retrospect', *Journal of Economic Literature*, **21** (June), pp. 518–50.

Hahn, F.H. (1987), 'Information, dynamics and equilibrium', *Scottish Journal of Political Economy*, **34**, (4) (November), pp. 321–34.

Hahn, F.H. (1988), 'Hicksian themes on stability', paper presented to the IEA Conference, '*Value and Capital* after fifty years', Bologna, pp. 1–24. Subsequently published in Lionel McKenzie and Stefano Zamagini (eds.) *Fifty Years of Value and Capital*, London: Macmillan, 1991.

Kaldor, N. (1934), 'A classificatory note on the determinateness of equilibrium', *Review of Economic Studies*, **1**, pp. 122–36; reprinted in *Collected Essays*, vol. 1, *Essays on Value and Distribution*, London: Duckworth, 1960, pp. 13–33.

Kaldor, N. (1966), 'Marginal productivity and the macroeconomic theories of distribution', *Review of Economic Studies*, **33**, pp. 309–19; reprinted in *Collected Essays*, vol. 5, *Further Essays on Economic Theory*, London: Duckworth, 1978, pp. 81–99.

Kaldor, N. (1985), *Economics without Equilibrium*, the Okun Memorial Lectures at Yale University, Cardiff: University College Cardiff Press.

Keynes, J.M. (1933), *Essays in Biography*, London: Macmillan; reprinted in *Collected Writings*, vol. X, London: Macmillan, for the Royal Economic Society, 1972.

Keynes, J.M. (1936), *The General Theory of Employment, Interest and Money*, London: Macmillan; reprinted in *Collected Writings*, Vol. VII, London: Macmillan, for the Royal Economic Society, 1973.

Leontief, Wassily (1966), *Essays in Economics: Theories and Theorising*, Vol. 1, Oxford: Basil Blackwell.

Lutz, F.A. and D.C. Hague (eds) (1961), *The Theory of Capital*, London: Macmillan.

Maloney, John (1985), *Marshall, Orthodoxy and the Professionalisation of Economics*, Cambridge: Cambridge University Press.

Mitchell, Wesley C. (1925), 'Quantitative analysis in economic theory', *American Economic Review*, **15**, (1) (March), pp. 1–12.

Pigou, A.C. (1929), 'The functions of economic analysis', Sidney Ball Lecture; reprinted in A.C. Pigou and D.H. Robertson, *Economic Essays and Addresses*, London: P.S. King & Son, 1931, pp. 1–20.

Robinson, Joan (1932a), *Economics is a Serious Subject: the Apologia of an Economist to the Mathematician, the Scientist and the Plain Man*, Cambridge: W. Heffer & Sons.

Robinson, Joan (1932b), 'Imperfect competition and falling supply price', *Economic Journal*, **42**, (168) (December), pp. 544–54.

Robinson, Joan (1933a), *The Economics of Imperfect Competition*, London: Macmillan; 2nd edn, 1969.

Robinson, Joan (1933b), 'A parable on savings and investment', *Economica*, **13**, (39) (February), pp. 75–84.

Robinson, Joan (1933c), 'Comment on Shove', *Economic Journal*, **43**, (169) (March), pp. 124–5.

Robinson, Joan (1933d), 'The theory of money and the analysis of output', *Review of Economic Studies*, **1** (October), pp. 23–6; reprinted in *Collected Economic Papers*, Oxford: Basil Blackwell, 1951, 1978, pp. 52–8.

Robinson, Joan (1953), 'A lecture delivered at Oxford by a Cambridge economist', in *On Rereading Marx*, pp. 10–18, Cambridge Students' Bookshops Ltd; reprinted in *Collected Economic Papers*, **4**, Oxford: Basil Blackwell, 1973, pp. 254–63.

Robinson, Joan (1956), *The Accumulation of Capital*, London: Macmillan.

Robinson, Joan (1960a), *Exercises in Economic Analysis*, London: Macmillan.

Robinson, Joan (1960b), *Collected Economic Papers*, Vol. 2, Oxford: Basil Blackwell.

Robinson, Joan (1962), *Essays in the Theory of Economic Growth*, London: Macmillan.

Robinson, Joan (1978), *Contributions to Modern Economics*, Oxford: Basil Blackwell.

Robinson, Joan (1979), *Collected Economic Papers*, Vol. 5, Oxford: Basil Blackwell.

Robinson, Joan and Dorothea Morison (1951), 'Beauty and the beast', in Robinson, *Collected Economic Papers*, **1**, Oxford: Basil Blackwell, 1951, pp. 225–34.

Shove, G.F. (1933), 'The imperfection of the market: a further note', *Economic Journal*, **43**, (169) (March), pp. 111–24.

Sraffra, Piero (1926), 'The laws of returns under competitive conditions', *Economic Journal*, **36**, (December), pp. 535–50.

Sraffa, Piero (1930), 'A criticism and rejoinder', *Economic Journal*, **40** (March), pp. 89–93.

Sraffa, Piero (1961), 'Interventions in the debate at the Corfu Conference on "The Theory of Capital"', in Lutz and Hague (1961), pp. 305–6.

Turner, Marjorie (1989), *Joan Robinson and the Americans*, London/Armonk, NY: M.E. Sharpe.

APPENDIX: dedications listed in the manuscript of *Economics is a Serious Subject*

This pamphlet is presented to

ACP [Pigou]	The first serious optimist – with the gratitude of all who will follow him.
JMK [Keynes]	To the optimist who showed that optimism can be justified.
GFS [Shove]	To the English pessimist who beat them at their own game.
DHR [Robertson]	To the serious economist who does not quite like serious economics.
HM [Helen Makower]	To the pessimist who likes facts, with the apologies of an optimist.
CG [Charles Gifford]	To the economist who knew it all, but never said so.
PS [Sraffa]	To the pessimist who knew he could not trust us but asked the technique.
Mrs TH [Marjorie Tappan Hollond]	To the economist who thinks that the shield is white.
RFK and EAGR [Kahn and Austin Robinson]	To the co-optimists and the optimistic pessimists and all serious economists.
MHAN [Newman]	And to the pure mathematician whose sympathy and well-deserved contempt have had a beneficial effect on the serious economist.

7   Accumulation and the rate of profits: reflections on the issues raised in the correspondence between Maurice Dobb, Joan Robinson and Gerald Shove*[1]

Introduction

One of Joan Robinson's favourite sayings was: 'As I never learnt mathematics, I have had to think.' A by-product of this characteristic is that her writings abound with striking intuitive propositions, often tossed off as asides from the flow of the main argument. Both Richard Goodwin and Frank Hahn have attested to her uncanny logical powers and 'feel'. Thus, Goodwin (1989, p. 916) writes:

> Schumpeter once said to me that Böhm-Bawerk was remarkable for the fact that he could see the resolution of complex logical and even mathematical problems without any knowledge of mathematics. This was also true ... for Joan ... Once I was giving a paper on a two-sector, dynamical model, in the course of which I said that both sectors would exhibit both motions. She interrupted to say that I was wrong: there was only one motion. I denied this ... But I was bothered and later ... discovered that she was right since the system was degenerate!

Hahn (1989, p. 896) is less generous, but he does concede that

> Joan had a number of very important things to say. If she had been trained in mathematics and had been technically more competent she could really have done more to clinch them. The things she had to say were: (1) That the future is very important to the present. That was all lost in the malleable neoclassical models with one capital good: one could always undo the capital good and consume it ... a very strong point ... (2) She was very good in trying to distinguish between equilibrium comparisons and causal stories ... comparative statics, or comparative dynamics, compared to genuine causal stories.

We mention this aspect of Joan Robinson's personality as the introduction to the history of one such aside. In his review article of Joan Robinson's 1942 *Essay on Marxian Economics*, Gerald Shove criticized her comment:

* Written with J.A.T.R. Araujo. A revised version of 'Maurice Dobb, Joan Robinson and Gerald Shove on Accumulation and the Rate of Profits' and 'An Addendum', both originally published in the *Journal of the History of Economic Thought*, Spring, 1993, pp. 1–24, pp. 24–30.

> The equilibrium rate of profit is that rate which induces zero net investment. But over the course of history since the Industrial Revolution began, net investment has always been going on. The actual rate of profit, therefore, good years with bad, has exceeded the equilibrium rate. Abnormal profits are the normal rule. (Joan Robinson, 1942, pp. 60–61)

Michael Lawlor found in the Keynes papers in the Library of King's College, Cambridge a batch of letters which contained fascinating exchanges between Joan Robinson and Shove, and Maurice Dobb and Shove, about this proposition and Joan Robinson's response to Shove's criticism of it following the publication of his review article in the March 1944 issue of the *Economic Journal*. As the letters are in the Keynes papers, may we suppose that Keynes as editor of the *Economic Journal* asked Dobb to look at Shove's article and Joan's response to it?

In this chapter we bring to the reader's attention the relevant aspects of the arguments of the letters. When we wrote Araujo and Harcourt (1993a), we had not yet been able to trace some of Shove's replies to Dobb's letters. We thought that, if they were anywhere, they would be in the collection of Dobb's papers which is housed in the Wren Library, but as they had not yet been catalogued we were not allowed access to them. As we mentioned in the opening endnote, they have now been found and catalogued. There are nine additional letters, eight by Shove, one by Joan Robinson, all to Dobb.[2] We try to show who was 'right', first within a Marshallian framework which Joan Robinson and Shove were using, slightly tinged by that of Keynes of *The General Theory*; then within an analytical framework based on the *The General Theory* and developed by Paul Davidson in *Money and the Real World* (1972); and, finally, within an analytical framework which has classical *cum* Marxian *cum* Keynesian/Kaleckian roots and which formed the basis of the central model of Joan Robinson's *magnum opus, The Accumulation of Capital* (1956) and later works. We show that it is possible to have growth maintained with positive net investment and the natural (if not the normal or equilibrium?) rate of profits being received. One of our aims is to illustrate some aspects of the transition in Joan Robinson's approach from her Marshallian–Keynesian framework period of the mid- to late 1930s to her mature 'vision' of the workings of capitalism in which the contributions of Keynes, Kalecki and Marx – and Piero Sraffa – are combined in a coherent whole, not least to give a convincing answer to her original claim – albeit *not* the answer which her initial intuition suggested it would be!

Procedure in the *Essay*

The procedure that Joan Robinson adopted in her 1942 *Essay* was to compare and contrast Marx's economic theories with the corresponding orthodox theories as she perceived them. Thus, when she came to the relationship between accumulation and the rate of profits, she discussed both the Marxian and the orthodox theories of accumulation and what determined the rate of profits in their respective accounts. This led to the proposition we noted above. Implied in this passage is an early statement of her views on Marshall's work, in particular what she perceived as a contradiction or inconsistency in his thought, an unresolved tension between his analytical framework which was basically static and his vision of an evolutionary, accumulating, changing system moving forward through actual time. It was not until she had persuaded herself that there was no coherent theory of profit in the orthodox theory but that there was in the classicals and Marx, especially as presented by Sraffa in his Introduction to the Ricardo volumes, Sraffa with Dobb (1951),[3] that she was able to postulate in principle a model of an accumulating, growing economy in which net investment was always positive, yet only the natural or competitive rate of profits was being received.[4] In doing so she partially reprieves Marshall and moves on from her 1942 interpretation.

Here is a typical statement, taken from *Economic Heresies*, Joan Robinson (1971):

> The notion of the supply price of capital being the 'reward of waiting' was invented by Marshall, but he never really reconciled himself to the confines of a stationary state. In his vision of contemporary capitalism, as opposed to his formal analysis, 'progress' is taking place. He can best be understood if we set his argument in a kind of near-enough golden age with steady overall accumulation going on and a more or less constant overall rate of profit. Profits in particular industries go up and down around a central 'normal' level, and the total stock of capital is continuously growing. This model (...) has something in common with the classics, since it depicts growth; but it is radically different in its theory of profits. For the classics, the real-wage rate is given in terms of the commodities that the workers consume; the rate of profit then emerges as a residual. For Marshall, the rate of profit is given and the real-wage rate in terms of all commodities emerges as a residual. (1971, pp. 13–14)

In a sense Joan Robinson's original proposition is the opposite of Keynes's theory of investment, as set out by Abba Lerner (1944), where Keynes's failure to distinguish between the marginal efficiency of investment (*mei*) and the marginal efficiency of capital (*mec*) is put right. In Lerner's analysis, full (stock and flow) equilibrium requires equality between the *mec*, the *mei* and the rate of interest (*i*). Net investment is zero because the *mec* equals the *mei* on replacement investment when the optimum stock of capital goods, for the given initial conditions including the value of *i*, has been established. The approach to this, in effect, Marshallian long-period equilibrium position is analysed by assuming a new lower level of *i* and then establishing the conditions for short-period flow equilibrium per unit of time, to wit, that net investment is such that the *mei* equals *i*, but both are *less* than the *mec* of the existing stock of capital goods which is, however, no longer the *desired* stock. (The lower i has made another, higher level optimal.) Full long-period equilibrium – but only after many periods – will be established again when the $mei = mec =$ the (now lower) i. Thus net investment over the interval has been induced by the need to deepen the stock of capital, as a result of the change in relative factor prices.

We should note that, in an article published in 1936, Joan Robinson set out an analysis which was similar in outline to Lerner's but differed in detail because she, like Keynes, did not distinguish explicitly between the *mec* and the *mei*. In Robinson (1936, 1937) there is an explicit attempt to apply the new Keynesian analysis of effective demand (combined with the neoclassical marginal productivity theory of distribution using the then fashionable concept of the elasticity of substitution) in a Marshallian long-period setting, to see whether some of the new results, such as the paradox of thrift, held also for the long period. Starting from a long-period equilibrium position, she supposes that the ruling rate of interest changes, usually that it falls. This induces a process of deepening:

> A fall in the rate of interest will increase capital per head, so that a given output is produced by fewer workers using more 'roundabout' methods. The marginal physical productivity of capital will be reduced and of labour increased, and the rate of real wages will rise. (Joan Robinson, 1937, p. 82)

The process continues until the new long-period equilibrium capital–labour ratio is established. Net investment is then zero and the then established *mec* equals the rate of interest. One question which she asks, which need not concern us further here, is whether this new equilibrium level of the economy will be associated with sustained unemployment. On the way to this equilibrium, the *mec* in her terms, the *mei* in Lerner's, is *above* both the ruling rate of interest and the ultimately established *mec*. She does not have an explicit analysis of the short-period equilibrium flow of net investment per period of time on the way to the full stock-flow long-period equilibrium position, but her story here is clearly consistent with what she wrote in her 1942 *Essay*.[5]

Although Keynes is not very explicit on all this, many commentators have interpreted his theory of investment as one of widening or expanding capacity regardless of changes in either methods of production or relative factor prices; or, perhaps more accurately, vaguely conceding their influence while concentrating more on stimulus to confidence, to a sense of improved sales in the future so as to encourage more investment now. Certainly, the Lerner process is not what is occurring in a simple Golden Age model when only a widening process occurs and we discuss the conditions whereby a steady advance with full employment of both labour and capital goods is possible, the impetus for growth being, say, the growth of the labour force. (We abstract from technical progress, though, obviously, with Joan Robinson's reference to the Industrial Revolution, that is something which in principle should not be done.)

We proceed as follows. In the next section we summarize the debate between Joan Robinson and Shove, and Dobb and Shove concerning the original proposition. In the fourth section we outline a possible solution to their debates using Davidson's approach. In the fifth section we digress on the aspects of the exchanges between Dobb and Shove which anticipate elements of the postwar theories of growth. In the sixth section we set out the solution implied in Joan Robinson's later work. We end with a short concluding section.

Basic proposition

Joan Robinson's basic proposition means that, *within the Marshallian framework*, the actual rate of profits would permanently exceed the 'normal' (equilibrium) rate of profits in an expanding system. The equilibrium situation is characterized by zero net investment, that is when 'the stock of capital is in equilibrium, tending neither to increase nor diminish' (Joan Robinson, 1942, pp. 54–5). Accordingly, the normal rate of profits 'is equal to the supply price of the existing stock of capital' (ibid.). (In Lerner's terms, this was to become $mec = mei = i$ in full stock-flow equilibrium).

Shove countered as follows:

> There is no *logical* inconsistency between an expanding system and the maintenance of an 'equilibrium' rate of profit. So long as the expansion of demand (or supply) is correctly estimated, the supply of capital and the demand for it keep in step, and the actual rate of profit ruling at any given moment is equal to the supply price of the stock existing at that moment. (Shove, 1944, p. 60)

Shove reiterated succinctly his basic objection in a letter to Dobb of 22/6/44 (Letter 8):

> By way of preface, I must explain that if Joan had said merely that, in an expanding system with the stock of capital growing, the rate of profit *may* be above the normal I should have had no quarrel with her. What I object to is her claim that it *must* be.

Thus according to Shove only unexpected changes in the demand or supply of capital would result in abnormal profits within the context of a growing economy. If demand or supply grows at a *foreseen*[6] rate, normal profits would be the rule from Shove's viewpoint.

Shove's *own* view is well illustrated in the passage below, which comes from his letter to Dobb of 7/7/44 (Letter 12):

> My contention is that in a system in which the future is foreseen correctly &, over the range with which we are concerned, all the relevant functions (curves) are continuous & show some elasticity, the stock of capital will grow (investment go on) at such a rate as to keep the demand price for the stock equal to its supply price.

In his opinion, this characterizes a *moving*, not a stationary, equilibrium. Shove points out in more than one letter that he is not concerned with the empirical relevance of Marshall's analysis, but with its logical consistency, as in the passage below:

> As I said before, I am not convinced that entrepreneurs do in fact behave in the way assumed. But that is irrelevant, since we are concerned with the question whether Marshall was wrong in his reasoning, not whether he was wrong in his facts. (Letter 12, 7/7/44)

He criticizes Joan Robinson for using two-dimensional diagrams in her third letter to him (Letter 3, 10/5/44; Letter 4, 12/5/44 and 19/5/44), because there is a third variable, time, as well as the rate of profits and the stock of capital goods to be taken into account. Nevertheless, his own argument is implicitly conducted in terms of a two-dimensional diagram, in which the demand for capital curve (represented by the marginal product of capital schedule) and the supply of capital curve (represented by the supply price of

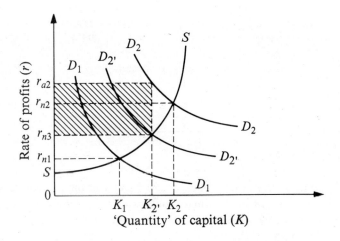

Figure 7.1

capital schedule, which is not precisely defined at this stage) are depicted: see Figure 7.1.

In Figure 7.1, which is based on Joan Robinson's diagrams (Letter 3, 10/5/44), the initial equilibrium configuration is given by the intersection of the supply curve SS and the demand curve D_1D_1. The subscript n in r_{n1} indicates that the latter is the normal rate of profits for the 'quantity' K_1 of capital. Suppose that the demand curve moves to D_2D_2; the new equilibrium configuration is (r_{n2}, K_2). If this change were to be foreseen, the expansion of demand (and the growth in the quantity supplied of capital) could be compatible with the actual rate of profits being equal to the normal rate of profits, for in this case a quantity K_2 of capital could actually be supplied. Abnormal profits could arise only if this change were not correctly estimated. Suppose that capital suppliers think that the new demand curve is $D_2D_{2'}$, so that they supply a quantity $K_{2'} < K_2$ of capital. The actual rate of profits is $r_{a2} > r_{n3}$ (the normal rate of profits on $K_{2'}$ in terms of the 'wrong' demand curve $D_2D_{2'}$). Abnormal profits are the shaded area, $(r_{a2} - r_{n3}) K_{2'}$. Shove concluded:

> Thus, profits in excess of the equilibrium rates will be 'normal' only if the expansion of demand is habitually under-estimated (or the expansion of supply habitually over-estimated) – a condition which Mrs. Robinson does not introduce into the argument, and which does not accord very well with the 'modern economists'' explanations of the trade cycle. (Shove, 1944, p. 60)

In her second letter to Shove (5/5/44), Joan Robinson argued that 'if he [the individual 'waiter'] is carrying out positive accumulation it must be because the current and prospective rates of profit are above his supply

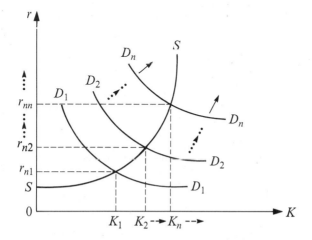

Figure 7.2

price', which is in turn equal to the normal rate of profits. Shove (Letter 4, 12/5/44 and 19/5/44) replied with an example in which the (upwardly sloping) supply curve of capital[7] is kept unchanging and the demand curve for capital moves out with the passage of time (see Figure 7.2).

This implies that the rate of profits is rising with the passage of time (because the capital supply curve *assumed for the purpose of illustration* rises to the right and is not changing). It is *not* necessary that the rate of profits should be above the investor's supply price (Letter 4, 12/5/44 and 19/5/44). In Shove's view, what is necessary for positive accumulation is that the points of intersection of the demand and supply curves are moving upwards to the right with the passage of time. In an expanding system, then, it would be more appropriate to refer to a *moving* equilibrium.[8]

Shove's definitions of equilibrium and 'normality', accordingly, were as follows: 'The system is in equilibrium when the demand price for the existing stock of capital is equal to its supply price' (Letter 12, 7/7/44). And he added:

> This amounts to be the same thing as saying that the rate of profit is normal, for it implies that the increment of probable quasi-rent just covers the rate of return on outlay required to induce the owner to provide the increment of capital, i.e. marginal efficiency of capital = rate of interest. (Letter 12, 7/7/44)

Finally, Shove based his definition of 'normality' on the following conception of the supply price of the stock of capital: 'For the supply price of a given stock of capital at a given moment of time is the marginal cost of building up that stock (...) in the *least costly way* i.e. (*inter alia*) at the rate at which includes the smallest real cost' (Letter 19, 5/8/44).

So, in the middle of the exchanges, Shove formulated, yet again, his 'crucial question':

> How can a situation such as you [Joan Robinson and Dobb] contemplate[d] come into being in a system in which the future is correctly foreseen & all the relevant curves (functions), over the range with which we are concerned, are continuous & show some elasticity?[9] (Letter 12, 7/7/44).

In his first letter to Shove (Letter 7, 15/6/44), Maurice Dobb argued that the proper supply curve of *investment* would be the locus of the *marginal supply price of investment* corresponding to each level of the rate of investment (defined as the rate of investment per unit of time). The marginal supply price of investment is defined (Letter 13, 10/7/44) as the

> inducement necessary to call forth a *given increment* of capital (stock) *per unit of time* ...; this supply price varying with the size of the increment of capital per unit

of time, so that the price associated with a rate of investment of any considerable positive quantity x is generally greater than that associated with an infinitesimal or zero rate.

With the assumption of a *given income*,[10] the marginal supply price of investment rises as the amount of investment per unit of time increases.

We assume, initially, that all capital is circulating capital, entirely used up in the course of a period of production, so we think of capital as a stock and of capital as a flow (investment = I) interchangeably. In his first letter to Shove (Letter 7, 15/6/44), Dobb observes that *if* the short-period demand curve for investment, which shows the expected rate of return at different levels of investment (or circulating capital) per unit of time, is a marginal curve, equilibrium is at the point at which the marginal expected rate of return equals the marginal supply price of investment. This marginal demand curve for investment is the marginal productivity curve of (circulating) capital. However, Dobb argues that the *average* rate of return (the average product of capital) is taken to be (possibly by the entrepreneur) the *actual* rate of return. Consider Figure 7.3.

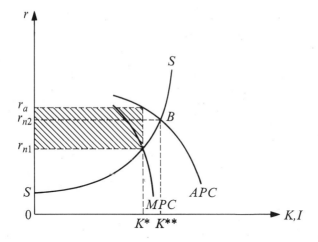

Figure 7.3

MPC stands for the marginal product of capital and *APC* for the average product of capital. *If MPC* is the appropriate demand curve for capital (investment), and if the normal rate of profits is defined as being equal to the marginal supply price of investment, the equilibrium level of capital is K^* $(= I^*)$, yielding a normal rate of profits, r_{n1}. But if the actual rate of profits corresponding to K^* is one given by the *APC* curve (r_a), at each point of time the average expected profits on investment would be above normal,[11] that is, abnormal profits $= (r_a - r_{n1})K^*$.

Dobb further observes that 'the reason why the existence of abnormal profits does not speed up investment to make abnormal profits disappear is that any further speeding up of investment reduces profitability of the investments that are in some sense marginal in any given period of time'. This, according to Dobb, would impose a limit to the growth of (annual) investment such as to 'prevent the growth of that stock from following close enough on the heels of the growth of the long-period demand for capital (marginal productivity of that stock) as to keep profits down to "normal" – and this *even* if the growth of demand is expected'.

This is *not* Dobb's main argument. He argues that the relevant short-period demand curve for investment should be the one indicating the *average* (rather than marginal) rate of profits. If the *APC* curve is the proper demand curve (see Figure 7.3) equilibrium would be at *B*, with a capital stock K^{**} and a rate of return, r_{n2}. The latter would be both actual and normal, so that normal profits would be the rule even for a growing economy. (This conclusion is valid only if normal profits are associated with the *marginal supply price of investment*.)

However, we may recall (as Dobb did) that Joan Robinson defined the normal rate of profits as being equal to the (marginal) supply price of capital. In Dobb's analysis of the determination of equilibrium there is no role for the normal rate of profits. He considered the marginal supply price of *investment* schedule to be the relevant supply curve of investment, whereas the normal rate of profits is defined by the supply price of the existing *stock* of capital.

In effect, Dobb defines the marginal supply price of the existing stock 'as the price at which, now that the existing stock is in existence, people are content to *leave it alone* – that is, to *refrain from reducing it*, or to add to their existing income by consuming it. This, I believe, is what Pigou means by maintenance-price of stock in his "Stationary States"' (Letter 13, 10/7/44). Thus Dobb identified this maintenance-price with the 'normal' price of capital. The marginal supply price of the existing capital, argues Dobb, is not compatible with positive accumulation, since it is appropriate to a *zero* rate of investment. If, as Joan Robinson did, we define the normal rate of profits as the marginal supply price of the existing capital stock, which in turn equals the maintenance-price of the stock, the actual rate of profits (which equals the marginal supply price of investment) cannot equal the normal rate of profits in an expanding economy. The marginal supply price of a positive amount of net investment must be *higher* than the marginal supply price of a *zero* amount of net investment. Otherwise, no rational capital owner would have any reason for 'waiting'.[12]

Dobb's conclusions may be summarized as follows:

(I) Expanding system (positive accumulation):
Actual rate of profits = marginal supply price of investment > marginal supply price of the existing stock of capital = maintenance-price of the stock = normal rate of profits.
(II) Stationary system (zero net investment) :
Actual rate of profits = marginal supply price of investment = marginal supply price of the existing stock of capital = maintenance-price of the stock = normal rate of profits.
(III) Contracting system (disinvestment):
Actual rate of profits = marginal supply price of investment < marginal supply price of the existing stock of capital = maintenance-price of the stock = normal rate of profits.

Dobb (Letter 20, 8/8/44) observes that, although he agrees with Joan Robinson that abnormal profits would be the rule in *any* expanding system, 'she didn't give any reasons, and I am curious to know whether the reasons she had in mind were the same as what have occurred to me or something quite different'. Indeed, it was not until Joan Robinson had absorbed Sraffa's message as well as Marx's that she had a clear-cut answer. This also makes clear why she could never find in Marshall's analytical framework a clear-cut definition of the supply price of the existing stock of capital.

We now consider Dobb's arguments and try to elucidate them in diagrams. According to Dobb (Letter 9, 27/6/44), 'I *meant* to assume as a minimum condition no more than a rising supply-curve of investment (i.e. less than perfectly elastic), and hence a marginal supply-price of investment (i.e. of the flow out of current income) that is *greater* than the marginal supply-price (Pigou's maintenance-price) of the stock existing at that period.' Dobb seems to have assumed that the maintenance-price of the stock would be constant over time (for example, Letter 9, 27/6/44). By contrast, the marginal supply price of the investment schedule (the investment supply curve) would be positively sloped because, *with the assumption of a given income*, as the amount of investment per unit of time grows, 'the marginal utility of (consumed) income rises as compared to the marginal utility of disposable income in all future years, and hence the reluctance to invest increases'. In a Keynesian world in which the growth of income (at least partially) stems from the growth of investment, a rising supply curve of investment would not necessarily follow, for the marginal utility of the consumed income may not be rising, as income itself is growing (so there is less sacrifice in saving a given proportion of income which could otherwise be consumed).

We now drop the assumption that all capital is circulating capital. The vertical axis of the diagram still shows the rates of return on invested capital, but the horizontal axis is unequivocally represented by a *continuum* of values of the amount of investment per period. We may deduce from Letter 13 (10/7/44) that Dobb and Shove apparently agreed that the demand price of investment should be defined as the 'increment in the sum of the (discounted) values of (probable) quasi-rent[s] associated ... with a *given increment in [the previously existing stock of capital] by an amount x* per unit of time. In Letter 7 [15/6/44] Dobb explained why the demand curve for investment should decline: because the investment opportunities are exhausted as the stock of capital grows and the cost of capital goods rises if the rate of investment increases (for example, as the result of both wage increases and falling productivity).

Dobb's version of the Marshallian system may be depicted as in Figure 7.4.

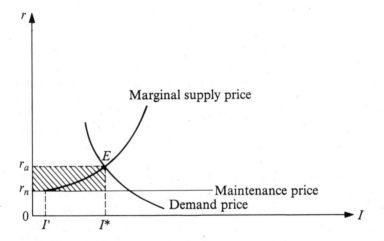

Figure 7.4

The marginal supply price of investment schedule in Figure 7.4 is assumed to be equal to the marginal supply price of the existing capital stock in the interval $0 < I < I'$; it starts to rise for values of $I > I'$. Here we follow Dobb in his interpretation of the 'supply-price of maintaining the existing stock unchanged (static stock-definition) as being identical with the supply-price of investment appropriate to a zero (or very small) rate of investment per unit of time (flow definition)'. While $0 < I < I'$, the realized rate of profits (r_a) equals the normal rate of profits (r_n). But this is a disequilibrium situation, and the amount of investment per unit of time tends to adjust to its equilibrium level, at point E, at which $r = r_a$ and $I = I^*$. Abnormal profits obtained from the newly-created capital goods I^* is the shaded area ($r_a - r_n)I^*$.

However, for most of the correspondence the authors drew attention to alternative definitions of the relevant variables involved in the present discussion. From Letter 19 (5/8/44) we note that Shove defined the normal rate of profits as being equal to the supply price of producing the stock of capital at the margin in *the least costly way*. The difference in these definitions reveals a more subtle difference between the authors with respect to their *approach* to capital accumulation.

As Dobb recognizes (Letter 16, 19/7/44), his definition of the supply price of the stock neglects the cost of producing the stock. Rather, it 'focusses attention on the price necessary to maintain that stock, once created, at an unchanged size' (Letter 16, 19/7/44). Dobb assumes that the process of accumulation starts from 'a day of creation', either the creation of the world, or capitalist society, or some such. According to him, during the 'early years' of the process of accumulation, the rate of growth of the stock of capital would be lower than the rate of growth of the demand for it, up to the point at which 'the rate of profits had *risen to a level* (i.e. above 'normal') sufficient from then onwards to *maintain a steady rate of investment*, and sufficient to increase the stock of capital as fast as the demand for it grew' (Letter 13, 10/7/44). Then, if 'normal' refers to the marginal supply price of maintaining the stock, the marginal supply price of producing additional capital goods would be above the normal rate of profits. The amount of investment per period (for example, a year) is *not* negligible, so that it raises the supply price of investment per year, which is equal to the actual rate of profits and is greater than the supply price of stock at each point of time (cf. Letter 22, 11/8/44).

Shove's approach is apparently based on a process of accumulation which proceeded from (minus) infinity, and not from a 'day of creation'. Therefore, the supply of capital goods adjusts smoothly to the demand for it, provided that the changes are foreseen. In this case, it can be said that the process of accumulation 'which spread over infinity involved only a negligible variation in the rate of investment of each *single* year' (Letter 22, 11/8/44). It follows that there is only a negligible difference between the marginal supply price of investment (when investment is realized in terms of very small additions to the capital stock) and the marginal supply price of producing the capital stock at the margin, as defined by Shove. The normal rate of profits would be (approximately) equal to both, and to the actual rate.

In three of his last four letters (Letter 16, 19/7/44; Letter 20, 8/8/44; Letter 22, 11/8/44), Dobb sets out two criticisms of Shove's approach. First, since the supply price of producing capital at the margin is usually higher, the greater is the investment rate per unit of time, Shove would have not been able to provide a *unique meaning for normal*, for the normal rate of profits would vary with changes in the amount of investment per unit of time. Secondly (and perhaps more importantly), Shove's definition of the marginal supply price of capital includes the proviso 'in the least costly way'. The 'least costly way', according to Dobb's interpretation, refers to the cost of producing a null or infinitesimally small amount of additional capital goods, that is, to the price appropriate to zero (or infinitesimally small) net investment. In this case, the normal rate of profits would be equal (or approximately equal) to Pigou's maintenance-price of the stock, and abnormal profits would again be the rule in a process of positive accumulation.

Dobb illustrated his argument by means of an unusual diagram, which was intended to represent the accumulation of capital *over time* (See Figure 7.5).

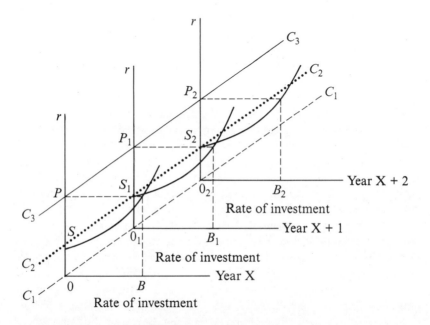

Figure 7.5

The dashed line $C_1 - C_1$ represents both the time axis and the growth of the capital stock through time. The three superimposed diagrams show how the process of accumulation takes place between specific years denoted by X, X + 1 and X + 2. They are identical, so revealing Dobbs' assumption of a constant absolute rate of investment[13] (an assumption also made by Shove). The supply curves SS, S_1S_1 and S_2S_2 relate different rates of investment to marginal supply prices of investment for years X, X + 1 and X + 2. The horizontal segments $0B = 0_1 B_1 = 0_2B_2$ show the constant amounts of investment being realized between the three years; these segments are equal to the distance between 0 and 0_1 and between 0_1 and 0_2, showing that the economy is changing in *scale* (*but not proportionately*) over time, and that this change in scale is due to the occurrence of positive accumulation. Since the supply curves are the same with the passage of time, no technical progress is taking place; even under conditions of growth and absence of technological change, Dobb's system shows that the actual rate of profits, required to maintain a rate of investment $0B = 0_1 B_1 = 0_2 B_2$ and given by the vertical segments $0P = 0_1 P_1 = 0_2 P_2$, is permanently above the normal rate of profits, compatible with *zero* net investment and given by the vertical segments $0S = 0_1 S_1 = 0_2 S_2$.

The evolution of the normal and actual rates through time is shown respectively by the dotted line $C_2 - C_2$ and the continuous line $C_3 - C_3$. As these lines are parallel to the time axis, the normal and the actual rates remain constant with the passage of time. Figure 7.5 is not qualitatively different from Figure 7.4; the latter represents a *specific* period of time in which positive accumulation is being observed.

In Letter 9 (27/6/44), Dobb made a concession to Shove, in the following terms:

> I can also see that this conclusion [that is, actual rate of profits > normal rate of profits] can be avoided if one assumes that the period of expanding demand for capital has followed upon some previous period of approximately stationary demand *during which* the expanding demand of the later period was fully anticipated. Then *any*-sized expansion in stock of capital required in the later (expanding) period can be assumed to have been provided by infinitesimal investments in each of the preceding years back to year I.

On this Shove (Letter 12, 7/7/44) commented: 'You have granted all that is necessary to establish my point against Joan (...) From which [that is, from Dobb's point above] it follows that a growing stock does not necessarily imply a rate of profits > normal.' Dobb's concession (which was not accepted by Robinson – see the final letter, 24, 17/8/44) is the basis for Shove's suggestion for a 'compromise peace' between Dobb and Shove (Letter 23, 14/8/44):

> I think we are now in position to draw up a compromise peace. 1) I agree that if an increase in the demand for capital is not foreseen in sufficient time ahead to allow the appropriate enlargement of the stock to be accumulated in the least costly way, demand price may be above supply price. 2) You [Dobb] agree that if it *is* foreseen long enough ahead to allow this, demand price will be above supply price.

The debate among Joan Robinson, Shove and Dobb is intimately connected with the unclear interpretation which Joan Robinson gave to what Marshall understood as the supply price of capital. In her article 'Marx,

Marshall and Keynes' (1955) , written 13 years after her *Essay* (1942), Joan Robinson recognized this difficulty: 'In his [Marshall's] view there is a *normal rate of profit* which represents the *supply price of capital*, but it is never clear whether this is the supply price of a certain amount of capital – the rate of profit at which there is neither growth nor decline in the total stock of capital – or whether it is the supply price of a certain rate of accumulation of capital' (1955, p. 62). That is to say, Joan Robinson was not sure whether Dobb's or Shove's definition captured correctly what Marshall meant by the supply price of capital.

In the Preface to the second Edition (1966) of her *Essay*, she wrote what perhaps could be seen as the 'final word' concerning this debate:

> The account which I gave of the orthodox theory of profits (...) in the setting of the stationary state, was challenged by Gerald Shove. He maintained that Marshall intended by 'normal profits' the rate of profits compatible with a steady, foreseen rate of growth. Abnormal profits then result from unexpected changes in the growth of demand for particular commodities. This reading of Marshall is certainly as plausible as the static interpretation. The trouble with Marshall is that he expects us to believe both at once; and in neither does he give a coherent account of what determines the 'normal' rate of profits. (Robinson, 1966, p. xvi)

The real difficulty is not so much with the definition of the supply price of capital, but rather what do we mean by the 'quantity of capital', the definition of which is a prior *logical* step in the determination of the normal rate of profits *within the neoclassical tradition*.

A solution

In this section we suggest a possible solution to the Robinson–Dobb v. Shove controversy. We argue that Davidson's (1968, 1972) model provides a solution, one which suggests that Shove's result is a very special case.

Keynes (1936, p. 135) defined the *marginal efficiency of a capital-asset* as the rate of discount that equates the demand price of the capital-asset under consideration to its (flow-) supply price. Keynes noted that the supply price of the capital asset did not necessarily equal its prevailing market price, but the price 'which would just induce a manufacturer newly to produce an additional unit of such assets, i.e. what is sometimes called its *replacement cost*' (Keynes, 1936, p. 135).[14] The demand price is the present value of the expected stream of quasi-rents per unit of capital, using the current rate of interest (which may be interpreted as the marginal convenience yield on money) as the appropriate rate of discount.

There will be positive net investment as long as the demand price is above the flow-supply price;[15] this is tantamount to saying that investment in a particular capital-asset will cease when its marginal efficiency equals the current rate of interest, reinforcing Keynes's notion that 'money rules the roost'.

This is a *scarcity theory* of investment: investment in a particular capital-asset is worthwhile only when it is relatively scarce. As Keynes (1936, p. 213) put it:

> For the only reason why an asset offers a prospect of yielding during its life services having an aggregate value greater than its initial supply price is because it is *scarce*; and it is kept scarce because of the competition of the rate of interest on money. If capital becomes less scarce, the excess yield will diminish, without its having become less productive – at least in the physical sense.

Davidson (1968, 1972) studied the process of adjustment to equilibrium, adopting a Marshallian three-period analysis. He derived the aggregate demand function for capital goods from the summation of the particular (that is, the firms') demand functions. For simplicity, Davidson assumed a 'representative capital good'.[16] The *stock* demand function for capital, D_k, may be represented as follows:

$$D_k = f_1(\bar{P}_k, \bar{\delta}, \overset{+}{\phi}, \overset{+}{E}) \tag{7.1}$$

where P_k is the market price of capital goods, δ is the rate of discount used by entrepreneurs in evaluating the present value of the expected stream of quasi-rents, ϕ is a set of profit expectations related to the (exogenous) growth in demand and E is the ability of firms to obtain finance. The symbols (–) and (+) denote the signs of the partial derivatives of D_k with respect to each independent variable. It is still a scarcity theory of the demand for investment although $f_1(.)$ is a more complex schedule than the simple Keynesian *mec* schedule.

At any point of time, the stock of capital goods inherited from the past constitutes the *stock* supply of capital goods (S_k), the result of past investment decisions and so predetermined:

$$S_k = \bar{S}_k \tag{7.2}$$

The *flow* demand for capital (d_k), which arises from depreciation per period of time of the existing stock, is assumed to be a constant fraction n of S_k,[17] that is,

$$d_k = nS_k = n\bar{S}_k \tag{7.3}$$

The *total* market demand for capital is

$$D_k + d_k = f_1(P_k, \delta, \phi, E) + nS_k \tag{7.4}$$

Finally, the *flow* supply function of capital (s_k) relates outputs of capital goods to their expected market prices. The flow supply function indicates the *gross* investment (I_g) realizable in each short period. It is upward sloping and convex to the origin because of short-term diminishing returns. There is also a minimum flow supply price (P_m) representing the shutdown price for the industry. Hence,

$$s_k = f_2(P_k) = I_g \tag{7.5}$$

and the *total* market supply of capital is

$$S_k + s_k = S_k + f_2(P_k) \tag{7.6}$$

The capital goods market clears when

$$(D_k + d_k) - (S_k + s_k) = 0 \tag{7.7}$$

There will be positive *net* investment (I_n) if gross investment exceeds depreciation, that is, if $s_k - d_k > 0$. Accordingly, the value of net investment $(P_k I_n)$ is

$$P_k I_n = P_k(s_k - d_k) \tag{7.8}$$

An economy is said to be 'growing' if $P_k I_n$ is positive. We retain Davidson's initial assumption: 'all increments in household wealth are retained only in money or placements and ... the Monetary Authority acts so that a shortage of finance is never a constraint on the rate of investment', Davidson (1972, p. 69).

If profit expectations, the rate of interest and the number of entrepreneurial investors able to obtain finance remain constant, and the demand price for capital goods equals their long-period supply price, all investment is allocated to the replacement of the existing stock, and a long-period equilibrium *stationary state* prevails. The situation is depicted in Figure 7.6

There is zero net investment, so that the horizontal distance between D_k and $D_k + d_k$ equals the horizontal distance between S_k and $S_k + s_k$ at the equilibrium price. Gross investment equals depreciation, the spot price P_s equals the long-period supply price P_{LP}, and only normal profits obtain. When the spot price P_s is higher than the short-period equilibrium (flow-supply) price or forward price (P_f), there is a situation of *backwardation*. As Davidson (1972, p. 88) notes, '[i]n a period where backwardation occurs, the flow of output during the period will exceed (or just equal) the quantity used up in

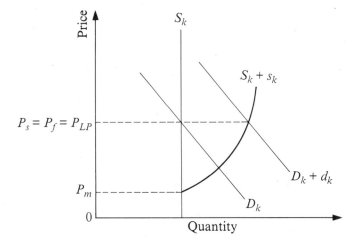

Figure 7.6

the production process and net investment will be positive (or zero). Thus, backwardation is associated with accumulation and a growing economy (or at the limit, with a stationary economy).' This case is depicted in Figure 7.7, where the horizontal distance between $D_k + d_k$ is shorter than the horizontal distance between S_k and $S_k + s_k$ at the forward price P_f.

Accumulation is thus associated with backwardation and, consequently, with the spot price P_s being higher than the forward price, so that *abnormal* profits obtain. Therefore, Davidson's model provides formal support for Joan

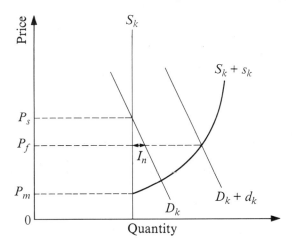

Figure 7.7

Robinson's contention that accumulation, within a *static* Marshallian frame-work, is associated with abnormal profits. In the process of adjustment to full equilibrium, the spot price asymptotically approaches the long-period equi-librium supply price. When the adjustment factor $(P_f - P_s)/P_s$ vanishes, there is no further net investment (Figure 7.8).

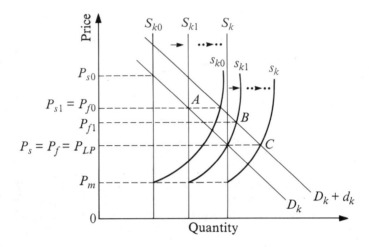

Figure 7.8

If the spot price (P_{s0}) of the 'representative' capital good in question is greater than its forward price (P_{f0}) at the beginning of a particular short period, there is room for profitable investment, so that capacity is not yet adjusted to demand; that is, we are in a *transition* to a situation of full stock-flow equilibrium. Short-period flow equilibrium is reached when S_{k0} (and $S_{k0} + s_{k0}$) shifts rightwards to a point A, when the increased level of output of the capital good is associated with a lower spot price P_{s1}, now equal to P_{f0}. At point A, the stock of capital is now S_{k1}.

At the beginning of the following period, the spot price P_{s1} is still greater than P_{f1}, the forward price associated with this new particular period (point B). Capacity is still insufficient to exhaust the possibilities of profitable output expansion, so that $P_{s1} > P_{f1} > P_{LP}$. P_{LP} is the long-period supply price, associated with normal profits. In each period, output expands, leading to successive reductions in the spot price; productive capacity also expands, causing the forward price to approach the long-period supply price. The process of capital accumulation will come to an end when only normal profits obtain, so that $P_s = P_f = P_{LP}$ (point C), a *stationary* state.

During the adjustment process to full long-period equilibrium, abnormal profits are the rule, and the moving stock supply curve is the essential ingredient of our answer to Shove's 'crucial question'. By the same token, Dobb's concession and Shove's 'compromise peace' are only acceptable if the increase in the stock of capital in each period is *infinitesimal*, implying that the actual rate of profits is *approximately* equal to the normal one, *even when the future is foreseen correctly.*

However, as soon as the other variables – δ, ϕ, E – are allowed to change, a stationary state is not the necessary outcome of the analysis. In particular, changes in ϕ as an incentive for increasing investment are stressed by Davidson:

> Since the interest rate is constrained to positive values, the ultimate source of continual capital accumulation for a profit-maximizing, market-oriented, monetary economy lies in investors believing in the continuous growth of profit opportunities over time ($\Delta\phi > 0$). (1990, p. 52)

Let us assume that a steady and foreseen growth of profit opportunities over time leads to a steady and foreseen growth in demand; that is, D_k moves to the right with the passage of time. This is the 'dynamic case' considered by Shove. However, in Shove's analysis, the final outcome – steady growth with normal profits – is based on his assumption – 'for the purpose of illustration' – that the capital supply curve does not change with changes in demand. In this case, the process of adjustment to each new equilibrium implied by the changing demand curves is rather smoother. When the stock of capital inherited from the past periods is taken into account, the capital supply curve will move with changes in demand. We have already shown that, with a *given* demand curve, abnormal profits obtain during the whole adjustment process – they only cease to exist when net investment is zero. If the demand curves are moving steadily to the right, the process of adjustment may be endless, and abnormal profits will be the rule. Therefore, Shove's assumption of an unchanging capital supply curve is essential for his results – it had more than 'illustrative' significance.

Shove's views on accumulation with normal profits seem to be denied by Davidson's analysis. Net investment only occurs, within this framework, when the demand price for capital goods exceeds the forward price, which implies abnormal profits during the process of accumulation. With respect to the 'dynamic case' Shove overlooked the capacity-creating role of investment, which leads to an ever-changing capital supply curve *vis-à-vis* growth in demand.

With the benefit of hindsight we can see that Shove blurred the distinction between a comparison of two long-period equilibrium positions, on the one hand, and the transition from one equilibrium to another, on the other. Or, as Joan Robinson wrote in the final letter,

On the profit question I think the whole trouble arises from stepping from a static to a dynamic system without working out the problems involved.[18] I was very much surprised at the line Shove took, as I thought my argument quite obvious – tho' of course rather shocking in its implications. (Letter 24, 17/8/44)

A digression

In the light of the postwar literature on the nature of golden ages and steady states, the following exchanges between Dobb and Shove are both fascinating and prophetic. Having set out his views on what the 'crucial question' was (see above), Shove went on:

> Of the two explanations you [Dobb] give, the second (viz. that 'the expectation of today's and tomorrow's expansion did not pre-date the start of the expanding phase') is surely inconsistent with the hypothesis that the system is one in which the future is correctly foreseen; since it implies that, before the expansion began, today's and tomorrow's conditions of demand &/or supply were not foreseen i.e., that the future was not foreseen correctly. If this is so, it does not show that the situation you contemplate can arise in a system in which the future is foreseen correctly.
>
> Your other explanation (viz. that 'the system has always expanded at a steady rate') is more elusive – to me at any rate. For it brings one up against quasi-metaphysical difficulties about the nature of time – which we must, I take it, conceive not only to be absolutely continuous but also to have no beginning (or end) in the sense that however far one goes back (or forward) one can always go further. (Letter 12, 7/7/44)

We gave the gist of Dobb's reply above. Here is the full version:

> As regards the 'metaphysics of time'. It may well be that my assumption about 'continuous expansion at a steady rate' is somehow self-contradictory unless I deal with infinities. I must admit that I had been thinking in terms of a year of creation somewhere (of the world, or of commercial society or something). The picture I had was that sometime in the course of the 'early years' of the process (if this concept is permissible) the rate of increase of stock had proceeded *more slowly* than the growth of demand until the rate of profit had *risen to a level* (i.e. above 'normal') sufficient from then onwards to *maintain a steady rate of investment*, and sufficient to increase the stock of capital as fast as the demand for it grew. This, I think, is all right, if one rules out the effect of growing income on the supply-price of investment. If the latter falls as income grows (or the curve becomes pushed to the right), then the rate of investment will *grow* as time goes on, & in later years the stock will increase *faster* than the demand for it. As this occurs, actual profit will fall over time & approach 'normal' – approach asymptotically but never quite reach.
>
> The reason why I made incidental reference to this change of income & its effects being unforeseen was because I thought *you* [Shove] were assuming merely that the growth of *demand* for cap. was foreseen. I now see you say in the E.J. 'so long as the expansion of demand (or *supply*) is correctly estimated', and perhaps

'or supply' covers such events as this, I haven't yet had time to think whether or not this does affect the above picture, & if so how. (Letter 13, 10/7/44)

A coherent account

Joan Robinson and Shove tried to offer different answers to the same basic question: 'How can perpetual accumulation be conceived to occur?' (Robinson, 1952, p. 47). Using a modern version of Marshallian comparative static analysis we have shown that Shove's argument was flawed.

A coherent account of what determines the 'normal' rate of profits is given by Joan Robinson herself. If the Keynesian *mec* schedule is replaced by the two-sided relationship between investment and profits (or between the *rate* of growth and the *rate* of profits) in the Kaleckian–Robinson style (cf. Asimakopulos, 1971), it is not difficult to conceive of a Robinsonian model of accumulation, Robinson (1956, 1962) which yields Shove's results, that is, a process of accumulation with normal profits obtaining. But now Shove's result would arise within a different theoretical framework,[19] where the notion of scarcity is no longer central to the argument. So Shove's position is not *intrinsically* incorrect.

Perhaps the simplest way to illustrate this proposition is to use Donald Harris's (1975) analysis of production, accumulation and distribution (see Figure 7.9). On the left-hand side, we show the Marxian sphere of production. At any moment of time, there is an inherited stock of capital goods and a given labour force. This allows us to define a relationship between possible real wage levels (w) and the accompanying surplus *potentially* available to constitute the corresponding rate of profits (r). The current state of the class war is argued to determine the actual w ($= w^*$) and potential r ($= r^*$). We then move to the right-hand side of the diagram where we show, in the sphere of distribution and exchange, the Cambridge equation, $r = g/s_c$; it shows the rates of profits implied by different rates of accumulation when the saving propensity of the capitalist class is given (and the price level is determined by either the normal mark-up analysis of Kalecki and the Post-Keynesians or by a competitive process). A dynamic version of Keynes's 'animal spirits' function, whereby desired rates of accumulation are related to expected rates of profits (themselves determined by existing rates), is shown as $g = f(r^e)$, where r^e is the expected rate of profits. If the 'animal spirits' function intercepts the Cambridge relationship at r^*, where r^* is the maximum rate of profits which may be created and received in the existing conditions of both spheres, what is potentially there as a result of the social and behavioural conditions of production is actually realized as a result of the conditions prevailing in the sphere of distribution and exchange. We have a snapshot of Marx's scheme of expanded reproduction allied with a dynamic version of Kalecki's and Keynes's solution of the realization problem.

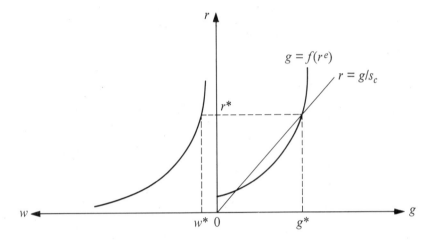

Figure 7.9

If, now, the feedback of actual accumulation on the relationship between w and r in the sphere of production is such as to allow r^* to be maintained (because w^* adjusts in line with movement outwards of the w–r relationship), the economy will remain in a steady state with a constant r which is both expected and realized. No wonder Joan Robinson called it a Golden Age! 'I used the phrase "a Golden Age" to describe smooth, steady growth with full employment (intending thereby to indicate its mythical nature)' (Joan Robinson, 1962, p. 52).

Concluding comment

We conclude by noting that the exchanges between Joan Robinson and Shove, and Shove and Dobb have provided a convenient link back to Marshall and the classicals, on the one hand, and forward to modern Cantabridgean growth theory on the other. It has also enabled us to watch the transition in and the development of Joan Robinson's thought and approach, as she moved from her Marshallian–Keynesian starting-points to her mature stance in which the classicals, Marx, Sraffa and Kalecki came to dominate her views.

Notes

1. The chapter is an expanded version of an article which is published in the spring issue of the *Journal of the History of Economic Thought*, Araujo and Harcourt (1993a); see also Araujo and Harcourt (1993b), an addendum to (1993a) in which the contents of some new letters which were found after we had received the proofs of (1993a) are discussed. We are most grateful to the Provost and Fellows of King's College, Cambridge, for allowing us to see the letters and to quote from the letters of Joan Robinson, and to Brian Pollitt for allowing us to quote from the letters of Maurice Dobb. We have been unable to find who is the executor of Gerald Shove's estate. We are also grateful to Prue Kerr, two anony-

mous referees for their helpful comments on a draft of this article, and to D. McKitterick and J. Smith, respectively the Librarian and the Manuscript Cataloguer of Wren Library, Trinity College, Cambridge, for drawing the discovery to our attention and allowing us to quote from the new letters. We also thank the editor for allowing us to reprint material from our original article and the addendum. J.A.T.R. Araujo also wishes to express his gratitude for the financial support from CAPES (The Brazilian Ministry of Education Agency for Grants).

2. The letters, 24 in all, run from May to August 1944 (the letters marked with KP are in the Keynes papers, and those marked with WL are in the Wren Library):

    1. Robinson to Shove, 1/5/44 (KP).
    2. Robinson to Shove, 5/5/44 (KP).
    3. Robinson to Shove, 10/5/44 (KP).
    4. Shove to Robinson, 12/5/44 (cont. on 19/5/44) (KP).
    5. Robinson to Shove, 30/5/44 (KP).
    6. Robinson to Shove, 2/6/44 (KP).
    7. Dobb to Shove, 15/6/44 (KP).
    8. Shove to Dobb, 22/6/44 (WL).
    9. Dobb to Shove, 27/6/44 (KP).
    10. Shove to Dobb, 28/6/44 (KP).
    11. Dobb to Shove, 30/6/44 (KP).
    12. Shove to Dobb, 7/7/44 (WL).
    13. Dobb to Shove, 10/7/44 (KP).
    14. Shove to Dobb, 16/7/44 (WL).
    15. Shove to Dobb, 18/7/44 (WL).
    16. Dobb to Shove, 19/7/44 (KP).
    17. Dobb to Shove, 21/7/44 (KP).
    18. Shove to Dobb, 22/7/44 (WL).
    19. Shove to Dobb, 5/8/44 (WL).
    20. Dobb to Shove, 8/8/44 (KP).
    21. Shove to Dobb, 9/8/44 (WL).
    22. Dobb to Shove, 11/8/44 (KP).
    23. Shove to Dobb, 14/8/44 (WL).
    24. Robinson to Dobb, 17/8/44 (WL).

3. 'These essays [1953] were written in a hilarious mood after reading Piero Sraffa's Introduction to Ricardo's *Principles*, which caused me to see that the concept of the rate of profit on capital is essentially the same in Ricardo, Marx, Marshall and Keynes; ... the essential difference between these ... and Walras, Pigou and the latter-day textbooks ... is that the Ricardians are describing an historical process of accumulation in a changing world, while the Walrasians dwell in timeless equilibrium where there is no distinction between the future and the past' (Joan Robinson, 1973, p. 247).

4. It was this conception which lay behind G.C.H.'s 'The Accountant in a Golden Age' (1965, 1992). In it he used standard accounting procedures to estimate accounting rates of profit, in order to see whether or not they gave the correct answers, answers which are already known in the conditions of a Golden Age (because what was expected is what actually happens).

5. The following quote contains the essence of her analysis:

    For, as long as capital goods continue to accumulate, their profitability at the margin declines and the incentive to further investment is continuously weakened. Investment is always tending to bring itself to an end, and in the stable conditions that we are considering nothing happens to revive the inducement to invest as it flags. In conditions of equilibrium the stock of capital is adjusted to the given rate of interest, and no further accumulation takes place. The marginal efficiency of capital corresponding to zero net investment is equal to the rate of interest and if, by chance, positive or negative investment were to occur, the marginal efficiency of capital would cease to be equal to the given rate of interest. If new investment were to take place capital would be increased and its earnings at the margin would fall. The marginal efficiency of capital would then be less than the rate of interest. The investment would turn out to have been unprofitable, capital goods would not be worth replacement and a movement back to equilibrium would set in with a decline in the stock of capital. On the other hand, if, in equilibrium, the stock of capital goods were allowed to deteriorate the marginal effi-ciency of capital would rise above the rate of interest and investment would take place until the stock of capital was restored to its former level. The familiar phrase 'long-period equilibrium' may be adopted to describe this situation. For, in the ordinary sense, a firm or an industry which is under an inducement to expand or to contract the plant which it employs is not in equilibrium, and long-period conditions are established only when investment has come to an end. (Joan Robinson, 1937, pp. 76–77)

6. People often write 'steady' as synonymous with 'foreseen'. We think this is too strict a proviso. In reaching this view, we have been much influenced by Claudio Sardoni's (1981) paper on expanded reproduction schemas in Marx.

7. There is a vagueness in all this: are we dealing with a long-period or a short-period supply curve? If the former, the supply price would include the normal rate of profits as a component and also the normal real wage, which would be paid to the (optimum) supply of labour per unit of output, and payments for the means of production in (optimum) quantities and valued at *their* long-period normal prices. If it is a short-period supply curve, presumably 'under' the curve is an amount for normal profit, now an absolute figure associated with the normal capacity-working of the existing stock of capital goods.

8. But is Shove correct in supposing that because the supply curve slopes upwards the normal rate of profits is 'rising' over time?

9. Shove's 'crucial question' is asked in different terms in another letter (Letter 21, 9/8/44):

Unless I have misunderstood, you [Dobb] maintain that if at any particular moment – call it 00.00 hours on D day – the stock of capital is increasing, the demand price for the then existing stock must be greater than its supply price. But if that were so the investors would surely be better off if they had a larger stock of capital: so that the crucial question arises *why haven't they accumulated a larger stock?*

10. This assumption keeps us in a Marshallian (Say's Law) world of full employment so that saving (= investment) is at the *expense* of consumption, rather than in a Keynesian world where there is unemployment so that there *is* the possibility of a free lunch – consumption and investment can both increase at the same time.

11. We assume that expected profits are determined by actual profits.

12. Contrast this with Lerner's statement of Keynes's theory where *mei* < *mec* (in an expand-ing economy) except at full equilibrium where they are equal. It is interesting to see the letter writers flowing back and forth in their arguments between the 'old' 'Classical' (in Keynes's usage) world of Marshall and the 'new' world of Keynes.

13. It is not therefore a steady state model of accumulation but one of a declining *rate* over time.

14. Note that this definition is similar to Shove's own definition, so that our solution does not rest on Dobb's definition of supply price of the stock of capital, that is, Pigou's mainte-nance-price. Therefore, we criticize Shove's position *on its own grounds*.

15. Davidson interprets the flow-supply price as the forward price of capital goods, and the demand price as the *notional* spot price, for there is no well-developed spot market for second-hand capital goods. See also Rogers (1989, p. 217, n.3).

16. Davidson, (1972, pp. 71–2, n.3) remarks:

This assumes that the stock of capital can be aggregated along the abscissa by homoge-neous physical units – an obviously unrealistic assumption. The alternative would be to provide separate demand and supply curves for each type of homogeneous capital goods – an unnecessary complication, as long as we discuss investment in a demand price v. supply price context, and not by reference to 'the rate of profit on physical capital'. Thus we are assuming some composite capital good.

Therefore, Davidson's model evades the problems related to the Cambridge criticisms of neoclassical capital theory; see Harcourt (1972).

17. This is clearly unacceptable – see, for example, Salter (1960, 1966) – but we retain it for simplicity.

18. Ironically, Shove thought this was the real cause of Joan Robinson's 'mistake'. In a P.S. to Dobb (Letter 8, 22/6/44), he wrote: 'My private opinion is that Joan did not fully appreciate the fact that when we are [working] with an expanding system we are concerned with a *moving* (*not a stationary*) equilibrium.'

19. Even within the Marshallian framework, Joan Robinson's position is ambiguous:

> Another solution of the problem is to graft Marshall's analysis of long- and short-period supply price on to the model. When an economy is expanding at the rate appropriate to the given conditions, all prices are equal to long-period average costs (including in cost, profit on capital at the given rate) and all capital equipment is working at the designed capacity. In each sector conditions of rising supply price obtain, so that any increase in output relatively to capacity would be accompanied by a rise in price above long-period average cost. The capitalists expect the rate of profit to continue in the future to rule at the present level. (1952, pp. 47–8)

She thus seems to admit the possibility of accumulation with normal profits within a Marshallian framework.

References

Araujo, J.A.T.R. and G.C. Harcourt (1993a), 'Maurice Dobb, Joan Robinson and Gerald Shove on Accumulation and the Rate of Profits', *Journal of the History of Economic Thought*, **15**, spring, pp. 1–24.

Araujo, J.A.T.R. and G.C. Harcourt (1993b), 'Maurice Dobb, Joan Robinson and Gerald Shove on Accumulation and the Rate of Profits: an Addendum', *Journal of the History of Economic Thought*, **15**, spring, pp. 24–30.

Asimakopulos, A. (1971), 'The Determination of Investment in Keynes's Model', *Canadian Journal of Economics*, **4**, (3), pp. 382–8.

Davidson, P. (1968), 'Money, Portfolio Balance, Capital Accumulation, and Economic Growth', *Econometrica*, **36**, April, 291–321; reprinted in Davidson (1990).

Davidson, P. (1972), *Money and the Real World*, London: Macmillan.

Davidson, P. (1990), 'Money and Employment', *The Collected Writings of Paul Davidson, Volume 1*, edited by Louise Davidson, London: Macmillan.

Feiwel, G.R. (ed.) (1989), *Joan Robinson and Modern Economic Theory*, London: Macmillan.

Goodwin, R.M. (1989), 'Joan Robinson – Passionate Seeker After Truth', in Feiwel (1989).

Hahn, F.H. (1989), 'Robinson–Hahn Love–Hate Relationship: An Interview', in Feiwel (1989).

Harcourt, G.C. (1965), 'The Accountant in a Golden Age', *Oxford Economic Papers*, **17**, (1), March, pp. 66–80; reprinted in Sardoni (1992).

Harcourt, G.C. (1972), *Some Cambridge Controversies in the Theory of Capital*, Cambridge: Cambridge University Press.

Harcourt, G.C., (1991), 'Marshall's *Principles* as seen at Cambridge through the Eyes of Gerald Shove, Dennis Robertson and Joan Robinson', *Quaderni di Storia dell'Economia Politica*, **IX**, pp. 355–72; reprinted in Sardoni (1992).

Harris, D.J. (1975), 'The Theory of Economic Growth: A Critique and a Reformulation', *American Economic Review*, **65**, May, pp. 329–37.

Keynes, J.M. (1936), *The General Theory of Employment, Interest and Money*, London: Macmillan.

Lerner, A.P. (1944), *The Economics of Control*, New York: Macmillan.

Marshall, A. (1890), *Principles of Economics*, London: Macmillan.

Robinson, Joan (1936), 'The Long-Period Theory of Employment', *Zeitschrift für Nationalökonomie*, Vol. VII, Heft 1; reprinted with alterations in Robinson (1937).

Robinson, Joan (1937), *Essays in the Theory of Employment*, London: Macmillan.

Robinson, Joan (1942), *An Essay on Marxian Economics*; 2nd edn, 1966, London: Macmillan.

Robinson, Joan (1952), 'The Model of an Expanding Economy', *Economic Journal*, **62**, March, pp. 42–53.

Robinson, Joan (1955), 'Marx, Marshall and Keynes', lectures delivered at the Delhi School of Economics, published by the School as Occasional Paper No.9; reprinted in Robinson (1959–79).

Robinson, Joan (1956), *The Accumulation of Capital*, London: Macmillan.

Robinson, Joan (1959–79), *Collected Economic Papers*, 5 vols, Oxford: Basil Blackwell.

Robinson, Joan (1962), *Essays in the Theory of Economic Growth*, London: Macmillan.

Robinson, Joan (1971), *Economic Heresies: Some Old-Fashioned Questions in Economic Theory*, London: Macmillan.

Rogers, C. (1989), *Money, Interest and Capital*, Cambridge: Cambridge University Press.

Salter, W.E.G. (1960, 1966), *Productivity and Technical Change*, Cambridge: Cambridge University Press, 2nd edn with addendum by W.B. Reddaway, 1966.

Sardoni, C. (1981), 'Multisectoral Models of Balanced Growth and the Marxian Schemes of Expanded Reproduction', *Australian Economic Papers*, **20**, December, pp. 383–97.

Sardoni, C. (ed.) (1992), *On Political Economists and Modern Political Economy. Selected Essays of G.C. Harcourt*, London and New York: Routledge.

Shove, G. (1944), 'Mrs. Robinson on Marxian Economics', *Economic Journal*, **54**, April, 47–61.

Sraffa, P. with the collaboration of M. H. Dobb (eds) (1951–5, 1973), *Works and Correspondence of David Ricardo*, 11 vols, Cambridge: Cambridge University Press.

8 Some reflections on Joan Robinson's changes of mind and the relationship of them to Post-Keynesianism and the economics profession*

I

Until her very last years, I think it is true to say that Joan Robinson's bark was often worse than her bite (both measured high on their appropriate Richter scales), that her *analysis* was not *that* far removed from the mainstream mould. It is true that Keynes in the 1930s wondered why she always had to be so fierce in debate and she (sort of) apologized for being so (she passionately believed in seeking truth); and Hayek reproached her for assuming that, if people did not agree with her, they must be of extremely low intelligence, with their morals probably not the best either, so that argument back and forward with her was often difficult, to say the least. Indeed, I can remember when Joan 'debated' with Bob Solow before the undergraduates in Cambridge after Solow's 1963 Marshall Lectures (on a mythical creature called 'Joan' and another called 'Nicky') they hardly ever joined up in argument. She would tell him that he had been knocked over on this point (often before he had had time to reply) and that they would now move on to the next point. But when we look at the *substance* of her analysis as she moved towards her final stance which put her well and truly within the Post-Keynesian rubric – of course it does, for, despite an unhealthy American Post-Keynesian attempt at hegemony to the contrary, Joan *was* an original pioneer – we find her Marshallian, even Pigovian, background tending to break through.

In order to argue for this point of view – and I do not want to push it too far, for often she would be demonstrating to the 'enemy' how they should have done their own dirty work – I shall concentrate on some key watersheds in her life's work, in order to show the nature of and the reasons for the movements towards her final stance.

II

To do this, it might be helpful if I briefly refer to the strands of Post-Keynesianism which Omar Hamouda and I identified in our 1988 survey

* A revised version of a paper, 'Joan Robinson and Post-Keynesianism', which was given at the Conference on Joan Robinson in Turin in December 1993.

article, 'Post-Keynesianism: from criticism to coherence?' (reprinted in Sardoni, 1992). As we said in the survey, the umbrella term, 'Post-Keynesian'[1] is useful for gathering in groups of economists who, historically, have interacted with one another's work (not always uncritically or positively), as well as being hostile to mainstream economics, both neoclassical microeconomics and bastard Keynesianism. In one sense, therefore, they are under this same umbrella for *historical* as much as for analytical, method of approach or purely logical reasons.

The attempted classification was based, first, on the 'vision' of the economies and societies they predominantly analysed and, secondly, on their principal method or methods of analysing them. As some of the people concerned changed their views over their lives (not least, Joan Robinson), their later views were taken as the evidence for their particular classification – a definite limitation when, as in Joan's case, they made radical changes over their lifetimes. In the survey article we identified as the three main strands, the American Post-Keynesians, the neo-Ricardians and the Kaleckians/ Robinsonians. In addition, we argued that Nicholas Kaldor, Richard Goodwin and Luigi Pasinetti could not be fitted into any one category, because they had (at least some of) the characteristics of two or even all strands, and that Wynne Godley and his colleagues were unique rather than easily classifiable. We should also have included a role for institutionalists and institutions, especially as John Kenneth Galbraith is the patron saint of the *Journal of Post Keynesian Economics* (*JPKE*) and Joan Robinson herself always put much emphasis on asking what were 'the rules of the game' of the economy being analysed, what were its institutions and how they arose.

Let me say emphatically at this stage, because Bruce McFarlane has recently taken me to task for giving the, quite unintended, impression (in the Introduction to the Essays in Honour of Luigi Pasinetti edited by Mauro Baranzini and me (1993, p. 38, n.2)) that Michal Kalecki was a minor Post-Robinsonian, that I am well aware that, though there was mutual and long sustained interaction between these two great friends, causation did, most of the time, run more *from* Kalecki *to* Joan Robinson than the other way around. Increasingly, I believe, her own mode of thought and analysis were moulded by her absorption of Kalecki's approach, to the propagation of which she lent her very considerable powers of exposition. I think this is as true of the main propositions of *The Accumulation of Capital* (1956) and the papers which run up to and follow it, as it is of her superb account of Kalecki on capitalism in the 1978 *Oxford Bulletin* Memorial Issue for Kalecki reprinted in *Collected Economic Papers* (*CEP*), (1951–79), Vol. V.

It is ironic that the economists most attacked by Joan Robinson – Hahn, Samuelson, Solow and Stiglitz, for example – were sympathetic to her points on methodology: witness the rise of path-dependent equilibrium models over the last 10 years or so. (Joan Robinson – and Kaldor, of course – were inclined in the end to argue that there may not even be equilibria 'out there' to be found.) But though their views on methodology may have overlapped, and Joan never accepted this, probably correctly, if Samuelson's way of putting of the case is at all representative,[2] their 'visions' only did in regard to Keynes, and even he – or his conjectures – were often wrongly included in a framework which was Walrasian/Fisherian, not classical *cum* Marxist. (Furthermore, we must be careful, even here, because Hahn, for example, does not regard general equilibrium as *descriptive* theory but as a reference point for truth.) By contrast, though Joan Robinson and the neo-Ricardians have largely overlapping 'visions' – Kalecki is not as acceptable to the neo-Ricardians as Keynes is – they were at loggerheads on method. Joan thought that their methods were at one with her view of neoclassical methods, of which she strongly disapproved, while they argued that she had thrown in her lot with the enemy as far as method is concerned, abandoning the one method, long-period positions, which allows general theoretical propositions to be derived. Thus, to them, it is not surprising that she became nihilistic at the end of her life, arguing that she had been doing theory for 50 years and that it had come to pieces in her hands; for if you did not do long-period analysis, you were left with the ephemera of the short period, about which no worthwhile generalizations could be made. The American Post-Keynesians overlapped with Joan Robinson's views as far as emphasizing the need to theorize about what reasonable people do in uncertain environments, and what are the systemic consequences of this, but, with the exception of Jan Kregel and the partial exception of Hyman Minsky, the agents in their stories are far too close to those of the neoclassical 'enemy' (even though they come from the work of Marshall and Keynes in particular) and too far away from the class society of the classicals and the Marxists, in which conflict is ever-present and profit making and accumulation are a way of life for the principal decision makers. *Analytically*, in the neoclassical schema, lifetime utility-maximizing individuals drive the system along and all the institutions of society – markets, stock exchanges and firms, for example – are but agencies, the better to allow the former to 'do their thing'.

III

In retrospect, Joan Robinson herself saw her early work, such as *The Eco nomics of Imperfect Competition* (1933a) and the papers surrounding it, as criticizing from within the Marshallian/Pigovian theory of the firm and industry, using their static method. This she was to call 'a shameless fudge' – the idea that business people could find by trial and error the equilibrium profit-maximizing, cost-minimizing prices on their downward-sloping demand curves without affecting *endogenously* the position of the curves themselves in the process. Here is a very succinct statement by her, one of many, this one dating from 1953; it is taken from her *Economic Journal* article, '"Imperfect Competition" revisited'.

> In my opinion, the greatest weakness of the *Economics of Imperfect Competition* is one which it shares with the class of economic theory to which it belongs – the failure to deal with time. It is only in a metaphorical sense that price, rate of output, wage rate or what not can move in the plane depicted in a price-quantity diagram. Any movement must take place through time, and the position at any moment of time depends upon what it has been in the past. The point is not merely that any adjustment takes a certain time to complete and that (as has always been admitted) events may occur meanwhile which alter the position, so that the equilibrium towards which the system is said to be *tending* itself moves before it can be reached. The point is that the very process of moving has an effect upon the destination of the movement, so that there is no such thing as a position of long-run equilibrium which exists independently of the course which the economy is following at a particular date. (CEP, 1951–79, Vol. II, p. 234)

This part of her early work concerned value and distribution. As she joined in the arguments of the 'Circus', 'spied' (with others) on Keynes's lectures, and wrote her progress reports on what was emerging in the discussions and lectures following the publication of *A Treatise on Money* (1930), she wrote (1933b) that Keynes was developing without realizing it a 'long-period analysis of output' (CEP, 1951–79, Vol. I, p. 56). Putting it this way was a hangover from the *Treatise on Money* in which full stock-flow equilibrium occurs when profits are at their *long-period* normal level, as also are wages, and saving is equal to investment on the *Treatise on Money* definitions, but the real and money dichotomy inherited from Marshall was beginning to break down. There is a remnant of all this left in *Introduction to the Theory of Employment* (1937a) where, in the chapter on the rate of interest, especially in the section on the rate of interest as the regulator of the economic system, she argues that it 'contains an important element of truth ... Within very broad limits the system does regulate itself. Very severe unemployment does, slowly and imperfectly, bring about its own cure' (1937a, pp. 83–4). There then follows a simple Keynesian argument of the impact of unemployment (and the reverse case, high employment) though the price level and activity, on the demand for money and the rate of interest, and of its feedback effects on aggregate demand. She concludes: 'For the discussion of problems involving broad changes over the course of generations, in population, the rate of technical progress or the general social forces influencing thriftiness, it is possible to regard fluctuations in employment as a secondary consideration, and to conduct the discussion in terms of a self-regulating system' (1937a, p. 84).

But that *The General Theory* itself was, for the most part, set in a short-period context was acknowledged by Joan when she tried out his system in a long-period setting – very much economics for the economists, but neverthe-less she was able to show that some of Keynes's most important results, such as the paradox of thrift, went through; see Robinson (1937b, 1947). Though Joan Robinson had taken on board with enthusiasm the revolutionary theory of output and employment as a whole (and the general price level), she was still prepared to use a neoclassical theory of distribution, marginal products and all that. The elasticity of substitution was all the rage at that time with many of the contributors to the pages of the youthful *Review of Economic Studies*. (This, incidentally, throws doubt on her retrospective claim that one of the principal explicit aims of *The Economics of Imperfect Competition* was to knock over the marginal productivity theory of distribution, 'the doctrine that wages are determined by the marginal productivity of labour' (Joan Robinson, 1973, p. x).)

She was also fending off, along with Keynes and Kahn, Piero Sraffa's criticisms of neoclassical capital theory – witness Piero Sraffa's letter of October 1936 to Joan, to which I have often referred, for example in Harcourt (1990, p. 49), in which he suggests, in effect, that she ask her gardener what a quantity of capital is, and other evidence in the *Collected Writings*, that Keynes, Joan and Kahn were trying to keep at a distance Sraffa's (1925, 1926) critique of the theory of the firm and industry, and of partial equilib-rium analysis generally, and also Sraffa's emerging(ed) views on value and distribution theory which he was discussing with, at least, Keynes. Keynes, Kahn and Joan regarded all these as side issues when considered alongside producing a clear and persuasive account of the theory of effective demand. (There is some evidence that Keynes did go deeply into capital theory in the early 1930s, following Hayek's criticism that one of the weaknesses of his system in the *Treatise on Money* was its lack of a coherent understanding of capital-theoretic puzzles. It seems reasonable to suppose that Keynes would have talked to Sraffa about this, for Sraffa was clearly aware of these puzzles when he wrote, at Keynes's request, his critique (Sraffa, 1932) of Hayek's *Prices and Production* (1931).)

IV

Now a sea-change occurs in Joan Robinson's thought as Karl Marx comes over the horizon, first (and at second hand), when she reviewed (1936) Strachey's *The Nature of Capitalist Crisis* (1935) and then with the begin-ning of her friendship with Michal Kalecki. This led to the making of her *Essay on Marxian Economics* (1942). This was subject to a critical review article by Gerald Shove (1944), not so much for either her understanding or exposition of Marx's views, as for her lack of understanding, in his opinion, of neoclassical economics – read, mostly, Marshall. There is also Keynes's evaluation of Marx, as a result of Keynes reading Joan's *Essay*, together with both Keynes and Joan reaffirming the short-period structure of the system in *The General Theory* and their sympathy with the classical political econo-mists' practice of measuring key concepts in terms of labour time. (Keynes was more sympathetic to the latter procedure than Joan Robinson, who al-ways had a blind spot about what the LTV (Labour Theory of Value) really entailed. This is as evident in her long preface to the second edition (see pp. vi–xi), written in 1965, 25 years on, as it was in the first edition of the *Essay*. Basically, she insisted on seeing the LTV as a theory of relative prices rather than as a portmanteau term for Marx's explanation of the origin of profits in capitalism, an explanation which entailed as a necessary corollary an analysis of the deviations of the prices of production around their underly-ing labour values.)

The relevant passages from Keynes's letter of 29 August 1942 to 'Mrs Austin Robinson' (who was, as well, 'My Dear Joan') are the following:

> I found it most fascinating – as well written as anything you have done. This is in spite of the fact that there is something intrinsically boring in an attempt to make sense of what is in fact not sense. However, you have got round it by making no undue attempt in this direction. I hope you will have done something to give the quietus to these discussions by doing Marx that justice he deserves. But I expect that the faithful will regard your attempt, such as it is, to make sense of him rather irreverent.
>
> I am left with the feeling, which I had before on less evidence, that he had a penetrating and original flair but was a very poor thinker indeed, – and his failure to publish the later volumes probably meant that he was not unaware of this himself.
>
> Your footnote about me on page 23 [I have not been able to find the footnote but the issue being discussed is clear, GCH]:– I do not plead guilty here. Certainly I never intended to suggest that the wage unit is a stable measure of real output for purposes of comparison between periods widely different in other respects. At the top of page 214, ... I said expressly that I am thinking of the unit of labour as 'operating in a given environment of technique, natural resources, capital equip-ment and effective demand'. How could I have protected myself more completely and more wordily from your accusation? I never connect the wage unit with real output, and merely remark that, subject to the above assumption as to the given environment, it is 'the sole physical unit which we require in our economic system apart from units of money and time'.
>
> Yours ever,
> JMK

In the *Essay on Marxian Economics*, after discussing Marx's definitions and the LTV, Joan went systematically through the 'big' issues in economic doctrine – long-period employment and falling rate of profits, for example – trying to set out and then contrast Marx's answers with those of the orthodox ('academic') economists. This way of proceeding was increasingly to characterize her mode of writing for the rest of her life. It led, as I have often pointed out, to some grievous misunderstandings, that she was in fact a closet neoclassical in her analysis when what she was trying to do in fact was to give the orthodox answers to some of the questions which the orthodox had posed. This is true, for example, of many of the papers which cluster around the publication of *The Accumulation of Capital*. Nevertheless, she did try in a number of places, including *The Accumulation of Capital*, to integrate the orthodox analysis of the choice of technique, emanating more from Wicksell than from Marshall, into her own positive analysis. She warned us that the difficulty of the analysis exceeded the importance of the issues in the whole scheme she had in mind – but it was there. Ultimately, of course, she was to reject it, even as a minor part of the analysis. She argued that the traditional distinction between the movement along a production function in a given state of knowledge and the movement of the function itself because of the influence of technical progress was to misspecify the investment process both at the level of the individual firm and industry and for the economy as a whole. In one of her many discussions of this point, she says: 'To discuss the choice of technique, we must look, not at total stock of capital as a point on a pseudo-production function, but at the investment plans which are being made at each moment' (1971, p. 104). Having analysed the accumulation process 'in an environment of near full employment' in which a large firm is not 'provided with a predigested "book of blue-prints" [but has to] find out what the possibilities are and assess them as best it may', she concludes: 'Since, as output per head rises, prices are likely to rise less than in proportion to wage rates, it is possible to see long spells of accumulation in which real wage rates are rising but the rate of profit is not falling. In this sense, "substitution of capital for labour" is the essence of industrial development, but it has nothing whatever to do with the factor prices shown on a pseudo-production function' (ibid. pp. 106–7). As I often pointed out to her, what she was saying here was, in essentials, much the same as what Salter had to say in his seminal work on productivity and technical change (Salter, 1960, 1965, 1966). She did not disagree for, despite all the evidence to the contrary, she never regarded his work as being in the neoclassical tradition!

V

As far as Joan Robinson's personal quest is concerned, there are a number of significant papers which follow *An Essay On Marxian Economics*. In particular, there is her booklet (1953) *On Re-reading Marx*. The third lecture is called 'An open letter from a Keynesian to a Marxist' – read Ronald Meek – in which she claimed that she understood 'Marx far and away better than you do … [because she had] Marx in [her] bones and you have him in your mouth' (*CEP*, 1951–79, Vol. IV, p. 265). From the point of view of our task in this essay, though, it is the 'Lecture delivered at Oxford by a Cambridge Econo-mist' (to one thoroughly scared tutor and his or her pupil) which is signifi-cant. Joan Robinson sets out her views on the nature of equilibrium, of how in her opinion you cannot get into it, or even tend towards it. Here I think she may have had Hayek in her sights as well. I recently reread his brilliant 1937 *Economica* article on economics and knowledge. It made me realize, first, how small and parochial the profession was then and, secondly, how funda-mental were the concepts with which they grappled, only to have both their questions and their attempted answers lost to the modern generation of econo-mists, especially those trained in the United States. In many ways Joan's discussion of the nature of time and equilibrium is more fresh and exciting (and insightful even) than it was to be in the 1953/4 *Review of Economic Studies* paper and *The Accumulation of Capital*. What *is* strange is that this aspect of her critique was rather neglected, even by herself, as people chased after the conundrum of measuring capital within the neoclassical framework, and the intricacies of Golden Age models and so on. Again, if she had published the preface to a subsequent edition of *The Accumulation of Capital* (see Harcourt, 1990, p. 51), her purposes would have been better understood and the sea-change in her views then emerging better realized, even by herself. For she certainly gave some fuel to the misconceived view of what she was doing, not least in her early response to the Introduction (1951) to the Sraffa with Dobb edition of Ricardo's works and correspondence and her 1961 review in *Oxford Economic papers* of Sraffa's 1960 book (Robinson, 1961a) and, later on, when the reswitching debate was in full swing, with her 1967 paper with K.A. Naqvi on it all in the *Quarterly Journal of Economics*. Not that her position was not covered by appropriate qualifications, it was, rather, that the significance of the latter was not understood by mainstream readers, nor by the neo-Ricardians and the American Post-Keynesians.

VI

At the same time as Joan Robinson was writing about 'high theory' from a critical point of view and attempting to generalize *The General Theory* to the long period, she was also being both philosophical and practical about China. This was partly a reflection of her view that to understand an economy we must always start from its history, institutions and 'rules of the game', espe-cially when the economist concerned is actually trying to influence the form which the latter two should take. There may be overlaps of analysis at certain points between one sort of economy and another; for example, her discussion of the choice of technique in *The Accumulation of Capital* which is derived from Wicksell has a part to play in her 1950s lectures in China (and her debate with Dobb and Sen over their rationalization of Stalinism), but the changed setting has to be – and it is – made explicit. Again, many of her exercises in *Exercises in Economic Analysis* (1960) reflect her thoughts on current issues in China.

Most of all, her difficult but profound essay, 'The Philosophy of Prices' (*CEP*, 1951–79, Vol. II) (which was too much for the Russians and Poles to take) reflect her musings on the nature of the society being analysed. Basically, she grappled with the inescapable facts of life of *any* society in which commodities are exchanged, having been produced by labour and commodities, and a price mechanism rules: that there is a two-way interchange between incomes and prices and that the appropriate price structure for the desired development of the economy may not throw up incomes for significant sections of the population which are consistent with society's perception of what is a decent, acceptable and humane standard of life. This problem is as acute for a planned economy as for a freely competitive capitalist one. The problem is made even more complicated by the fact that in one form of (pure) price system incomes arise from prices which are related to commodities produced by specific factors, while, in the other form of pure price system which she identifies, factors are not specific and can operate in *any* sector.

VII

By the late 1960s, Joan Robinson herself was putting all the emphasis on the methodological critique of neoclassical theory and arguing for a change to process analysis in historical time in a Kaleckian mode. This distanced her from the approach taken by the neo-Ricardians. She recognized this and had many a brawl with Garegnani and, to a lesser extent, with John Eatwell, Murray Milgate and Krishna Bharadwaj. She remained appreciative of Luigi Pasinetti's work. For example, she wrote a most favourable review (1975) of his 1974 collection of essays. She said that he had 'played a notable part in the development and exposition of ... "Post-Keynesian" theory'. She quoted, with approval, Pasinetti's main theme: 'Keynes' theory of effective demand, which has remained so impervious to reconciliation with marginal economic theory, raises almost no problems when directly inserted into the earlier discussions of the Classical economists' (1975, p. ix) and, even more perhaps, the resemblance which Pasinetti discerned between Ricardo's method of analysis and that which Keynes had revived: looking for fundamentals, direct stating of assumptions, singling out the variables believed to be most important, 'freezing out' the others – for the moment – by simple assumptions, so as to produce 'a system of equations of the "causal type" as opposed to a completely interdependent system of simultaneous equations' (Pasinetti, 1974, pp. 43–4). Joan Robinson goes on to show how thought experiments may be done with this approach and how the point of Pasinetti's 'Golden Age' analysis, for example, in his 1962 *Review of Economic Studies* paper, 'belongs to the sphere of doctrine' – it shows that there is no room for a theory of profits based on the "marginal productivity of capital" or the "rate of return" on saving' (Robinson, 1975, p. 398).

Her final assessment of Sraffa's purposes and contributions is contained in two papers, 'Spring Cleaning' (1980, 1985) and her 1980 *Cambridge Journal of Economics* paper with Amit Bhaduri on 'Accumulation and Exploitation', in which they attempt to link up Sraffa and Kalecki's modes of analysis. The latter paper is more optimistic in tone than the former, urging the coming generations to discuss 'the influence of changes in technology on demand for labour, on accumulation and on effective demand' (Bhaduri and Robinson, 1980, p. 111), a request which is even more pertinent today than when it was first published. In both papers, Joan Robinson distinguished between, on the one hand, the first two parts of Sraffa's 1960 book where change was explicitly ruled out, and the third part (on choice of technique), on the other. She interpreted the first two parts as an attack on 'the amorphous moralising Marshallian theory of "factors of production" receiving "rewards" consonant with their respective productivities' (Bhaduri and Robinson, 1980, p. 111), but I think that Krishna Bharadwaj, Garegnani and Pasinetti have shown that Sraffa's prelude to a critique was intended to encompass the entire corpus of supply and demand theories of distribution. In Part III, the choice of technique is discussed and changes are allowed – the latter she found unable to accept. Sraffa himself saw it as a critique of the concept of price as an index of scarcity in the theory of distribution – here the rate of profits (r) – by showing that there was no *necessary* inverse relation between r and the 'quantity' of capital.

Their viewpoints mesh, however, when, having argued that 'the given position in an economy is a purely logical structure', she adds that such a construction may be used to answer the question 'what would be different if ...?' (Robinson, 1980; 1985, p. 161). 'Keynesian' analysis, by contrast, is developed by making predictions about the consequences of change: 'what would follow if ...' (ibid.). It 'starts ever afresh from the short-period position that past history has brought into existence "today" and attempts to understand what consequences will follow from recent changes in it' (ibid.). Kalecki, using this method, allows us to operate in 'historical time' because 'We know something about how the share of wages in the value of net output is affected by monopoly power and the pricing policy of corporations, by particular scarcities, by effective demand, by bargaining power and the social and political climate in which it operates; and about the "inflation barrier" which drives money wages irresistibly upward when real wages are pushed too low' (Bhaduri and Robinson, 1980, p. 111). We have already noted above, the underdeveloped set of questions which complement this, and which Joan Robinson argues may be tackled by 'Sraffaesque' models which encompass 'distribution according to Marx and realisation according to Kalecki' (Bhaduri and Robinson, 1980, p. 104).

VIII

In 1979, Joan Robinson contributed a Foreword (Robinson, 1979), to Alfred Eichner's edited collection of the papers on various aspects of Post-Keynesianism which were originally published in *Challenge* (Eichner, 1979). There she identified Keynes's realization, set out most explicitly and succinctly in his 1937 answers to his critics in the *Quarterly Journal of Economics*, that

> the main distinction [between him and the school from which he was struggling to escape] was that he recognized...the obvious fact that expectations of the future are necessarily uncertain.
>
> It is from this point that Post-Keynesian theory takes off. (Robinson, 1979, p. xi)

From this starting-point she tells us that the authors of the papers in the volume are 'exploring, from various points of view, the problems of prices, employment, accumulation, distribution, growth and stagnation in the actual, historical evolution of an ever-changing world. In the nature of the case, definitive answers cannot be found quickly. There is plenty of work still to do'[3] (Robinson, 1979, p. xxi). This seems to me a good place to leave off, more optimistically than Joan herself was to be in her last year, or rather last months in Cambridge. Her spell of teaching at Williams in the autumn of 1982 had cheered her up (see Turner, 1989, pp. 204–7); it was the return to Cambridge in late December 1982 that disoriented her. She told me that for the first time in her working life she had no new projects to get on with. I tried to reassure her by suggesting that she look through what she had accomplished and that I get the research students to come and meet her, individually or in small groups, so that they could be inspired to carry on the torch that she had so decisively lit. I was not, I'm afraid, successful. Nevertheless, I believe, passionately, that Joan Robinson has set out for us a vital Post-Keynesian agenda – and an approach with which to implement it.

Notes

I am most grateful to Philip Arestis, Jan Kregel and Cristina Marcuzzo for their comments and suggestions but, of course, take responsibility for the final product, also to be published in Christina Marcuzzo, Luigi Pasinetti and Alessandro Roncaglia (eds), *The Economics of Joan Robinson*, London: Routledge, 1995.

1. I was rather surprised to be reminded that Joan wrote in the Introduction to *CEP*, 1951–79, Vol. II, in December 1959 that 'The bulk of the present volume was written within the last five years and all ... within the last eight. It belongs to the field of what is sometimes called post-Keynesian economics' (p. v).
2. Samuelson writes: 'I do not think that the real stumbling block has been the failure of a literary writer to understand that when a mathematician says, "*y* rises as *x* falls", he is implying nothing about temporal sequences or anything different from "when *x* is low, *y* is high".' He goes on to argue that, though it is possible in theory to design efficient transition paths between one long-period position and another, it is nevertheless legitimate to doubt

whether either a planned economy or a competitive capitalist economy could have the skills 'to *approximate* in real life such warranted paths' (*CEP*, 1951–79, Vol. V, p. 85). Joan Robinson commented that Samuelson had reminded us

> that a plane diagram can show relations between only two variables ... [that] a mathematician knows that a functional relationship is timeless ... makes no reference to history or to the direction of change [so that] there cannot be a movement between points on a plane diagram.... However, Professor Samuelson continues to use his construction to describe a *process* of accumulation that *varies* wages, *alters* technology and *changes* a stock of inputs made, say, of wood into one made of iron and then into copper. (CEP, 1951–79, Vol. V, p. 88).

3. I hope that those who join the chase will read Joan and Richard Kahn's work on money and the rate of interest in the 1950s and early 1960s. There, as well as expositing and extending Keynes's insights, they show by example (that is, by not doing so) the incoherence of modelling systemic behaviour by the use of *one* representative agent; see Robinson (1961b) on 'Own Rates of Interest' for a good example of what I have in mind.

References

Baranzini, Mauro and G.C. Harcourt (eds) (1993), *The Dynamics of the Wealth of Nations. Growth, Distribution and Structural Change. Essays in Honour of Luigi Pasinetti*, Basingstoke: Macmillan.

Berg, Maxine (ed.) (1990), *Political Economy in the Twentieth Century*, New York/London/Toronto/Sydney/Tokyo/Singapore: Philip Allan.

Bhaduri, Amit and Joan Robinson (1980), 'Accumulation and Exploitation: An Analysis in the Tradition of Marx, Sraffa and Kalecki', *Cambridge Journal of Economics*, **4**, pp. 103–15.

Eichner, Alfred S. (ed.) (1979), *A Guide to Post-Keynesian Economics*, New York: M.E. Sharpe.

Feiwell, George R. (ed.) (1985), *Issues in Contemporary Macroeconomics and Distribution*, London: Macmillan.

Hamouda, O.F. and G.C. Harcourt (1988), 'Post Keynesianism: From Criticism to Coherence?', *Bulletin of Economic Research*, **40**, pp. 1–33; reprinted in Sardoni (1992).

Harcourt, G.C. (1990), 'On the Contributions of Joan Robinson and Piero Sraffa to Economic Theory', Chapter 3 of Berg (1990), pp. 35–67; reprinted in Sardoni (1992).

Hayek, F.A. (1931), *Prices and Production*, London: Routledge & Kegan Paul.

Hayek, F.A. (1937), 'Economics and Knowledge', *Economica*, **4**, pp. 33–54.

Keynes, J.M. (1930), *A Treatise on Money*, 2 vols, London: Macmillan, *CW*, Vols V, VI.

Keynes, J.M. (1936), *The General Theory of Employment, Interest and Money*, London: Macmillan, *CW*, Vol. VII.

Keynes, J.M. (1937), 'The General Theory of Employment', *Quarterly Journal of Economics*, **51**, pp. 209–23; reprinted in *CW*, Vol. XIV.

Kregel, J.A. (1973), *The Reconstruction of Political Economy. An Introduction to Post-Keynesian Economics*, New York: Wiley, Holsted Press.

Pasinetti, L.L. (1962), 'Rate of Profit and Income Distribution in Relation to the Rate of Economic Growth', *Review of Economic Studies*, **XXIX**, pp. 267–79; reprinted in Pasinetti (1974).

Pasinetti, L.L. (1974), *Growth and Income Distribution. Essays in Economic Theory*, London: Cambridge University Press.

Robinson, E.A.G. (ed.) (1965), *Problems in Economic Development*, London: Macmillan.

Robinson, Joan (1933a), *The Economics of Imperfect Competition*, London: Macmillan.

Robinson, Joan (1933b), 'The Theory of Money and the Analysis of Output', *Review of Economic Studies*, **1**, 22–6; reprinted in *CEP*, Vol. I (1951).

Robinson, Joan (1936), 'Some Reflections on Marxist Economics', review of Strachey (1935), *Economic Journal*, **46**, pp. 298–302.

Robinson, Joan (1937a), *Introduction to the Theory of Employment*, London: Macmillan, 2nd edn, 1969.

Robinson, Joan (1937b), *Essays in the Theory of Employment*, London: Macmillan, 2nd edn, 1947, Basil Blackwell.

Robinson, Joan (1942), *An Essay on Marxian Economics*, London, Macmillan, 2nd edn, 1966.

Robinson, Joan (1953), *On Re-Reading Marx*, Cambridge Students Bookshop; reprinted in *CEP*, Vol. IV (1973).

Robinson, Joan (1951–79), *Collected Economic Papers*, 5 vols. Oxford: Basil Blackwell.

Robinson, Joan (1953–4), 'The Production Function and The Theory of Capital', *Review of Economic Studies*, **XXI**, pp. 81–106; reprinted in *CEP*, Vol. II (1960).

Robinson, Joan (1956), *The Accumulation of Capital*, London: Macmillan.

Robinson, Joan (1960), *Exercises in Economic Analysis*, London: Macmillan.

Robinson, Joan (1961a), 'Prelude to a Critique', *Oxford Economic Papers*, **13**, pp. 53–8; reprinted in *CEP*, Vol. III (1965).

Robinson, Joan (1961b), 'Own Rates of Interest', *Economic Journal*, **71**, pp. 596–600.

Robinson, Joan (1971), *Economic Heresies. Some Old-fashioned Questions in Economic Theory*, London: Macmillan.

Robinson, Joan (1973), 'Foreword' to Kregel (1973).

Robinson, Joan (1975), 'Review of Pasinetti (1974)', *Economic Journal*, **85**, pp. 397–99.

Robinson, Joan (1979), 'Foreword' to Eichner (1979).

Robinson, Joan (1980, 1985), 'Spring Cleaning', mimeo, Cambridge, published as 'The Theory of Normal Prices and the Reconstruction of Economic Theory', in Feiwell (1985), pp. 157–65.

Robinson, Joan and K.A. Naqvi (1967), 'The Badly Behaved Production Function', *Quarterly Journal of Economics*, **LXXXI**, pp. 579–91.

Salter, W.E.G. (1960), *Productivity and Technical Change*, London: Cambridge University Press, 2nd edn, 1966.

Salter, W.E.G. (1965), 'Productivity Growth and Accumulation as Historical Processes', in E.A.G. Robinson (1965).

Samuelson, Paul A. (1975), 'Steady-State and Transient Relations: A Reply on Reswitching', *Quarterly Journal of Economics*, **LXXXIX**, 40–47; reprinted in Robinson *CEP*, V (1979), pp. 83–7.

Sardoni, Claudio (ed.) (1992), *On Political Economists and Modern Political Economy. Selected Essays of G.C. Harcourt*, London: Routledge.

Shove, G.F. (1944), 'Mrs Robinson on Marxian Economics', *Economic Journal*, **54**, pp. 47–61.

Sraffa, Piero (1925), 'Sulle relazione fra costo e quantita prodotta', *Annali i Economia*, **3**, pp. 277–328.

Sraffa, Piero (1926), 'The Laws of Returns under Competitive Conditions', *Economic Journal*, **36**, pp. 535–50.

Sraffa, Piero (1932), 'Dr Hayek on Money and Capital', *Economic Journal*, **42**, pp. 42–53.

Sraffa, Piero (1960), *Production of Commodities by Means of Commodities. Prelude to a Critique of Economic Theory*, London: Cambridge University Press.

Sraffa, Piero with Maurice Dobb (eds) (1951), *Work and Correspondence of David Ricardo*, Vol. I, London: Cambridge University Press.

Strachey, John (1935), *The Nature of Capitalist Crisis*, London: Victor Gollancz.

Turner, Marjorie S. (1989), *Joan Robinson and the Americans*, Armonk, New York: M.E. Sharpe.

9   George Shackle and Post-Keynesianism*

I

George Shackle is to Post-Keynesianism what John Hicks (or, rather, JR) was to mainstream neoclassical economics. Both made fundamental contributions and provided deep insights which were accepted and acted upon, often by people who knew not from whence (or whom) they came. In Shackle's case, his general influence is associated with the treatment of time, expectations and uncertainty, with which is associated as well, his unique interpretations of both Keynes and Walrasian general equilibrium analysis. He hoped that his own major analytical contributions, the theory of potential surprise, would be taken up and extended by others. His biographer, Jim Ford, is inclined to argue that with the exception of a small group (including himself), this has not happened and that in so far as such a gentle and unassuming person as George Shackle could have had a disappointment, this was it. But they might have been too pessimistic in their assessment.[1] George's ideas are both respected and being looked at anew within the mainstream itself.[2] But as this is not our main story in this essay we shall not follow it up any further here.

To write this essay we looked at the writings of a number of people who come under the Post-Keynesian umbrella and who have explicitly acknowledged the influence of Shackle on their work. They include the late Alan Coddington (an observer rather than a Post-Keynesian), Victoria Chick, Paul Davidson, Sheila Dow, John Hicks and Jan Kregel. By looking up their references to Shackle's work, we gained an impression of how his ideas have permeated their work and the work of others. In addition, we read or reread much of Shackle's work. We found especially helpful the 1957 de Vries Lectures, *Time in Economics* (1958), *The Years of High Theory* (1967) (our favourite Shackle book), *Epistemics and Economics* (1972), and George's superb essay in the Arestis/Sawyer volume of dissenting economists (1991). In addition, Jim Ford very kindly let us see his forthcoming obituary essay on George for the *Economic Journal* and some of his papers on Shackle's early work on the trade cycle, together with Ford's interpretation and extension of it (Ford and Peng, 1993).

* Although this is a joint essay, the first versions of Sections I, II, III, IV and VI were written by G.C. Harcourt and C. Sardoni wrote the first version of Section V. We are indebted to Stephan Boehm, Jim Ford, Wendy Harcourt, Prue Kerr and Jochen Runde for helpful comments on a draft of this essay, which was first published in Stephen Boehm, Stephen F. Frowen and John Pheby (eds), *Economics as the Art of Thought: Essays in Memory of G.L.S. Shackle*, London: Routledge, 1995.

II

When writing on Shackle's influence on Post-Keynesianism we need to remember that 'Post-Keynesianism' is a portmanteau term which embraces a diversity of ideas and a collection of heterogeneous people. In Hamouda and Harcourt (1988), they were divided into three broad groups, with some individuals, including Shackle himself, spanning more than one group, and so contributing to more than one strand. The principal groups include the American Post-Keynesians, the Neo-Ricardians and the Kaleckians *cum* Robinsonians. Shackle's influence on most members under the Neo-Ricardian grouping is minimal for they do not regard uncertainty or expectations as central to either their understanding of the economy or the nature of economic theory.

We feel that in this regard they are unfaithful to themselves. For they argue that, because *general* theory may only relate to an account of the possible interrelationships between sustained, persistent, dominant and permanent features of an economic system, the long-period method is the only possible mode of theorizing. The concept of the long-period position which is central to their approach carries a connotation of realized expectations so that uncertainty and reactions to it seemingly have no role to play in this theoretical schema. Yet what could be more sustained and all-pervading than the inevitable, inescapable presence of uncertainty? It is true that each individual uncertain event is unique and once-and-for-all. Yet an *environment* of a continuous stream of such unique uncertain events is, paradoxically, a certain, obvious and inescapable fact of life, about the effects of and responses to – and surely an inescapable task of a theorist is to tackle these? – George Shackle had more profound things to say than most economists in the twentieth (or any other) century.

No more so is this relevant than in the theories of investment and theories of the rate of interest in Keynes and, then, the Post-Keynesians. Shackle had the highest regard for Hugh Townshend (who reviewed his first book) and who wrote a remarkable article in the *Economic Journal* in 1937, 'Liquidity-Premium and the Theory of Value'. The article drew out the implications of the theory of liquidity preference and of the arguments of Chapter 17 of *The General Theory*, which Keynes himself initially had missed; or, at least, he had not taken in their full significance. Victoria Chick has put the essence of all this very well in her *New Palgrave* entry on Townshend:

> [Townshend's] note takes issue with Hicks' [subsequent] attempt ... to transform the theory of liquidity preference into a mirror image of the loanable funds theory by Walras's Law. Townshend saw that this was an attempt to retain the link between prices and the flow concepts of cost and demand.... [He argued] that it was in the nature of Keynes's ... theory that expectations of the future could change the value of assets overnight and be reflected in the market prices

of those assets even in the absence of actual trading. Thus current prices could be determined by subjective as well as objective factors and future prices were indeterminate. (1987, p. 662)

Shackle himself enlarged on these themes in a number of places, especially in *The Years of High Theory*:[3]

> The interest-rate in a money economy. This was the enigma that led Keynes to the nihilism of his final position, made explicit by him in the *Quarterly Journal of Economics*, and by his interpreter Mr Hugh Townshend in the *Economic Journal*, virtually at the same moment. The interest-rate depends on expectations of its own future. It is expectational, subjective, psychic, indeterminate. And so is the rest of the economic system. The stability of the system, while it lasts, rests upon a convention: the tacit general agreement to *suppose* it stable. This stability, once doubted, is destroyed, and cascading disorder must intervene before the landslide grounds in a new fortuitous position. Such is the last phase of Keynesian economics. But Keynes had shown governments how to prolong the suspension of doubt. (Shackle, 1967, p. 217)

Shackle and Townshend are here expositing a theme which Nicholas Kaldor was to set out in 1939 in what is generally regarded as his greatest theoretical article, 'Speculation and economic stability'. The theme relates to those markets in which stocks dominate flows, and speculations dominate tangible economic factors, in the determination of prices. The market for financial assets is a prime (but alas, not the only) example. Related to these characteristics is the importance, for the stability of the system, of adoption of certain conventions which in turn, in some concrete situations, can prove to be very fragile.

Again, because of uncertainty and the need to cope with it when making spending and wealth-holding decisions, aggregate demand, especially the component accounted for by investment expenditure, could falter. Because of the peculiar properties of the liquidity variable, themselves attributable in turn to the presence of uncertainty, the faltering demand could be siphoned off into the holding of a non-employment and non-employment-creating asset.[4] If moreover, at the same time as the desire to accumulate was falling off, the desire to hold the liquidity variable was increasing, there would be a directly reinforcing effect on the initial contractionary forces, for not only would the marginal efficiency of capital schedule move to the left (or even collapse) but one effect of the liquidity preference schedule moving to the right could be to tend to raise the rate of interest (complex of) which in turn would have a further contractionary effect on investment spending.

Of course, the whole thrust of Shackle's arguments was that, in these realms, the effects of movements of schedules were not only qualitatively and quantitatively much more important than the effects of movements *along* schedules – hence his dislike of IS/LM Keynesianism – but also much harder, if not impossible, to predict. Carried to its logical extreme this insight has the nihilistic implications of the sort which Alan Coddington detected in the work of both Shackle and Joan Robinson and which created the sense of terrible, unresolved tensions in the pages of his last book, *Keynesian Economics: The Search for First Principles* (1983). Coddington fervently hoped that the contributions of Robert Clower and Axel Leijonhufvud would provide a safe route out of the impasse which he saw threatening economics as a discipline, but we do not believe that he persuaded himself that it was a creditable one. He was thus faced with accepting

> a position that [appeared] to be consistent but analytically nihilistic... If subjectivist logic is followed to the point of becoming convinced that there is nothing for economists to do but to understand certain (praxiological) [*sic*] concepts, then the only problem that remains is that of subjugating one's conscience long enough to draw one's salary in exchange for imparting this piece of wisdom. One could, of course, having got into this state of mind, spend a good deal of time and energy in trying to convince those who engage in macroeconomics, econometric model building, mathematical economics, general equilibrium theory and so on, of the folly of their ways. But, that task accomplished, there would be nothing left but for the whole profession to shut up shop. (Coddington, 1983, p. 61)

Although such inferences also led Shackle to be ambivalent concerning macroeconomic policy and its chances of success, reinforcing a scepticism borne out of his wartime experiences (see Ford, 1992, p. 4) and to Joan Robinson feeling that, after over 50 years as an economic theorist, economic theory had come to pieces in her hands, that she no longer believed in it, Shackle also offered some interesting insights concerning the way in which macroeconomic policy *could* be at least partly successful. He did this by referring to Keynes's own position in *The General Theory*. Keynes's conviction that the inducement to invest is 'capricious and incalculable' and that there is a tendency for the economy to remain below full employment required policy interventions. But the 'capricious and incalculable' nature of the inducement to invest also implies an improbable ability to control and foresee such a volatile variable. He tried to solve this dilemma in a 'Marshallian' way. In dealing with investment in a formal way by using the marginal efficiency of capital schedule, Keynes adopted the Marshallian method of *ceteris paribus*.

> He adopted the method, natural and obvious to a Marshallian, of regarding the marginal efficiency of capital, for the analytic purpose in hand, as dependent only on the size of the aggregate flow of investment, and of treating that size itself as determined by that numerical value of the marginal efficiency at which the latter was equal to the prevailing rate of interest. This analytical scheme had a number

of advantages. A superficial one was the suggestion it offered for influencing the size of the investment flow by manipulating the interest-rate. (Shackle, 1972, p. 432)

But all the *cetera* of the analysis are extremely unstable and precarious. If they change the marginal efficiency schedule shifts 'bodily, abruptly and widely'. If the schedule is subject to such movements how can we hope to control the economy through the rate of interest?

> The legitimate answer seems to be that no matter what the shape and position of the curve, we can always try to push investment one way or the other along the curve. If the curve shifts, the effect of this on the size of investment flow must be counteracted, if desirable, by a movement along the new curve. Keynes was justified, we may think, in urging that monetary policy should do what it can in any circumstances to bring the aggregate investment-flow to an appropriate full employment level. (Shackle, 1972, p. 433)

Shackle's approach here differs from that of the general equilibrium and mechanical business cycle models, both with respect to theory and to policy.

> The method implicit in the *General Theory* is to regard the economy as subject to sudden landslides of re-adjustment to a new, precarious and ephemeral, pseudo-equilibrium, in which variables based on expectation, speculative hope and conjecture are delicately stacked in a card-house of momentary immobility, waiting for 'the news' to upset everything again and start a new dis-equilibrium phase. (Shackle, p. 433)

III

We have mentioned Shackle's view that many of the relationships in economics are prone to, *in principle*, unpredictable instability. A corollary of this is, of course, his scepticism, to put it at its mildest, concerning general equilibrium analysis principally as a means of capturing the essence of the economic process, just because it excludes the essential characteristics of time as he saw them as a human being and as an economist. We quote Shackle himself at this point:[5]

> In the classical dynamics of the physicist, time is merely a mathematical variable. The essence of his scheme of thought is the fully abstract idea of function, the idea of some working model or coded procedure which, applied to any particular and specified value or set of values of one or more independent variables, generates a value of a dependent variable. For the independent variable in a mental construction of this kind, *time* is a misnomer ... The solution to the differential equation, if it can be found, is complete in an instantaneous and timeless sense.
> This timelessness ... abolishes the distinction between past and future. The physicist has, within the stated limits of his problem, complete, perfect and indisputable *knowledge* of where his particle will be at any instant; the very nature of

human consciousness ... depends ... upon *ignorance* of the future ... upon the necessity to live in one moment at a time. (Shackle, 1958, pp. 23–4; italics in the original)

Later on, he amplified this last insight.

For the individual human consciousness time is not a mathematician's space nor a historian's panorama but a moment. In this solitary moment all the consequences that the decision-maker seeks or accepts must necessarily be contained. These consequences must therefore be experiences by imaginative anticipation. As the basis of these anticipations the individual cannot avail himself of a unique self-consistent picture free of doubts or counter-suggestions, but has in mind a set of rival diverse hypotheses ... [which, in Shackle's view, should be regarded as] the essential freedom of the individual imagination to create afresh from moment to moment .... [I]f this freedom were unbounded, if there were no discernible links between action and consequence, decision would be needless and useless. To afford enjoyment by anticipation, imagination must work within a sense of the possible, of the rules of the game, of the essential artistic constraint.

In speaking of freedom, what do we imply? That decisions can be creative acts each injecting something essentially new into the world process: we imply the possibility of *inspiration*. In the universe without inspiration, decisions are empty; in the universe without order, without links between action and consequence, decisions are meaningless. Between these two extremes ... is there room for the world of inspiration and order, the world of continuing creation by the instrument of decisions made by men? (1958, pp. 33–4)

The essential weakness of general equilibrium analysis, as Shackle understood it, stemmed from these views. His is a rather idiosyncratic interpretation of general equilibrium, certainly not one which accords either with what Walras himself thought it was or with the view of the best modern practitioners, for example, Frank Hahn.[6] But Shackle's interpretation does go right to the heart of the weakness and abuse of general equilibrium theory in the hands of those less gifted than either its founder or its leading modern expositors. For Shackle it

is the natural and even the logical arrival point of that procedure of theorizing which assumes that men pursue their interests by applying reason to their circumstances ... reason can only be applied to circumstances in so far as those circumstances are taken as known. But the circumstances relevant to the choice of actions include other men's chosen actions. If the solution is to be general or symmetrical; if it is to accord to any and every person, no matter whom, a freedom and knowledge formally identical with those of every other person, if the rules of the games are to be precisely the same for all, the various actions of all these persons must be pre-reconciled. But choices which are pre-reconciled are effectively simultaneous.... Sequential actions, transformations of one situation into a subsequent and different one, occurring successively, are excluded in the nature of things from being studied as the consequences of pure reason, unless these successive transformations all belong to simultaneously pre-reconciled plans. (Shackle, 1972, pp. 90–92)

In Victoria Chick's critique (1978) of Clower's attempt to derive Keynesian results starting from a Walrasian general equilibrium framework which is then modified, she expressed succinctly a view which would have been dear, we believe, to Shackle's heart. Having outlined the main features of Walras's exchange model, she notes:

> In contrast, the *General Theory* presents a model of a *production* economy, using *money*, moving through *time*, subject to *uncertainty* and the possibility of *error*. Is it any wonder that Walras' Law does not hold? ... Production, unlike exchange, *necessarily takes time* ... it imposes an *ordered sequence of economic decisions*, necessarily overlapping continuously in time at the macroeconomic level but quite distinct at the micro level. (Chick, 1978, 1992, p. 59)

Perhaps the most profound comment made on Shackle's understanding of the inappropriateness of ancient and modern general equilibrium analysis for illumination of actual economic processes is to be found in Jan Kregel's paper at the Shackle Conference in 1986 (Kregel, 1990). There Kregel links Shackle's highly original work on imagination, and its central role in economic decision making and the functioning (or malfunctioning) of the economic system (parts and whole), to Adam Smith's similar discussion. In doing so, Kregel argues, convincingly in our view (see especially pp. 81–9) that modern general equilibrium theorists have misunderstood Smith's views on the roles of self-interest, the invisible hand and the price mechanism, so that modern general equilibrium theory is as illegitimate an heir of our founder's *Theory of Moral Sentiments* and *Wealth of Nations* as the bastard Keynesians are of Keynes's *General Theory*. The link with Shackle arises from Smith's argument that we can only *know* what we ourselves think and feel; therefore, we build into our behaviour the supposition that others have similar sensations and functions and that this gives rise to both norms in, and constraints on the working of the system, especially with regard to price formation, distribution and accumulation. Shackle took this insight further, concentrating his sights principally on business people's decision making under uncertainty and the process of accumulation, inspired, in Kregel's view, implicitly by Smith and, of course, explicitly by Keynes.

> It is in the explanation of the nature of the motivation of human action that Shackle takes up his investigations, providing the most important extension of the Smithian conception, which he calls 'the human predicament', to the analysis of the predicament facing business enterprise in modern capitalist economies. This represents the shift in the source of the desire for accumulation from Smith's time to the present day, from individual acquisition predominated by exchange, to

business enterprise in which the investment decision dominates accumulation. (Kregel, 1990, p. 93)

Paul Davidson found in Shackle's work staunch support for Davidson's spelling out of the implications of the economic system being made up, in large part, of non-ergodic processes. In recent years Davidson has stressed that this insight is one of Keynes's principal contributions. Non-ergodic processes are characteristic of systems of relationships where the stability of key parameters cannot be guaranteed and where both cross-section and time series averages are spurious measures – spurious in the sense that the values of the variables in the system have no necessary tendency to converge on the values of the averages. As Davidson puts it, 'the outcome of an economic process can never be forecast with statistical accuracy at the start of the process'. He adds: 'it is only in a non-ergodic environment, where people recognize that the future may be non-predictable in any stochastic sense, that the sensibility of human beings prevails. Sensible expectations rely on diverse organizations that have evolved to permit human beings to cope with the unknowable. Only in such a world are the attributes of dignity and human motivation necessarily geared *not to rationality* but to sensibility' (Davidson, 1990, p. 327; italics in original).[7]

This distinction between 'sensible' and 'rational' is both Marshallian and Shacklean.

IV

It would be wrong to allow Shackle's deep intuitions and influence to be reduced to the bare bones of 'movements of are more important than movements along schedules'. We know that his genes and his intelligence made him in principle a capable mathematician. He has left us some fine technical articles in which both algebra and geometry are exploited in the best possible way by a master craftsman in complete command of his tools of trade. But he did not think mathematics *was* the appropriate language for large parts of economics. He thought that the written language could best indicate the multidimensional aspects of key factors at work in the economic system. Because he was such a kind and generous person, when he distinguished between two sorts of economics (and economists!), he refrained from saying, at least very emphatically, which he preferred. Thus in his 1983 autobiographical essay in the *Banca Nazionale del Lavoro Quarterly Review*, he wrote: 'I think there are two kinds of economics. One of them aims at precision, rigour, tidiness and the formulation of principles which will be permanently valid: an economic science. The other is ... rhetorical ... often used disparagingly [–] a modern unscholarly abuse. The rhetorician employs reason and appeals to logic, but he is a user of language at its full compass, where words are fingers touching the keyboard of a hearer's mind. I do not believe that human affairs can be exhibited as the infallible and invariable working of a closed and permanent system' (Shackle, 1983, 116).

But increasingly it became clear from his writings that he preferred the second sort of economics. Sheila Dow especially has taken up this theme in her writings on the economics of the tower of Babel (see, for example, Dow, 1990). She argues that

> In practice, this mode of thought [the Babylonian approach] involves approaching any issue from a variety of starting-points, using a range of partial analyses in order to build up a picture. Each chain of reasoning may be said to start from axioms, but the axioms of one chain of reasoning may be the conclusions of another. One aspect of Babylonian thought is the rejection of formalism in the sense that not all knowledge can be expressed formally.
> ... For example, Feynman ..., who applied the term 'Babylonian' to a style of mathematical reasoning, demonstrated that three statements of the law of gravitation which are mathematically equivalent are philosophically and psychologically unequivalent. To express all economic theory in terms of a common language, as advocated by Hahn, would thus be to eliminate knowledge. (Dow, 1990, pp. 146–7)

In his earliest work Shackle argued that Keynes's ideas needed to be presented in a framework which included the concepts of *ex ante* and *ex post* (to which he had been introduced by Brinley Thomas's 'thrilling' lectures on the Swedish School at the LSE (see Harcourt, 1990, p. xix)). But, then, his emerging views on time made him very critical indeed of deterministic mechanical period analyses of economic processes, including the trade cycle. Especially was this so of any analysis past one period – the next. Jim Ford has succinctly described Shackle's principal objections:

> The interpretation of time germane to economics [as] 'inside' or 'subjective' time, rather than 'outside' or 'mechanical' time led Shackle to make two related contentions: the first was that it was impossible to construct a dynamic model of an economic system except for one period at a time; and the second was that the formal, mathematical models of growth and of business cycles which were based upon such mechanisms as difference equations were otiose, having no meaning, being necessarily built on mechanical, non-expectational, time. (Ford, 1992, p. 10)

He adds: 'The implication that economics would not be a predictive science was not entirely welcome', a view that is nevertheless being reached from such diverse sources as the critical realists, Frank Hahn, and the evangelical wing of the modern Austrian School![8]

What Shackle seems to have in mind is that, though each moment of time is a separate miracle, if we know what has led up to it we can discuss what may happen next, in the sense of next period. However, after that, the number of possible interrelated scenarios for each decision maker taken in isolation and then looked at collectively are so many and so complex that they may not be handled intelligently even by the onlooking economist. This viewpoint is related to an argument which Tom Asimakopulos had with Joan Robinson, an argument that goes back to Keynes's own despair of ever finding a determinate time unit with which to analyse obviously interrelated economic processes, the component parts of which nevertheless take different stretches of actual historical or calendar time to work themselves out. Asimakopulos did not like her later argument, in *Economic Heresies*, for example, that 'Marshall's short period is a moment in a stream of time ... It is better to use the expressions "short period" and "long period" as adjectives, not as substantives. The "short period" is not a length of time but a state of affairs' (Robinson, 1971, pp. 17–18). Asimakopulos by contrast insisted that both Marshall and Keynes (one in a partial setting, the other in an economy-wide setting) did have a definite length of actual time in mind so that there was 'time available to permit variations in the utilisation of productive capacity in response to changing short-term expectations' (Asimakopulos, 1988, p. 196). The simplification then required for Keynes's theory (which he shied away from) is to suppose that most production periods and gestation periods in the economy are of similar lengths and that decisions about production, and about investment, are synchronized.[9]

This was basically Kalecki's solution and it allowed him to string together successions of short periods in order tell his many stories of cyclical growth in capitalism and, as Richard Goodwin also did, to dismiss the distinction between trend and cycle as bogus.[10] Thus, these Post-Keynesians are not held back, or at least explicitly troubled by Shackle's basic misgivings. It would be fascinating to know whether Shackle and Kalecki ever broached this theme when they worked together in London in the 1930s (see Harcourt, 1990, p. xxi). It would have been even more fascinating to have eavesdropped if they had.

We are aware that temperament has much to do with which stand is taken. Because Shackle thought that liquidity preference was Keynes's most profound contribution, and because Shackle had such respect for Townshend's insights, he may have let his consequent understanding of finance capital dominate his views on the boundaries and limitations of theory.[11] Kalecki was more influenced by the characteristics of industrial capital, partly because of his early personal experience, partly by inclination, and so Shackle's hesitations would not have been such a clamp on his attitudes to and mode of theorizing.

V

We began this essay by comparing the role George Shackle played for Post-Keynesians with the role Hicks played for mainstream economists. In this section we consider briefly the relationship between Shackle's and Hicks's positions concerning some crucial aspect of Keynesian economics.

J.R. Hicks and George Shackle first met in 1930 at LSE. They were two of the group of young economists who worked with Lionel Robbins and Friedrich von Hayek: a group of eminent economists who, in Hicks's words, shared a common 'faith' from which most of them were soon to depart:

> We seemed at the start, to share a common viewpoint, or even, one might say, a common faith. Some of us, especially Hayek, have in later years maintained that faith, others, such as Kaldor, Abba Lerner, George Shackle and myself, have departed from it, to a greater or less extent. (...) The faith in question was a belief in the free market, or 'price-mechanism' – that a competitive system free of all 'interferences', by government or by monopolistic combinations, of capital or of labour, would easily find an 'equilibrium'. (Hicks, 1982, p. 3)[12]

Keynes's *General Theory* of course played a decisive role in making them depart from the old faith. However, despite this initial common faith and the common factor that contributed to its loss, Hicks has been very spare in his reference to Shackle's work, whereas Shackle has always emphasized the importance of Hicks's contributions to economics (see, for example, Shackle, 1967).

In fact we have to wait until *John* Hicks came to reconsider *J.R.* Hicks's IS–LM model in 1980–1 to find an explicit reference to Shackle's work and an acknowledgement of its relevance.[13] The reference to Shackle is only a short footnote but it is significant because of the relevance of the topic being examined: the interpretation of the concept of equilibrium in relation to Keynes's theory.

In his 1980–81 article, Hicks was concerned with the conceptual difficulties raised by his 1937 IS–LM model with which he had by then become dissatisfied. In particular, he dealt with the time dimension of the IS–LM model and the compatibility of the *flow-equilibrium* in the commodity market and the *stock-equilibrium* in the money market.

The equilibrium method plays an important role in *The General Theory*; therefore the IS–LM model which is based on the equilibrium method cannot be regarded as a totally misleading interpretation of Keynes. Such a model, in the same way as *The General Theory*, raises a number of difficulties especially connected with a coherent treatment of time and of stocks and flows. They are difficulties that are inherent in the equilibrium method itself, which is based on contemporaneous causality. The way out from all this is to abandon altogether the method. For Hicks,

If one is to make sense of the IS–LM model, while paying proper attention to time, one must, I think, insist on two things: (1) that the period in question is a relatively long period, a 'year' rather than a 'week', and (2) that, because the behaviour of the economy over that 'year' is to be *determined* by propensities, and suchlike data, it must be assumed to be in an appropriate sense, *in equilibrium*. (Hicks, 1980–81, pp. 147–8)

To assume equilibrium in the product market (that is, a flow-equilibrium) makes it possible to establish a Keynesian functional relationship between current output and current input.[14] Equilibrium in the product market (the *IS* side of the model) is a flow equilibrium which refers to a span of time, a period. In considering equilibrium in the money market (the *LM* side) we are concerned with stock relations and equilibrium must be in a point of time rather than in a period. Thus the IS–LM model must necessarily combine two different sorts of equilibrium. A way to reconcile these two different kinds of equilibrium might imply converting the stock relation into a relation which holds over the whole period to which the flow equilibrium applies.

If we adopt the equilibrium interpretation, on the IS side, the economy must be treated as *if* it were in equilibrium over the period; that means, on the IS side, that the economy must remain in flow equilibrium, with demands and supplies for the flows of outputs remaining in balance. It would be logical to maintain that on the LM side the economy must be treated similarly. There must be a *maintenance* of stock equilibrium. (Hicks, 1980–81, p. 151)

A stock equilibrium over the period implies the flow equilibrium over the period.[15] This is the concept of full equilibrium over time. This concept of equilibrium, however, is not acceptable in the Keynesian context; it is at odds with the very notion of liquidity preference – on which the LM schedule is based.[16]

Thus the notion of equilibrium seen above must be amended. Hick's amendment derives from his analysis in *Causality and Economics* (1979). In order to make liquidity compatible with equilibrium,

We must evidently refrain from supposing that expectations as they were before April of what is to happen after April, were precise expectations, single-valued expectations; for in a model with single-valued expectations, there can be no question of liquidity. And we must also refrain from the conventional representation of uncertain expectations in terms of mean and variance, since that makes them different in kind from the experiences which are to replace them. There is, however, a third alternative. Suppose we make them expectations that the values that are expected (...) will fall within a particular range. This leaves room for liquidity, since there are no certain expectations of what is going to happen, but it also makes it possible for there to be an equilibrium in the sense that what happens falls within the expected range. A state of equilibrium is a state in which there are no surprises. (Hicks, 1979, p. 85; quoted in Hicks, 1980–81)

This, for Hicks, is the only notion of equilibrium over time which is compatible with the concept of liquidity. It is in this respect that he acknowledges Shackle's contribution: 'I should here make an acknowledgement to G.L.S. Shackle, who in much of his work has been feeling in this direction' (Hicks, 1980–81, p. 330n).

Before looking at Shackle's reply to Hicks, it is interesting to look at how Hicks proceeded in his analysis after introducing his 'amended' notion of equilibrium over time. In *Causality in Economics*, having introduced the notion of equilibrium depicted above, Hicks argues that, if the equilibrium method is to be used within the Keynesian model, such a notion of equilibrium must be adopted but,

> Even so, it appears that the weakest part of the Keynesian model; the conventional Keynesian model, is after all the Liquidity Preference relation, which from other points of view, perhaps more important points of view, is its characteristic feature. Liquidity, it turns out, is not at home with Equilibrium; and is therefore not at home with Contemporaneous Causality. (Hicks, 1979, pp. 85–6)

Hicks finds a 'better place' for liquidity in the context of sequential causality in which effect follows cause. Sequential analysis is the analytical method followed by the Swedish economists and is regarded by Hicks as the most promising way forward:

> the further development of theory, which I agree is required, should begin with an attempt to identify the questions it will have to be concerned with. These, I have tried to show, are in essence questions of sequential causality. We have so far no more than the beginning of a theory which will help us with such questions; but we do have a beginning. (Hicks, 1979, pp. 101–2)

In a short comment on 'Hick's explanation', Shackle (1982) returns to his distinction between the two approaches to economics; he ascribes to Hicks great merits in the construction and development of equilibrium economics; and clearly puts himself in the other camp, where the 'theme of the unknowable or not yet originated future' is dominant. More specifically, on Hicks's 1980–81 paper, Shackle argues that there Hicks has not yet fully acknowledged the incompatibility between Keynes's theory and equilibrium economics.[17]

As for the reference to his own work, Shackle, not surprisingly, discards Hicks's interpretation:

> I do not think his suggestion in footnote 12 that 'Shackle ... has been feeling in this direction' at all represents my course of thought. I am not sure what 'this direction' is; but the conception I described in Chapter 28 of *Decision, Order and Time* (1961) ... was not meant to underpin any notion of equilibrium. My proposal ... was part of an attempt to elucidate the nature of uncertain expectation.

Perhaps my repudiation of the equilibrium frame of analysis can best be summarized by saying *all markets are in some degree speculative*. (Shackle, 1982, p. 438)

In Shackle's view the truest interpretation of Keynes's thought is to be found in his 1937 article in the *Quarterly Journal of Economics* (Keynes, 1937)[18] as *The General Theory* was still largely affected by Keynes's struggle to escape from old ideas. It is in the light of Keynes's position in this article that the equilibrium method of *The General Theory* must be interpreted.

It was Marshall's influence upon Keynes which led him to use the equilibrium method in *The General Theory*.[19]

The *General Theory* was necessarily at odds with itself. For its author had been brought up to believe that in order to make sense of things we must have 'as many equations as there are variables', we must have a determinate 'equilibrium'. But equilibrium was the antithesis of the *General Theory*'s inward vision of business life. (...) How could the two 'necessities' be reconciled? Only by the method of studying the abstract adjustment which the expectations and beliefs (...) prevailing at some moment would lead to, given a breathing-space or moratorium to work out their logical inter-active consequences, and then of imagining, so far as possible, the cascade of real events which must flow from the inevitable upset of any such state of rest accidentally attained. (Shackle, 1972, p. 435)

This is what Shackle called the 'kaleidic' method. Such a method provides us with a notion of equilibrium.

It presents us with descriptions of equilibrium positions for the economic society as a whole, which differ from those of the value-construct in not being optima, but merely positions which do not contain within their structure an immediate source of movement. It shows how in the nature of things, and in their own nature, these 'equilibria' are vulnerable in the extreme to any expectation-changing news; for they rest upon expectations which naturally and necessarily conflict with each other (speculative prices can only stay at rest on conditions of conflict expectations) and are ready at a touch to break up and dissolve. (Shackle, 1972, p. 437)

If this is the only acceptable notion of equilibrium ('kaleidic' equilibrium), what role is left for economic theory to play? Is, in particular, theory able to provide us with answers concerning the way in which relevant variables move and change when such fragile positions of rest are upset?[20] Such a view of the economy and the consequent vision of economics can

offer diachronic insights of a very tentative, modest and short-range kind, not seeking to show what must happen, but what is the range of diversity of the immediate developments that various situations are capable of. (...) The notion of kaleidic equilibrium is an explicit recognition of, and draws attention to, the overwhelming evident fact that *economic* affairs of society are not self-contained and independent. They may be compared to a sailing-boat in tempestuous and tide-swept waters. Certainly the boat itself has unity of structure, but what happens to it will be the outcome not only of its design (its capacities for response to impacts of various kinds, its *elasticities*) but the policies, training and local knowledge of the crew and the behaviour of vast forces of the environment (...) We may be able to gain knowledge of how the economic boat will respond to this or that shift of the surrounding forces, we cannot hope to know what those shifts will be. (Shackle, 1972, p. 438)

Both Hicks and Shackle see the difficulties that are inherent in the method which Keynes uses in *The General Theory*, in particular the difficulty to reconcile the notion of liquidity preference and a traditional notion of equilibrium. However, they point to and develop alternative approaches. Hicks, once he became convinced that the IS–LM model represents an unsatisfactory representation of the essential spirit of Keynes's theory, moved towards the sequential approach which was first started and developed by the Swedish economists. Shackle developed a vision of economic theory according to which it is impossible to capture the richness and unpredictability of actual economic systems by recourse to any rigid formal model. It is from this point of view that Shackle criticized also the sequential approach which Hicks regarded as the way out from the difficulties of the equilibrium method. As we have seen, in his critique of the sequential approach, Shackle remained closer to Keynes than Hicks was to Keynes.

VI

In the appendix to *Time in Economics* (Shackle, 1958, p. 92), Shackle set out the five qualities 'which an economic theory should possess in some degree'. They were:

1. logical rigour,
2. realism,
3. immediacy,
4. inclusiveness and
5. human reference.

These five qualities may be recognized in all strands of Post-Keynesianism, though clearly different weights are given to them in each. Again, Post Keynesians differ very much in their attitudes to policy and with regard to what policies are morally and politically acceptable. Shackle himself became more and more passive concerning policy as he grew older. An essential clue as to why may be contained in the conclusion to this appendix. He wrote: 'In sum, we have our choice, *predicted man* is less than human, *predicting man* is more than human. I conclude, in an expression of mere personal conviction, that man in his true humanity can neither predict nor be predicted' (Shackle, 1958, p. 105).

Keynes worried about whether it was possible both to do good and to be good. His own life suggests emphatically that it is. That George Shackle was a good man has been attested to over and over again. Provided, therefore, that proper note is taken of his caution and reservations, we believe that Post-Keynesians should try to do good, and that, in this endeavour, we would surely have the blessing of the person whose example, wisdom and insights have so profoundly affected us all.

Notes

1. Jochen Runde for one confirms this in his fine paper in this book [*Economics as the Art of Thought*].
2. Fernando Carvalho recently published a paper (Carvalho, 1992) which spans Shackle's work, the work of two maverick mainstreamers, Bob Clower and Alex Leijonhufvud, and Post-Keynesianism. He has linked Shackle's concept of potential surprise to Clower and Leijonhufvud's economy-wide concept of the 'corridor' in order to give precision to the latter. His main results are, first, that the disappointment of individual's expectations is related to the degree of convergence between the expectations of different individuals, and, secondly, that the width of the corridor may be defined in terms of this divergence.
3. See also Shackle (1972, pp. 206–19).
4. As Shackle told G.C. Harcourt in their 1980 talk, 'investment is a highly hazardous business, a gambling question, for the businessman at the time of his decision does not know whether he will make profits or not, especially in future years. In these circumstances, businessmen are swayed by the current state of the news and can lose their nerve, keep their money in the bank and so unemployment starts – it's as simple as that' (Harcourt, 1990, p. xxi).
5. We fervently agree with Jim Ford (1992, p. 9): 'I let Shackle's words speak for themselves, for I am unable to improve upon them.'
6. But, as general equilibrium analysis is intrinsically linked to and based upon the hypothesis of perfect competition, Shackle's critique of general equilibrium seems to recall Schumpeter's denotation of perfect competition as a hypothesis which implies the exclusion of any strategy. Prices in the competitive framework are determined by 'the mass effect of the actions of all households and all firms in "markets", the mechanism of which are relatively easy to describe as long as the households and firms have no choice but to adapt the quantities of commodities and services they wish to buy or to sell to the prices that rule. We may call this the Principle of Excluded Strategy' (Schumpeter, 1954, p. 972). And Schumpeter concluded: 'But exclude "strategy" as much as you please, there still remains the fact that this adaptation will produce results that differ according to the range of knowledge, promptness of decision and "rationality" of actors, and also according to expectations they entertain about the future course of prices, not to mention the further fact that their action is subject to additional restrictions that proceed from the situations they have created for themselves by their past decisions' (Schumpeter, 1954, p. 973).
7. Jochen Runde has pointed out to us that Shackle allows for degrees between zero and one in the 'epistemic interval', that is, there is a place in his system for *degrees* of belief. Davidson's dichotomy does not – which seems to sever the link between Davidson and Shackle.
8. Stephan Boehm, however, has pointed out to us that 'the evangelical wing of the modern Austrian School' is not the only one to reject the notion of economics as a predictive science. All non-instrumentalists, such as realists, hermeneuticists, proponents of rhetoric and moderates like himself, reject such a notion.
9. Something that, as Jim Ford reminds us, 'assumes away the problem'.

10. It is ironic that the real business cycles theorists also make this argument, for we are sure they would be horrified to know that they had *anything* in common with the subversives above, if only they had ever heard of them.

11. This is *not* to say that he did not make important contributions to the theory of the firm and of investment, for example.

12. Shackle talked of this period in the following terms: 'Chance brought me to the London School of Economics at the moment when Hayek was reforming and reformulating Böhm-Bawerk's theory of capital; when Hicks was (in that very term) going to propound the production plan and the role played in it by the rate of interest; when Brinley Thomas (in that very term) was going to tell a minute class how the seeds sown by Wicksell were blossoming in the work of Lindhal and Myrdal; and when rumours about the book that Keynes was writing were drifting up from Cambridge. Thus by a blessing of chance I entered L.S.E. to begin my PhD dissertation at an electric moment of charged and tingling intellectual excitement (Shackle, 1983, pp. 112–3).

13. An exception is a reference to Shackle's work in a footnote to *Capital and Growth* (1965), where J.R. Hicks, in dealing with the relationship between the concept of temporary equilibrium and uncertainty, mentions Shackle's alternative approach to the treatment of uncertainty and expectations (Hicks, 1965, p. 70n).

14. 'For once we assume that production plans, during the period, are carried through consistently we have the relation between current input, during the period, and current output, during the period (which has been made equal to effective demand within the period) for which we have been looking' (Hicks, 1980–81, p. 148).

15. By quoting from *Capital and Growth*, Hicks states: 'Equilibrium over time requires the maintenance of stock equilibrium; (...) Thus when we regard a "long" period as a sequence of "short" periods, the "long" period can only be in equilibrium over time if every "short" period within it is in equilibrium over time. Expectations must be kept self-consistent; so that there can be no revision of expectations at the junction between one "short" period and its successor (...) That can only be possible if expectations – with respect to demands that accrue within the "long" period – are *right*. Equilibrium over time thus implies consistency between expectations and realisations within the period. It is only expectations of the further future that are arbitrary (exogenous) as they must be' (Hicks, 1965, pp. 92–3, as quoted in Hicks, 1980–81, p. 151).

16. 'There is no sense in liquidity, unless expectations are uncertain. But how is an uncertain expectation to be realised? When the moment arrives to which the expectation refers, what replaces it is fact, fact which is not uncertain (Hicks, 1980–81, p. 330).

17. 'In this "explanation" Sir John still does not seem to me to acknowledge the essential point: the elemental core of Keynes' conception of economic society is uncertain expectation, and uncertain expectation is wholly incompatible and in conflict with the notion of equilibrium' (Shackle, 1982, p. 438).

18. A point of view shared by several Post-Keynesians. See, for example, Minsky (1975, pp. 55–68).

19. Keynes gave a wide berth to both the achronic method of general equilibrium, and the pan-chronic method of supposing that all dates have an equal and co-valid reality, and are in a peculiar sense contemporaneous with each other, so that there are two kinds of time, one for the all-seeing analyst and one for the participant painfully crawling from one sudden contingency to another with no bird's-eye view' (Shackle, 1972, p. 430).

20. 'Can theory or measurement throw light on the character of the disintegrative movements which flow from the break up of a kalcidic equilibrium? Can such an equilibrium be described in such terms as will suggest the directions in which variables will move, and how fast and far their reactions will go?' (Shackle, 1972, p. 437).

References

Arestis, P. and S.C. Dow (eds) (1992), *On Money, Method and Keynes. Selected Essays. Victoria Chick*, Basingstoke: Macmillan.

Arestis, P. and M. Sawyer (eds) (1991), *A Biographical Dictionary of Dissenting Economists*, Aldershot: Edward Elgar.

Asimakopulos, A. (1988), *Investment, Employment and Income Distribution*, Cambridge: Polity Press.

Carvalho, F.J., (1992), 'Equilibrium and co-ordination with Shacklean expectations', *Revista Brasileira de Economia*, **46**, 319–37.

Chick, V. (1978), 'The nature of the Keynesian revolution: a reassessment', *Australian Economic Papers*, 1978; reprinted in Arestis and Dow (1992), pp. 55–79.

Chick, V. (1987), 'Townshend, Hugh (1890–1974)' in Eatwell, Milgate and Newman, Vol. 4, p. 662.

Coddington, A. (1983), *Keynesian Economics: The Search for First Principles*, London: Allen & Unwin.

Davidson, P. (1990), *Money and Employment. The collected writings of Paul Davidson*, Volume 1 (edited by Louise Davidson), Basingstoke: Macmillan.

Dow, S.C. (1990), 'Beyond dualism', *Cambridge Journal of Economics*, **14**, 143–57.

Eatwell, J., M. Milgate and P. Newman (eds) (1987), *The New Palgrave. A Dictionary of Economics*, Basingstoke: Macmillan.

Ford, J.L. (1992), 'G.L.S. Shackle (1903–1992): a life with uncertainty', Birmingham, mimeo.

Ford, J.L. and Wen Sheng Peng (1993), 'Shackle on expectation, investment, the business cycle and economic development', *Review of Political Economy* (G.L.S. Shackle Memorial Issue), **5**, pp. 138–64.

Frowen, S.F. (ed.) (1990), *Unknowledge and Choice in Economics. Proceedings of a conference in honour of G.L.S. Shackle*, Basingstoke: Macmillan.

Hamouda, O.F. and G.C. Harcourt (1988), 'Post-Keynesianism: from criticism to coherence?', *Bulletin of Economic Research*, **40**; reprinted in Sardoni (1992, pp. 209–32).

Harcourt, G.C. (1990), 'Introduction: notes on an economic querist – G.L.S. Shackle', in Frowen (1990), pp. xviii–xxvi.

Hicks, J.R. (1965), *Capital and Growth*, Oxford: Clarendon Press.

Hicks, J.R. (1979), *Causality in Economics*, Oxford: Basil Blackwell.

Hicks, J.R. (1980–81), 'IS–LM – An Explanation', *Journal of Post-Keynesian Economics*, winter, 139–54.

Hicks, John (1982), *Collected Essays on Economic Theory, Volume II. Money, Interest and Wages*, Oxford: Basil Blackwell.

Kaldor, N. (1939), 'Speculation and economic stability', *Review of Economic Studies*, **7**, 1–27.

Keynes, J.M. (1937), 'The general theory of unemployment', *Quarterly Journal of Economics*, February: reprinted in *Collected Writings*, Vol. XIV, pp. 109–23.

Kregel, J.A. (1990), 'Imagination, exchange and business enterprise in Smith and Shackle', in Frowen (1990), pp. 81–95.

Minsky, H.P. (1975), *John Maynard Keynes*, New York: Columbia University Press.

Robinson, Joan (1971), *Economic Heresies: Some Old-fashioned Questions in Economic Theory*, Basingstoke: Macmillan.

Sardoni, C. (ed.) (1992), *On Political Economists and Modern Political Economy. Selected Essays of G.C. Harcourt*, London: Routledge.

Schumpeter, J.A. (1954), *History of Economic Analysis*, New York: Oxford University Press.

Shackle, G.L.S. (1958), *Time in Economics*, Amsterdam: North-Holland.

Shackle, G.L.S. (1967), *The Years of High Theory. Invention and Tradition in Economic Thought 1926–1939*, Cambridge: Cambridge University Press.

Shackle, G.L.S. (1972), *Epistemics and Economics: A Critique of Economic Doctrines*, Cambridge: Cambridge University Press.

Shackle, G.L.S. (1982), 'Sir John Hicks' "IS–LM: an explanation": a comment', *Journal of Post Keynesian Economics*, **IV**, 435–8.

Shackle, G.L.S. (1983), 'A student's pilgrimage', *Banca Nazionale del Lavoro Quarterly Review* (145), 107–16.

Shackle, G.L.S. (1991), 'George L.S. Shackle (born 1903)', in Arestis and Sawyer (1991), pp. 505–10.

10 The structure of Tom Asimakopulos's later writings*

I

Tom and I knew one another for 35 years. Our close friendship dates from the late 1960s after Tom had made a major shift in his approach to economics, following his year at MIT in 1965–6 where, listening to Bob Solow's lectures, the significance of Joan Robinson's critique of neoclassical theory and method fell into place (see Harcourt, 1991, p. 42, and Abe Tarasofsky's moving account of this episode quoted in the Preface of Harcourt, Roncaglia and Rowley, 1994, p. xii). When Tom and I were research students together at King's in the 1950s, he worked with Harry Johnson. I started with Nicky Kaldor and then went to Ronald Henderson, but I was very much influenced by Joan Robinson, and especially by *The Accumulation of Capital* (1956). I read her *magnum opus* in my second year as a research student, having been to her lectures on it the year before (with Tom and our mutual friend and my former teacher at Melbourne University, Keith Frearson). I did not have many talks with Tom about economics but I did observe with awe the work sheets for his PhD dissertation in the (old) Marshall Library; they were an appropriate index of his systematic thoroughness and command of technique.

I know now that his first mentor was Jack Weldon and that Murray Kemp was also an important influence (see Harcourt, 1991, 42, n. 2). I imagine (but I don't know) that Tom was taught Keynes from the *Treatise on Money* and *The General Theory* and Marshall from the *Principles*, by Jack, together with Joan Robinson and Edward Chamberlin from the originals and Piero Sraffa from the 1926 *Economic Journal* article, just as I was in Melbourne. I expect that he came to know J.R. Hicks from *Value and Capital* (and the *Trade Cycle*?), Roy Harrod from his 1939 article and 1948 book, Paul Samuelson from the *Foundations* (1947) and his published articles, and, I also imagine, some original D.H. Robertson. Reading Jack Weldon's superb chapter on the classical theory of distribution in Tom's book on income distribution (1988a), in retrospect I am not surprised that Tom came to the later views that he did, for the crucial seeds were sown early on by Jack. Nevertheless, in the 1950s and early 1960s, his overall structure of analysis differed from what it was to become, now fully reflected in the volume of selected papers (Asimakopulos,

* First published as Chapter 1 of Geoffrey Harcourt, Alessandro Roncaglia and Robin Rowley (eds), *Income and Employment in Theory and Practice*, Basingstoke: Macmillan, 1994, pp. 1–16.

1988b), the introduction to and his chapter in the edited book on income distribution, his microeconomics text (1978a), and his last book (1991) in which the views he had developed over the years in teaching Keynes, Harrod and Joan Robinson to his students were set out lucidly and in full for posterity.

Tom's published writings show more than any other scholar's work I know well[1] the great value of developing books and articles from teaching material, which is how the bulk of Tom's published work originated. The need to explain explicitly and clearly the assumptions of the analysis, to understand and to quote representative references which support the generalizations about other authors' views, the need to present a perspective and to explain the origins and relevance of concepts – all the demands on a good teacher were supplied in Tom's writings and they were built up from years of experience of lecturing on the issues, often at different levels.

Another characteristic of Tom's work was his ability to retain the essential message and thrust of great authors, to pass their message on, fully and fairly, while at the same time ironing out mistakes, inconsistencies, muddles and the blurred vision which inevitably must characterize the work of innovative original thinkers, charting new and/or unfamiliar territories. And because Tom did this for each of the great authors whose work he read, analysed and taught, the structure of his own thought is a model of coherence, clarity and logical consistency.

Tom wrote to me on 26 April 1984, soon after the death of Joan Robinson, that he had written 'a "critical" review [of her contributions (Asimakopulos, 1984), because she was] too important an economist to be treated any other way, but the basis for [all his] criticism [came] from her own critical writings'. Joan was as hard on herself as she was on others; that is to say, she was very hard indeed. Tom too had exacting standards and the more he liked and respected a person, especially a student, the harder he would be. I am sure, therefore, that he would wish the same attitudes to be present in evaluations of his contributions. I must say straight away that it is more difficult to fault him by these standards than it was Joan Robinson. I attribute this partly to differences in temperament, especially as Joan grew older, but mainly to Tom's conscientious attention to detail in his classes, where, it has to be said, he would often be teaching less gifted pupils than those whom Joan taught for most of her life.

II

The first thing to say about Tom's approach was that he insisted that all discussions of economic issues be grounded in the nitty-gritty of reality, of a recognizable economy with its specific history, institutions and 'rules of the game', as Joan Robinson used to put it. This was true not only of his discussions of employment and growth theories but also of his microeconomics lectures and the textbook (1978a) that grew out of them. All of its chapters are scattered with real-world examples and the theory is assessed by how well (or ill) it illuminates them. Tom deplored the habit in modern macroeconomics of ceasing to distinguish, in models which are supposed to relate to capitalist economies, between the capital goods sector and the consumption goods sector, with the different motives and financial power of the decision makers in, and the purchasers of the products of, each sector. This failure meant that the differential impacts of their behaviour as a group or class on economic processes were missed out. He was very critical of Martin Weitzman's influential article in 1982 on increasing returns and involuntary unemployment (which Nicky Kaldor loved – or, at least, he loved its conclusions), just because the model in the article was not recognizable as one of a capitalist economy because these essential features were missing in its specification. Thus: 'There is no investment in this model ... and it thus cannot even begin to analyze the question of the determinants of the levels of, and fluctuations in, output and employment in modern economies' (Asimakopulos, 1985, p. 352). 'The model does not contain workers or capitalists, but only units of a single "composite" factor of production, and there can thus be no wages or profits, even though the terms are used' (p. 352). The production units are referred to by Weitzman 'as "firms or plants" (p. 795) but they are no more ... than a combination of factor units come together to produce goods.... There is [therefore] no factor unit doing the "hiring" with the others being "hired".... Weitzman ignores the specification of his model and uses the verb "to hire" (p. 788)' (Asimakopulos, 1985, pp. 352–3). Tom points out that Weitzman attributes 'persistent involuntary under-utilisation of the major factors of production' to insufficient overall demand, itself traceable in turn to the unemployed lacking 'the means to communicate or make effective their potential demands' (Weitzman, 1982, p. 787). But for Keynes, such communication was not sufficient 'for an increase in employment to be self-sustaining, because the value of the increased output contains a profit component. Investment, as well as consumption, must increase in order to establish a higher equilibrium level of output and employment' (Asimakopulos, 1985, pp. 353–4). Tom concludes: 'Weitzman is unable to deal with Keynes's approach, or to examine its micro-foundations because there is no investment in Weitzman's model' (p. 354).

Again, when Tom (1978b) contrasted the model(s) of the firm implied in Wicksell's and Marshall's writings, he much preferred Marshall's model because its essential features were more recognizably those of actual firms in an historically real, capitalist economy. One of Wicksell's specifications, by contrast, was much more abstract and idealized and so did not give rise to categories of income and classes of persons to be found in actual firms, or to results which were legitimately comparable with those from Marshall's model. The setting for Tom's critique was the discussion in the modern literature 'concerning the appropriate criterion for firms to use in choosing the optimal technique for investment ... maximization of the internal rate of return on the amount invested and maximization of the present value of the investment' (Asimakopulos, 1978b, p. 51). Tom points out that 'The decision-makers in each of these models have different roles [and so] each ... refers to a different reality' (p. 51). He adds: 'the failure to appreciate this difference is due to the absence in much of current economic theory of specifications of the institutional settings for the analyses.... A necessary element in a theoretical model, if it is to be used to gain insights into the operation of actual economies, is the specification of the social relations of production which pertain to those economies' (pp. 51–2). Tom argued that Marshall included two important features of modern economies in his model: first, the concept of ownership of the means of production by a minority (the 'capitalists') which allowed them to organize and control production and purchase the labour power of the majority (the 'workers'); secondly, two types of capitalists, entrepreneurs who use their own as well as borrowed capital to organize production, and rentiers who lend their capital but are otherwise passive as far as production is concerned. Wicksell had only one, or sometimes, none of these features in his model.[2]

III

I mentioned that I was not surprised that in his later approach Tom would take a stance which reflected that of his first mentor, Jack Weldon, as well as of his second major mentor, Joan Robinson and, through her, Kalecki. In his chapter on the classical theory of distribution (Weldon, 1988), Jack stresses that there were recognizable macroeconomic processes in classical thought to which was linked the crucial organizing concept of the surplus, its creation, extraction, distribution and use. This was to become central to Tom's thought, too, though he was most interested in what was happening in the sphere of distribution and exchange. There he traced the interrelationships between the theory of effective demand, especially of investment, and employment and distribution, their links back to underlying pricing mechanisms, and also (with John Burbidge) how a theory of tax incidence could be developed within this framework.

The crucial change in Tom's structure of analysis occurred when he fully comprehended Joan Robinson's distinction between logical time and historical time, with which was associated her methodological critique of neoclassical theory – as she saw it, the illegitimacy of applying propositions drawn from a comparison of differences to an analysis of processes involving actual changes occurring. (She was eventually to sum this up in the graphic phrase,

'History versus Equilibrium'.) Joan wrote about all this in an intuitive manner, criticizing those economists who argued for a tendency towards equilibrium, whereas, she argued, either an economy (or a market or an industry or a firm) is *in* equilibrium and has been for a long time, logically since the expulsion from the Garden of Eden, *or* it is not. In the latter case, economists observe a specific situation with a particular history, structure and set of expectations and their role is to analyse what happens next when a change is imposed on the existing situation. Joan often used the analogy of a pendulum, the ultimate resting place of which is independent of whether it is given a slight nudge or arbitrarily lifted high and let go. In physics it does end up at the same place but in any economic system the analogy does not apply. Even in the first case it might not be true that an economy (*et al.*) would return after a slight nudge, unless the traders responsible for making the market and setting the prices had had such a long time to experience the realization of equilibrium prices that they did not panic when the (small) nudge occurred. But if the economy had never reached an equilibrium in the past, how could it be argued that people will ever have the experience to know that they will reach one in the future? Analytically, Joan Robinson (and Kaldor) were talking about path-dependent equilibria – where an economy ends up depends on the path taken on the way. In Joan Robinson's case, she thought that it was often unlikely that it would *ever* end up in an equilibrium though it might remain in a tranquil position for a while, one which superficially seemed to have equilibrium characteristics.

It was these insights which underlay much of Tom's later work. An early example is Tom's article, 'Keynes, Patinkin, Historical Time and Equilibrium Analysis' (1973). Here Tom contrasts the economic model examined in Patinkin's 1956 book (which acknowledged an 'obvious dependence ... on the ... concepts and techniques [of *The General Theory*])' with

> the model underlying *The General Theory*. This difference is reflected in the treatment of historical time, expectations, and the forces leading to positions of full-employment equilibrium. Keynes' model is ... a causal model ... deals with a particular situation at a particular period of time. Given ... the ... features of the particular situation examined,... the model works out what will happen next ... may not be one of full employment ... expectations may be disappointed with repercussions on behaviour in future periods. Patinkin's model ... is an equilibrium model. Attention is concentrated on equilibrium relations ... embodies the assumption that forces will move the system to equilibrium if the position examined [is] one of disequilibrium. (Asimakopulos, 1973, p. 179)

Keynes's 'essentially static' analysis is nevertheless 'concerned with a segment of actual, historical time.... The *memory* of past states and previous transaction prices affect present attitudes ... Patinkin's model ... deals with a very different "world" ... more readily described in terms of simple equations' (p. 180). In particular, expectations continue to be held with certainty, even though they may be disappointed and 'the basis on which expectations are formed' is seen to be responsible. 'Patinkin's model is ... essentially "timeless", with the economy's history having no role in [its] development ... [it] does not provide a useful theoretical basis for understanding the workings of the economies for which Keynes' model was developed' (p. 181).

We may also see these arguments reflected in Tom's discussion of local and global stability in his microeconomics textbook (1978a). He gives a very clear account (pp. 82–7) of the differences between Marshallian and Walrasian stability in a competitive market and then points out the limited nature of the concepts – local and global, Marshallian or Walrasian, or any combination of these. For *always*, the equilibrium sits there waiting to be found while the stability analysis does its thing, whereas the essence of the Robinsonian critique is that the very act of seeking changes the equilibrium itself. In the section 'limitations of standard stability analysis' Tom writes:

> The standard methods ... are mechanical. Expectations and the passage of time are ignored ... the experience of non-equilibrium situations does not affect the positions of the demand and supply curves ... the experience of changing prices does not change the expectations about future conditions.... There is no time ... other than a representation of demand and supply conditions for [a] particular slice of time. They cannot be used to trace a movement over a series of such slices, or during this particular period ... if the initial price is not an equilibrium price, without additional assumptions concerning ... the foundation of expectations, the holding of stocks, and possible changes over time in the values of the parameters. (Asimakopulos, 1978a, pp. 86–7)

In terms of Jan Kregel's classic paper on the various models in *The General Theory* and the papers after it (1976), the shifting equilibrium method emerges as the dominant one. In Keynes's theory, not only were short-term expectations not immediately fulfilled, but also their very non-fulfilment was allowed to feed back into the formation of long-term expectations and so change the implied equilibrium (rest state) position associated with the point of effective demand itself. It was grappling with this issue that led to some of Tom's most incisive work, such as his critique of Keynes's theory of investment and the two-sided relationships between accumulation and profit which he put in its place (scrupulously acknowledging the influence of Kalecki and Joan Robinson on his 1971 paper); his exposition of Kalecki's theory of investment (1977), whereby, by the time the chain of reasoning had been gone through, he had returned again to the arbitrary position from which, for convenience, he had started the analysis and had explicitly handled any problems raised by his discussion at each point on the way, so making sure that the analysis *was* set in historical time. Again, if we were to read (or reread) Asimakopulos and Burbidge on tax incidence (1974, 1988b), we would see all these issues being raised, faced fairly – and dealt with. The conclusion is a model of clarity and modesty:

> We have obtained results on the incidence of taxation by concentrating on situations of short-period equilibrium. This is appropriate for comparisons with the neoclassical models because they deal only with equilibrium positions, and it is in line with Kalecki's work in this area. It is only a first step, however, and a fuller treatment of the subject would require the tracing of the effects of tax changes over time. A change in tax at the beginning of a short period, even if we assume that it does not affect current investment, would probably work itself out over more than o.ie short period. The resulting changes in output, prices, profits etc. will affect investment decisions and these will lead to further changes. In order to assess the longer-term effects of tax changes the analysis must be carried out within the context of a fully articulated growth model that permits the effects of the changes to be traced out over time. (Asimakopulos, 1974; 1988b, p. 70)

Finally, in his 1983 paper for the Joan Robinson Memorial issue of the *Cambridge Journal of Economics*, which precipitated one of the most prolonged controversies of the 1980s in post-Keynesian theory, Tom discussed the deficiencies of Keynes's and Kalecki's modes of attack on the interrelationship between finance, saving and investment. In Keynes's case, in his 1937 articles on the rate of interest (*CW*, XIV, 1973), in which he discussed his neglect in *The General Theory* of the finance motive as an additional reason for demanding money, he reached the startling conclusion that: 'the investment market can become congested through shortage of cash [but] never ... through shortage of saving ... the most fundamental of my conclusions within this field' (*CW*, XIV, 1973, p. 22). This led Tom to re-examine Keynes's arguments and also Kalecki's, for he discerned a similarity between Keynes's concept of a 'revolving fund' of finance and Kalecki's 'image' of the circle of finance which closes itself, (Kalecki, 1935, p. 343). Tom wished to show that their models were not general but rather assumed a situation of considerable unemployment and undercapacity utilization of existing plant, with ample unused finance in the banking system, so that output and prices (perhaps) could be changed without pressure on interest rates. Moreover, it would be legitimate to proceed as if income had risen to give the new desired saving equal to the new desired investment straightaway. That is to say, it was allowable to slide over the distinction between the existence of a short-period rest state (with unemployment) and the process by which it was attained, a procedure which was not generalizable to all situations of the economy. In a sense Tom was to side with Ralph Hawtrey and, later, Hicks (in *The Crisis in Keynesian Economics*, 1976), in their reluctance to accept Keynes's short-cut method whereby the short-period rest state point could be used to 'explain' critical observations on the economy (see Harcourt, 1981, 1992, pp. 250–64).

Moreover, Tom remained insistent that, for Post-Keynesian analysis to be operational, it must be done in terms of periodic analysis. He criticized Joan Robinson's later views in which she changed the definition of the short period so that it became 'not a length of time but a state of affairs' and she argued that the expressions, 'short period' and 'long period', should be used 'as adjectives, not as substantives' (Joan Robinson, 1971, pp. 17–18). Tom objected to this approach because it took away 'the setting for Keynes's theory since there is no time available to permit variations in the utilization of productive capacity in response to changing short-term expectations' (Asimakopulos, 1988b, p. 196). (The simplification then required for Keynes's theory, which he himself shied away from, is to suppose that most production and gestation periods in the economy are of much the same length and that decisions about production, and about investment, are synchronized.) Joan Robinson's views are, I think, connected to the insights contained in Hugh Townshend's 1937 paper in the *Economic Journal*, 'Liquidity-Premium and the Theory of Value' and to those in Nicky Kaldor's 1939 paper, 'Speculation and Economic Stability'. The arguments of both of these papers, together with those of Keynes himself in his 1937 papers, lie behind, for example, Snippe's 1985 critique of Tom's article. Victoria Chick, in her entry on Townshend in the *New Palgrave*, has put the essence of the position very well indeed:

> Townshend's note takes issue with Hicks's [subsequent] attempt to transform the theory of liquidity preference into a mirror image of the loanable funds theory by Walras's Law. Townshend saw that this was an attempt to retain the link between prices and flow concepts of cost and demand ... [He argued] that it was in the nature of Keynes's ... theory that expectations of the future could change the value of assets overnight and be reflected in the market prices of those assets even in the absence of actual trading. Thus current prices could be determined by subjective as well as objective fact and future prices were indeterminate. (1987, p. 662)

This leads into Kaldor's analysis in which he discusses, in effect, the characteristics of those markets where stocks dominate flows, and expectations dominate tangible economic factors, in the determination of prices, so that the analysis must concentrate on a moment in time before being extended to illuminate periods of time. Tom drew on Kaldor's analysis in order precisely to define those conditions which must hold in the financial sectors in order that the simple multiplier story of Keynes and Kalecki went through. It involves taking a view of what is the typical way in which an investment project is financed over its lifetime; that is, both to get it off the ground in the first place and, then, to build the financial aspect of it into the liability side of the firm's balance sheet in a permanent form. For the economy as a whole, this requires consideration of both how banks behave in aggregate and how new saving from newly-created income associated with both new investment expenditure and secondary rounds of consumption expenditure is held. This requires, in turn, a consideration of the term structure of interest rates (and, increasingly, the factors which lie behind the holding of equities and the issue of new ones). Kaldor postulated a group of speculators who needed to take a view on the long-term rate of interest (and presumably the prices of equities) in order that they could 'do their thing' and keep the long-term rate of interest at levels it would have attained anyway, had there not been a rise in aggregate investment expenditure in the first place.

Tom was very careful to distinguish between the identity, $S \equiv I$, and the equilibrium condition, $S = I$, something which neither Keynes nor Kalecki ever had really clear in their own minds. But there was a faint blur in Tom's discussion of saving which literally is a decision not to spend; it is not a provision of finance as such. Kregel points this out in his comment in the *Journal of Post Keynesian Economics* (1986), where he argues that what Tom identified as temporary or undesired savings are in fact cash balances arising from decisions to hold or to disgorge (p. 96; see also Kregel's essay in Harcourt, Roncaglia and Rowley, 1994.) This pushes the argument back to the crucial role of the banks in allowing the new investment process to go through in its entirety, that is, to Keynes's original position. To help settle the arguments, may I suggest that we ask whether the following statement can be given a rigorous, precise meaning within the context of these exchanges? '"Yesterday's" saving may influence "today's" investment, and "today's" saving may influence "tomorrow's" investment, but it is "today's" investment which is responsible for "today's" saving".' I believe this both reveals a deep Keynesian insight and is *not* precise, for the distinction between 'desired' and 'actual' remains blurred. It was in sorting this out that Tom's approach was so invaluable, even if, as I believe, he lost sight of some of the elements in the argument whereby a 'moment' of time really was the proper vantage-point from which to begin the analysis.

IV

In his last book (Asimakopulos, 1991), Tom dealt with the contributions of Keynes, Harrod and Joan Robinson. He examined the work of the last two scholars because both of them, in their own distinctive ways, were attempting to 'generalise the *General Theory* to the long period'. In Tom's reading, both conceded, in the end, that they failed, basically because, while it could plausibly be argued that the analysis of *The General Theory* is directly applicable to actual economies in the here and now[3] even when simplified to rest state analysis, Tom nevertheless agreed with Keynes's judgement: 'I should, I think, be prepared to argue that, in a world ruled by uncertainty with an uncertain future linked to an actual present, a final position of equilibrium, such as one deals with in static economics, does not properly exist' (*CW*, XXIX, 1979, p. 222). From this standpoint, both Harrod's warranted rate of growth and Joan Robinson's Golden Ages were *not* the operational counterparts in growth theory of the aggregate demand and supply schedules (and their intersection) of *The General Theory*. Kalecki's (and Goodwin's) cyclical growth models, in which long-period and short-period factors impinge *simultaneously* on the economic decisions of the here-and-now to create activity, employment and distribution, were, I believe, Tom's favoured way forward.

Because of this, Tom was impatient with, and sceptical of the neo-Ricardian long-period method (outside the domain of doctrinal debates, where even Joan Robinson would allow its use if it exposed lack of logic in her opponents' propositions, even on the most abstract plain). Far from accepting that general theory could only be done using the long-period method, whereby general propositions could be made about the interrelationships between persistent and dominant forces at work in economies, Tom denied that, in general, there could be either convergence on or fluctuations around such centres of gravitation. He thus rejected the Milgate–Eatwell–Garegnani interpretation on *The General Theory* as a long-period theory (only to be labelled an imperfectionist for doing so!). In doing so, he also was rejecting Marshall's view that short-period normal equilibrium positions could be regarded as stations on the way to the central long-period normal equilibrium cross – a view held by Marglin (1984), in what would otherwise be an approach with which Tom would have sympathized.[4]

What then of Tom's relationship to the work of our mutual pastor of Cambridge research students from the 1950s, Piero Sraffa? I have deliberately separated this from his attitudes to the approach of the neo-Ricardians for, while they explicitly claim kinship with Sraffa, they have moved on in directions which are not obviously associated with Sraffa himself. Sraffa's writings are relevant for Tom's approach in two ways. First, Tom took on board the technical aspects of Sraffa's 1926 article in the *Economic Journal*; that is, the conditions which have to be satisfied in the real world for Marshall's partial equilibrium procedure legitimately to be applied. As a result of this, Tom is one of the few economists who have tackled successfully the aggregation problems in *The General Theory*, by making explicit the conditions which have to be satisfied before both the aggregate demand schedule and the aggregate supply schedule may be regarded as coherent concepts. In doing this, Tom expunged the confusions in Keynes's presentation of aggregate demand in *The General Theory* – the two different concepts, only one of which survives as coherent (see Asimakopulos, 1991, pp. 20–23), as well as explaining how the aggregate supply curve could be built up without running foul of, amongst other things, the Sraffa critique (see, in particular, Asimakopulos, 1988b, pp. 104–13).

Tom thus carefully absorbed the technical critique but he did not go the whole way with Sraffa in the latter's conceptual critique of supply and demand theory. This is clear in Tom's 1988b chapter on Sraffa and Keynes. Tom comments (p. 129) that, in the system of *Production of Commodities by Means of Commodities* (1960), Sraffa had left 'formally open' the question whether demand could affect the prices of production in a complete economic system 'even though the general thrust of Sraffa's work implied that demand is not important in this context or, at least, that its influence on price is "not comparable" with those of labour and material inputs'. In a footnote (n.3 p. 142), Tom amplifies this and reports Sraffa's response:

> I had written to Sraffa in 1971 and had observed that his theoretical framework did not permit any conclusions about the effects of demand on prices unless the assumption of constant returns to scale were added. He responded in a letter dated 11 July 1971: 'You say "I don't see how demand can be said to have no influence on prices, unless constant returns...." I take it that the drama is enacted on Marshall's stage where the claimants for influence are utility and cost of production. Now utility had made little progress (since the 1870s) towards acquiring a tangible existence and survives in textbooks at the purely subjective level. On the other hand, cost of production has successfully survived Marshall's attempt to reduce it to an equally evanescent nature under the name of "disutility", and is still kicking in the form of hours of labour, tons of raw materials, etc. This, rather than the relative slope of the two curves, is why it seems to me that the "influence" of the two things on price is not comparable.'

I suspect that Tom was too sympathetic to the approaches of Marshall and Keynes completely to agree with Sraffa, even though, in Tom's later writings, agreement with Marx and Kalecki on other matters was evident.[5] This *may* have meant – but this is only conjecture – that Tom would have agreed with Joan Robinson's (nearly final) statement on the connection between Sraffa's approach and those of Marx and in 'Accumulation and Exploitation: an Analysis in the Tradition of Marx, Sraffa and Kalecki' (Bhaduri and Joan Robinson, 1980). Here it is argued that Sraffa's target (in his prelude to a critique) was not 'current neoclassical teaching rooted in general equilibrium and "scarce means with alternative uses" [but] the amorphous moralising of Marshallian theory of "factors of production" receiving "rewards" consonant with their respective productivities'. It is claimed that Sraffa showed 'that the influence upon distribution in capitalist industry must be divided into two separate elements. On the one side are the technical factors ... [on the other] the share of wages in net output (and therefore the potential ratio of profit on capital) [which] depends upon commercial, social and political influences and the class war' (p. 111). Production potential and actual output coincide or diverge according to the state of effective demand, itself affected by the distribution of income. Sraffa's particular contribution was to establish that

'In principle, a given technical situation is compatible with any proportion of relative shares [thus ruling] out the notion of earnings determined by productivity' (p. 111). In Joan Robinson's view, the second half of the story is easily released into historical time. It is the challenge of the 'first half of the story – the influence of changes in technology on demand for labour, on accumulation and on effective demand – [which needs to be taken up afresh]' (p. 111). Those scholars who respond to this challenge will be continuing in a tradition to which not only Tom's two mentors contributed so much but also, very much so, Tom himself.

Notes

1. The one possible exception is Eric Russell, but I can assure you that that is praise indeed!
2. I was relieved to see, if we may judge from the bibliography of Tom's article, that my writings on the choice of technique (for example, 1968; 1992; 1972, pp. 55–63), escaped his criticisms.
3. We have seen that there is a dispute as to whether we mean a moment or a stretch of actual time.
4. For an alternative view, see the essays by Heinz Kurz and Alessandro Roncaglia in Harcourt, Roncaglia and Rowley (1994).
5. For another view on these issues, see the essay by Neri Salvadori in Harcourt, Roncaglia and Rowley (1994).

References

Asimakopulos, A. (1971), 'The Determination of Investment in Keynes' Model', *Canadian Journal of Economics*, **4**, pp. 382–8.

Asimakopulos, A. (1973), 'Keynes, Patinkin, Historical Time, and Equilibrium Analysis', *Canadian Journal of Economics*, **6**, pp. 179–88.

Asimakopulos, A. (1977), 'Profits and Investment: A Kaleckian Approach' in G.C. Harcourt (ed.), *The Microeconomic Foundations of Macroeconomics*, London: Macmillan, pp. 328–42.

Asimakopulos, A. (1978a), *An Introduction to Economic Theory: Microeconomics*, Oxford: Oxford University Press.

Asimakopulos, A. (1978b), 'The Non-Comparability of Criteria for the Choice of Optimal Technique', *Australian Economic Papers*, **17**, pp. 51–62.

Asimakopulos, A. (1983), 'Kalecki and Keynes on Finance, Investment and Saving', *Cambridge Journal of Economics*, **7**, pp. 221–33.

Asimakopulos, A. (1984), 'Joan Robinson and Economic Theory', *Banca Nazionale Del Lavoro Quarterly Review*, December, pp. 381–409.

Asimakopulos, A. (1985), 'The Foundations of Unemployment Theory: A Comment', *Journal of Post Keynesian Economics*, **7**, pp. 352–62.

Asimakopulos, A. (ed.) (1988a), *Theories of Income Distribution*, Boston: Kluwer Academic.

Asimakopulos, A. (1988b), *Investment, Employment and Income Distribution*, Oxford: Polity Press.

Asimakopulos, A. (1991), *Keynes's General Theory and Accumulation*, Cambridge: Cambridge University Press.

Asimakopulos, A. and J.B. Burbidge (1974), 'The Short-Period Incidence of Taxation', *Economic Journal*, **84**, pp. 267–88; reprinted in Asimakopulos (1988b).

Bhaduri, Amit and Joan Robinson (1980), 'Accumulation and Exploitation: An Analysis in the Tradition of Marx, Sraffa and Kalecki', *Cambridge Journal of Economics*, **4**, pp. 103–15.

Chamberlain, E.H. (1933), *The Theory of Monopolistic Competition*, Cambridge, Mass.: Harvard University Press.

Chick, Victoria (1987), 'Townshend, Hugh (1890–1974)', in John Eatwell, Murray Milgate and Peter Newman (eds), *The New Palgrave. A Dictionary of Economics*, Vol. IV, London: Macmillan, p. 662.

Harcourt, G.C. (1968), 'Investment Decision Criteria, Investment Incentives and the Choice of Technique', *Economic Journal*, **78**, pp. 77–95, reprinted in Claudio Sardoni (ed.) (1992), *On Political Economists and Modern Political Economy. Selected Essays of G.C. Harcourt*, London: Routledge, pp. 27–47.

Harcourt, G.C. (1972), *Some Cambridge Controversies in the Theory of Capital*, Cambridge, Cambridge University Press.

Harcourt, G.C. (1981), 'Marshall, Sraffa and Keynes: Incompatible Bedfellows?', *Eastern Economic Journal*, **7**, pp. 39–50; reprinted in Sardoni (1992), pp. 250–64.

Harcourt, G.C. (1987), 'Theoretical Methods and Unfinished Business', in David A. Reese (ed.), *The Legacy of Keynes. Nobel Conference XXII*, San Francisco: Harper & Row; reprinted in Sardoni (1992), pp. 235–49.

Harcourt, G.C. (1991), 'Athanasios (Tom) Asimakopulos 1930–1990: A Memoir', *Journal of Post Keynesian Economics*, **14**, pp. 39–48.

Harcourt, Geoffrey, Alessandro Roncaglia and Robin Rowley (eds) (1994), *Income and Employment in Theory and Practice*, Basingstoke: Macmillan.

Harrod, R.F. (1939), 'An Essay in Dynamic Theory', *Economic Journal*, **49**, pp. 14–33.

Harrod, R.F. (1948), *Towards a Dynamic Economics*, London: Macmillan.

Hicks, J.R. (1939), *Value and Capital*, Oxford: Clarendon Press.

Hicks, J.R. (1950), *A Contribution to the Theory of the Trade Cycle*, Oxford: Clarendon Press.

Hicks, John (1976), *The Crisis in Keynesian Economics*, Oxford: Clarendon Press.

Kaldor, N. (1939), 'Speculation and Economic Stability', *Review of Economic Studies*, **7**, pp. 1–27.

Kalecki, M. (1935), 'A Macrodynamic Theory of Business Cycles', *Econometrica*, **3**, pp. 327–44.

Keynes, J.M. (1930), *A Treatise on Money*, 2 vols, London: Macmillan.

Keynes, J.M. (1936), *The General Theory of Employment, Interest and Money*, London: Macmillan.

Keynes, J.M. (1937a, 1937b, 1973), *Collected Writings*, Vol. XIV, London: Macmillan.

Keynes, J.M. (1979), *Collected Writings*, Vol. XXIX, London: Macmillan.

Kregel, J.A. (1976), 'Economic Methodology in the Face of Uncertainty: The Modelling Methods of Keynes and the Post Keynesians', *Economic Journal*, **86**, pp. 209–25.

Kregel, J.A. (1986), 'A Note on Finance, Liquidity, Saving and Investment', *Journal of Post Keynesian Economics*, **9**, pp. 91–100.

Marglin, Stephen A. (1984), *Growth, Distribution and Prices*, Cambridge, Mass.: Harvard University Press.

Patinkin, Don (1956), *Money, Interest and Prices*, New York: Row Peterson.

Robinson, Joan (1933), *The Economics of Imperfect Competition*, London: Macmillan.

Robinson, Joan (1956), *The Accumulation of Capital*, London: Macmillan.

Robinson, Joan (1971), *Economic Heresies: Some Old-fashioned Questions in Economic Theory*, Basingstoke: Macmillan.

Samuelson, P.A. (1947), *Foundations of Economic Analysis*, Cambridge, Mass.: Harvard University Press.

Snippe, J. (1985), 'Finance, Savings and Investment in Keynes's Economics', *Cambridge Journal of Economics*, **9**, pp. 257–69.

Sraffa, Piero (1926), 'The Laws of Returns under Competitive Conditions', *Economic Journal*, **36**, pp. 535–50.

Sraffa, Piero (1960), *Production of Commodities by Means of Commodities. Prelude to a Critique of Economic Theory*, Cambridge: Cambridge University Press.

Townshend, Hugh (1937), 'Liquidity-Premium and the Theory of Value', *Economic Journal*, **47**, pp. 157–69.

Weitzman, M.L. (1982), 'Increasing Returns and the Foundations of Unemployment Theory', *Economic Journal*, **92**, pp. 787–804.

Weldon, J.C. (1988), 'The Classical Theory of Distribution', in Asimakopulos (1988a), pp. 15–47.

PART III

INTELLECTUAL
BIOGRAPHIES

11 Political arithmetic in Cambridge: talking to Richard Stone[1]

One of the discipline's most creative and productive applied economists, Richard Stone, was a classicist at school. His father, a lawyer who subsequently became a judge in India, wanted Stone to read classics at Westminster so that he too could be a lawyer, reading Law at Cambridge (Caius) as his father had done before him. Stone went along with this wish – with the result that he was bored out of his mind at school. He was not able to do the science subjects that would have interested him and he only took maths – geometry, arithmetic, algebra, no calculus or matrix algebra – up to school certificate. Thus there was no hint in his school performance of the brilliance he was to show over his four years at Cambridge (1931–5): two firsts, one in the Law tripos, and one in the Economics tripos. Indeed, he went to India for a year with his parents because, as his headmaster said, there was not much point in him staying on at school. (Looking back now, he says he was glad to have had that year off and wonders now why he, in turn, did not go along wholeheartedly with his daughter's desire to do the same.)

At Cambridge, though he did brilliantly at law, Stone became increasingly disenchanted with it as a discipline and especially as a potential way of life. With the prolonged depression around him as an undergraduate, like many idealistic young people of that time, he increasingly became drawn towards economics as a means of understanding what was happening and what might be done about it. This produced the first serious clash with his parents and resulted in Stone having a nervous breakdown. He was then, as always, a kindly, loving and considerate person for whom personal clashes were traumatic experiences which took a 'tremendous' amount out of him.[2] His father reluctantly gave way and Stone read economics for two years, again performing brilliantly. He remembers Joan Robinson as the best lecturer he went to – exceptionally clear and lucid, with none of the flourishes he feels she went in for in later years. He twice went to Keynes's lectures on the embryonic (though quite advanced by then) *General Theory* and was 'most impressed'. Colin Clark lectured on statistics. Richard Kahn was Stone's supervisor. Caius did not have a teaching fellow in economics in those days; indeed, it took an outstanding performance by an economics undergraduate to persuade them to elect Hicks to a teaching fellowship when he lectured at Cambridge in the mid-1930s, too late, of course, to teach Stone himself. So Kahn supervised Stone except when Kahn had to examine, when he went to J.W.F. Rowe at Pembroke.

On graduation, Stone went into the City, working as an insurance clerk at C.E. Heath & Co., Lloyds Brokers. He did this primarily to please his father, Stone having won the first round, as it were – his father felt that if you could not be a lawyer then to work in the City was at least acceptable! Stone's first job was to change the directors' towels and by the end of the four years he reckons he had done every job that an insurance clerk could do. Although he did not like the work, it gave him the chance, which otherwise would never have come his way, to meet a cross-section of people, often at the many dinner parties which he both went to and gave himself. Moreover, he worked very hard at his economics in the evening, reading, publishing papers, looking after 'Trends' (articles in *Industry Illustrated*), which involved getting the paper out once a month with statistics up-to-date and a specialist article on virtually anything and everything. This task was bequeathed to Stone and his first wife, W.M. Stone, by Colin Clark when he left for Queensland. Clark and Stone had now become great friends, going on holidays together. It was Clark who first awakened what was to be Stone's abiding interest in national income accounting, of which approach Stone was to become the profession's most influential and elegant practitioner, and for which influence and practice he received the Nobel Prize in 1984.[3]

When the war came, Stone went into the Ministry of Economic Warfare, where he stayed for a year. In 1940, at the suggestion of Austin Robinson, he was transferred to the Central Information Services of the Offices of the War Cabinet to join James Meade,[4] who was already there, setting out the structure of the national accounts for the war effort. He said he needed someone 'to fill in the figures'. This was the origin of the Meade–Stone partnership which resulted in the white paper (Cmd 6261) on the sources of war finance and estimates of national income and expenditure in 1938 and 1940 and the well known *Economic Journal* paper of 1941, 'The construction of tables of national income, expenditure, savings and investment'. When the department was split into two parts, Meade went into the Economic Section of the Cabinet Office,[5] while Stone joined the newly formed Central Statistical Office. There he continued on national income statistics until Harry Campion, the CSO director, said he had done enough on this and put him onto oil statistics. Stone told Keynes (he had known him from Cambridge days, especially from Keynes's Political Economy Club, at which the brightest third-year undergraduates met regularly in Full Term). Keynes said: 'I'll soon stop that' and took Stone on as his assistant. Stone comments: 'This saved the national income and in all respects was a very good arrangement since Keynes showed immense interest in the development of the work' (Stone, 1978, p. 26).

Stone would see Keynes mostly at 6 o'clock in the evening. Stone himself was young and healthy and did not realize then how tired Keynes, a sick man since 1937, would have been. Often there were explosions: Stone has described this with masterly understatement in his British Academy Lecture: 'The meeting would frequently end by Keynes telling me that he never wanted to see me again ... rather worrying when it first happened but there was really nothing to worry about' (ibid., pp. 26–7). Stone confirms the conventional wisdom that Keynes generally was extraordinarily kind to the young but could be rude to and overbearing with, possibly even take pleasure in putting down, his contemporaries. He was sometimes impatient with people who were neither as quick nor as clever as he was himself – Keynes was remarkably quick at grasping an idea, to which he would add speculations and fantasies at a breathtaking pace. Stone also confirms my own favourite Keynes story. When reproached by someone for being inconsistent, Keynes is reported to have said: 'When someone persuades me that I am wrong, I change my mind. What do you do?' Stone adds (in his British Academy Lecture, p. 14) that 'Keynes' reaction to anything new was to look for weak spots and shoot them full of holes ... only a way of gaining time ... he usually thought things over and either came up with some really good arguments or changed his mind ... seldom said so in so many words, but one discovered that the insuperable objections to the frightful rot one had been talking ... had somehow melted away ... never mentioned again'.

Stone worked with Keynes all through the war. At the same time he was running the National Institute for Economic and Social Research (NIESR) in London (of which his second wife, Feodora, was the secretary) a project on national accounting for the inter-war years. In 1944, to his surprise and delight, he was offered the directorship of the still embryonic Department of Applied Economics (DAE) at Cambridge.

Just before the war, principally through the instigation of Keynes, permission had been granted by the University to set up the DAE. This went into cold storage during the war, but towards its end Keynes got American finance in the form of a Rockefeller grant; in typical Cambridge fashion, the university was delighted to have a new initiative, provided that it did not cost it anything (except the director's salary). So the DAE started in the summer of 1945 with Stone as its first director. He was elected to a fellowship in Kings at the same time, with no teaching duties. (Kahn did get him to do a few hours when Shove died. Stone said he was no good at it and that Kahn was relieved when he 'gave up'. I wonder whether he was being too modest – certainly the many research students who have been supervised by him responded very positively to his care and guidance.)

Before entering actively into his new duties at the DAE, Stone accepted an invitation to visit the Institute of Advanced Study at Princeton. There he spent his time writing for the League of Nations a memorandum on national accounting methods which was to become the foundation of the Standard System of National Accounts (SNA) as we know it today.

From the beginning the DAE and the NIESR were closely entwined. There were constant interchanges between the two, and also between the NIESR and the Treasury,[6] as a glance at the list of people who have been associated with one or the other will show – Prais, Dow and Paige, for example. The first ten years of the DAE's existence were remarkable both for their output and for the people who worked there, many in the first flush of their scholarly youth. They include Durbin, Watson, Orcutt, Farrell, Tobin, Alan Prest, Tintner, Phyllis Deane, Alan Brown, Brian Reddaway and, of course, presiding over-all and making a distinctively generous intellectual contribution of his own to each research project, was Stone himself. He led by example – no less than 43 entries in Stone's bibliography date from those ten years. These include the first of the great red books, *The Measurement of Consumers' Expenditure and Behaviour in the United Kingdom, 1920–1938*, Vol. I (with D.A. Rowe *et al.*, 1954); the work on linear expenditure systems – Stone said that they suspected the limitations that Angus Deaton was to make explicit many years later; and the 1945 *Journal of the Royal Statistical Society* (*JRSS*) paper on market demand which used confluence analysis (and which was the bane of my undergraduate life at Melbourne when we were taken through it by Don Cochrane, who had been Stone's first research student).

Stone said that he had always been interested in quantification and meas-urement, that he had little use for complex and obstruse arguments that got nowhere just because quantification was not possible, even in principle.[7] He claimed, too modestly, that theory was where he started from, that if you knew Henry Schultz's 1938 book on demand, you could predict where Stone would go on to make his own contributions in this area; that, later on, when he and Alan Brown started on the growth project, they were only putting together the previous work (much of it from the DAE, of course) on national accounts and input–output tables, that most growth theory of that time was of little use to them. (They themselves made important contributions to it as the model developed.) I asked him about optimum growth theory because he told me that he supervised Jim Mirrlees's PhD dissertation. He said he was a great admirer of Ramsey's 1928 paper, though he doubted whether the further developments and refinements would ever be able to be applied.

Stone's papers are noted not only for their emphasis on quantification and measurement but also for innovative and difficult (in the Frisch sense of not dodging difficulties) mathematical analysis. These techniques Stone acquired as an avid reader and also from discussions with friends who were good mathematicians: David Champernowne, for example, another of Stone's con-temporaries.

The performance of the DAE over these years was in a sense the cause of Stone's leaving the directorship. Too many of the older guard at Cambridge absorbed in a silly and undigested way Keynes's own (supposed) views on econometrics – of course, Keynes's views were not always *that* sensible (see his *Economic Journal* review in 1939: *CW*, XIV, p. 306–18) of Tinbergen's work on econometric estimation of investment functions and the business cycle generally).[8] They thought that the DAE had strayed too far from one of its original intentions (it was in fact a relatively minor aspect) which was to provide, in effect, the labour for the research projects of the teaching members of the faculty. So when P.D. Leake endowed a Chair of Finance and Accounting at Cambridge in 1955 (Oxford refused to have it) Stone reluctantly accepted it, pushed by his management committee and pulled, he says, by the much larger salary. (The director of the DAE now gets a professorial salary and also a Chair as well – but it was not so in those days.) He kept a group for research and worked in harmony with the new director, another old friend, Brian Reddaway, who also maintained the link with the NIESR.

In 1960, in collaboration with the late Alan Brown, Stone started the Cambridge Growth Project. It attracted over the years a succession of brilliant young people, among them Angus Deaton, Graham Pyatt, Terry Barker, William Peterson, Rick van der Plocg and Martin Weale, and became one of the most complex and sophisticated models in the world. Stone spoke of the difficulties which they had in getting the financial sector into the model, that they got bogged down in data collection and classification, illustrating how hard it is in work of this kind to be comprehensive in the short run. After Stone's retirement in 1980, the direction of the work was taken up by Terry Barker, who developed, very much with Stone's blessing, a dynamic version of the model which is still going strong. With the model so well established, with its thousands of equations and their complex interrelationships, Stone told me that he had thought of trying to write down a small model which was manageable, in which you could see reasonably well what was going on, the sort of exercise that can be done only after you have absorbed yourself for years in the processes of constructing a huge model.

Stone's contributions cover a wide area. He has put his stamp on the way in which most of the world now does its national accounts. He regrets the passing of small units whereby, in the old days, you could get a substantial amount done 'in a hot July in New York' and have it out early the next year virtually as it was drafted. Nowadays, he said, it takes five to seven years, drafts go back and forwards through innumerable committees all over the world, and while few points of substance are changed, often the compactness and unity of structure of the original draft are lost in the process.

Stone pioneered much of the modern applied work on demand theory and estimation and there is the Growth Project, itself enough for the working lifetime of one person. His papers and books are marked by a lack of controversy, by generosity and good manners, by a desire to get on with solving problems rather than scoring points off opponents. His elegant personality is reflected in the clarity of his style and the pride that he and his wife took in the appearance of the published works themselves. The effect is one of polished, positive, good humoured endeavour, a refreshing contrast to the often acrimonious and bad tempered exchanges that were occurring in the Cambridge faculty and beyond over the same period.

Stone lived in retirement in Millington Road, with his third wife, Giovana (Feodora Stone died in 1956). He had a room in the DAE but he also converted and extended a garage of their home into a library for his books and journals; his run of the *JRSS* goes back to the beginning. There, in elegant splendour, typical of Stone himself, he continued to work and write, a happy and fulfilled person for whom the award of the Nobel Prize put a seal on his outstandingly productive achievements. (The news of the award was received with delight in the faculty building itself – spontaneous grins broke out all over as it was relayed down the corridors.) Stone rightly stressed the quantification and measurement aspects of our trade, yet agreed with the late Maurice Dobb that we should return to those boundaries 'more generously drawn by the classical pioneers' (Dobb, 1973, p. 11). So in the 1980s he worked on national accounts and their relationship to social demography, and on other aspects of the national accounts themselves, including their consistency. All these and his other efforts were intended to provide a thorough scientific back-up to the task of improving the lot of ordinary men and women – his ultimate goal when, as a young idealist, he had that first serious clash with his more conventional father concerning his desire to change from law to economics.[9]

Notes

1. The sad news of Dick Stone's death on Friday 6 December 1991 prompted me to reread an essay I wrote on him in April 1983 but never published. I did not know Dick well but I liked and admired him tremendously. I publish the essay now as a tribute to a superb person and economist who had lots of friends and admirers, and no enemies. It is based on notes of conversations I had with Dick Stone in April 1983. I am most grateful to Giovana Stone for her helpful comments on the essay and for correcting a number of factual errors. I am also grateful to James Meade for pointing out some mistakes in my initial account of the work by Meade and Stone on the national accounts during the Second World War.

2. Stone was to say this also of his period (1970–72) as Chairman of the Faculty of Economics and Politics at Cambridge. These were years of student revolt and political upheaval generally, which caused additional stresses in what has rarely been a happy or united faculty, so that the chairman's role of seeing fair play and of reconciling the irreconcilable *is* a traumatic one to play for even the toughest minded.

3. In the early draft of this essay in April 1983, I wrote: 'Robert Dorfman, in writing on the nature of Leontief's contributions which gained him the Nobel Prize, says that "a dominant theme ... runs through Leontief's four decades of professional work.... It is that economics is an empirical and applied science ... The only valid test of economic research is its empirical significance and its practical implications.... It was Leontief, who first saw the practical potentiality of an input–output *table* and who learned how to really put one together' (Dorfman, 1973, pp. 430–31). Stone's impact and influence on national income accounting ought to be similarly acknowledged.

4. The Meades and the Stones subsequently became close friends.
5. Nevertheless, Meade worked with Stone until the April 1941 budget.
6. Two NIESR directors – Bryan Hopkin and Andrew Britton – and one DAE director – Wynne Godley – have come from the Treasury.
7. His basic philosophy was set out in his essay, 'The *a priori* and the empirical in economics' (1966), where he concluded that 'The *a priori* and the empirical are completely intertwined in the development of the subject ... [that] modern developments have come about largely through breaking down the barriers between excessive specialisms' (p. 32).
8. Stone (1978, pp. 13–15) explains that the contrast between Keynes's initial reaction to and final judgement of Tinbergen (in a letter to Alfred Cowles in July 1945) 'that there is no-one more gifted or delightful or for whose work one could be more anxious to give every possible scope and opportunity', was probably due to the three factors: Keynes's 'irresistible urge to overstate', the 'rusty' state of his mathematics by the 1930s and his usual reaction to anything new (which is described in the text above, see pp. 154–5).
9. Fittingly, the reading at the funeral service in King's chapel on Tuesday 10 December was from Revelations 21: St John describes the coming of the New Jerusalem.

References

Dobb, M.H. (1973), *Theories of Value and Distribution Since Adam Smith. Ideology and Economic Theory*, Cambridge: Cambridge University Press.

Dorfman, R. (1973), 'Wassily Leontief's contributions to economics', *Swedish Journal of Economics*, **75**, (4), pp. 430–39.

Keynes, J.M. (1939), 'Professor Tinbergen's Method', *Economic Journal*, **XLIX**, pp. 558–68, *C.W.*, Vol. XIV, 1973, London: Macmillan, pp. 306–18.

Meade, J.E. and J.R.N. Stone (1941), 'The construction of tables of national income, expenditure, savings and investment', *Economic Journal*, **LI**, pp. 216–31.

Ramsey, F .P. (1928), 'A mathematical theory of saving', *Economic Journal*, **XXXVIII**, pp. 543–59.

Stone, J.R.N. (1945), 'The analysis of market demand', *Journal of the Royal Statistical Society*, **108**, pp. 1–98.

Stone, J.R.N. (1966), *Mathematics in the Social Sciences and other Essays*, London, Chapman & Hall.

Stone, J.R.N. (1978), 'Keynes, political arithmetic and econometrics', Keynes Lecture in Economics, 1978, published in *Proceedings of the British Academy*, **LXIII** (1980).

Stone, J.R.N., D.A. Rowe *et al.* (1954), *The Measurement of Consumers' Expenditure and Behaviour in the United Kingdom, 1920–38*, Vol. I, Cambridge: Cambridge University Press.

12 Krishna Bharadwaj, 21 August 1935 – 8 March 1992: a memoir*

Krishna Bharadwaj died on 8 March 1992 at the age of 56. For many years she was Professor of Economics at the Centre for Economic Studies and Planning at Jawaharlal Nehru University in New Delhi. She spent several years in the United Kingdom, as a Fellow of Clare Hall and as a Research Officer of the Department of Applied Economics, Cambridge, in the 1960s and 1970s, and at Trinity College, Cambridge, in the 1980s. She also taught at Bombay, Stanford and the New School for Social Research in New York and often visited Italy, both the University of Rome and the annual International Summer Schools at Trieste in the 1980s.

Krishna was one of the persons I loved best in all the world. She had complete integrity combined with the ability to inspire and support others. Thus she was a warm and supportive friend, supportive in the best sense of being fearlessly honest and straight, realistic and tough, capable of telling people to get on with things, if that was what was needed. Krishna was not only a fine scholar with a wide range of interests and contributions, she was also a disinterested scholar who despised egotism and careerism. Don Harris (31 March 1993) asked that I add: 'She was herself a modest person, completely without airs and pretension, and of gentle manner in both personal and professional relations'. Of course I concur. Most of all, Krishna was a clear-headed, instinctive patriot who applied her intellectual gifts to the understanding of her country's economy and society and to how its malfunctioning could best be overcome and development encouraged. These, together with her teaching, were always her top priorities. Her students revered her, for, though Krishna was not a good lecturer, she was a sympathetic and insightful critic in a small group and especially one to one. Several of her students subsequently became mine and they all confirmed this evaluation of her. Moreover, they too, like Krishna's daughter Sudha, are imbued with Krishna's idealism.

Krishna was born on 21 August 1935 at Karwar, the youngest of the six children of Maruti Chandawarkar, 'a highly motivated educationalist'. Two years later the family moved to Belgaum where North and South Indian traditions intermingled in a region 'known particularly for its music, dramatic arts and folk culture'. Music and dance became and remained very

* First published in *Journal of Post Keynesian Economics*, winter 1993–4, **16**, (2), pp. 299–311.

important parts of Krishna's life.[1] Belgaum was also a politically active place. In Krishna's autobiographical essay (Bharadwaj, 1992), she tells us that an important achievement of Gandhi's 'strategy of nationalist struggle' was the niche it created for the involvement of women and children 'of all ages and ranks' in direct action. This instilled in Krishna herself as a young person 'an urge for social and economic action towards independent self-reliant development'. Krishna's father died when she was 17, but he had clearly imbued her with a love of learning and a passionate commitment to political and social causes to complement her outstanding intelligence. Krishna had an extremely hard early life; moreover, she always worked extraordinarily hard and she had more than her fair share of personal disappointment and frustrations. But none of these ever broke her indomitable spirit or resilience of mind.

II

From her earliest days as an economist she was in rebellion against orthodox mainstream economics; but it was not until she was given Piero Sraffa's *Production of Commodities by Means of Commodities* (1960) to review for the influential *Economic Weekly* that her instinctive misgivings found a fully coherent framework within which to be expressed. She had come to economics, despite a fascination with mathematics and sciences, because it 'mundanely' allowed her to combine study with the 'potentialities it held for employment'. She was an undergraduate (starting in 1951) and graduate student at the University of Bombay. Her dissertation (1960) was on 'Techniques of Transportation Planning, with Special Reference to Railways'. She was already critical of the diagnosis of underdevelopment in terms of 'a departure from the competitive resource utilization model'; and she was introduced to and used herself the interdependent production models which, inspired by Leontief's work, were used for framing consistency plan models in India.

In the early 1960s, she went to the United States with her husband, Ranganath Bharadwaj, who had been awarded a 'Post-Doc' at Harvard. She joined the Center for International Studies at MIT, under the directorship of Rosenstein Rodan. Krishna was at MIT when Joan Robinson made her (in)famous visit, attacking the aggregate production function and the neoclassical theory of distribution – to Joan, if not to the attacked, overlapping sets. The controversy between the two Cambridges 'rekindled' Krishna's interest in distribution theory and she became 'more pointedly aware of the capital-theoretic debate. [But she] did not then know of the more fundamental critique of economic theory heralded by Piero Sraffa's work' (Bharadwaj, 1992, p. 38). This came in 1962, when 'Sachin Chowdhury, the editor of *The Economic Weekly* [which subsequently became *The Economic and Political*

Weekly], ... drew out of his drawer [Sraffa's] slim volume ... [which Krishna, who had recently returned to India, to a lectureship at the University of Bombay] agreed to review ... in a month or so!' (p. 39).

In fact, it took two years: the review, 'Value through Exogenous Distribution', appeared in August 1963. In order to write it, she followed a demanding intellectual pilgrim's progress, taking the same journey that Sraffa himself had taken over the 30 to 40 years prior to the publication of the book. She read, as he did, Smith, Ricardo, Malthus, Marx, Jevons, Marshall, Walras and Wicksell. The result was her outstanding review article, which she too modestly described as 'a novice's effort to state in simple terms what appeared to ... be astonishingly challenging and original' (1963, p. 39).

In my view, Maurice Dobb's, Ronald Meek's and Krishna's reviews stand out from all the others (the less said about some of them, the better) for most perceptively revealing the structure and the purpose of the book. (Joan Robinson's reviews were fine analytical pieces and expositions but too idiosyncratic, in that Joan always tended to read into others their support for her own current preoccupations.) The very title of Krishna's article showed that she had understood the nature of the method of classical political economic theory, and of its modern revival, for which the structure and the analysis of Sraffa's book was an integral part of the foundation.

Harald Hagemann (3 March 1993) reminds me that, in a much neglected but, in his and now my view too, 'outstanding, highly innovative, more technical' follow-up to her review (Bharadwaj, 1970), Krishna cleared away some fundamental misconceptions about the nature and purpose of Sraffa's distinction between basic and non-basic commodities. Sraffa had shown Krishna the exchange of letters between himself and Peter Newman over the latter's perceptive review (of Part I) of Sraffa's 1960 book (Newman, 1962), in which, nevertheless, Newman had missed the point of the distinction. Sraffa allowed Krishna to publish the letters in the appendix to her article. Though she set the argument in the context of the reswitching debate, itself then all the rage, her purpose was to emphasize that, in an interdependent production system, basics are price-determin*ing* and non-basics are price-determin*ed*. It followed that Newman's puzzle about having to have negative prices for some classes of non-basics, a possibility Sraffa had already conceded in his appendix B, 'Note on self-reproducing non-basics', in which he invented a hypothetical commodity called 'beans', was really beside the point. The correspondence itself is fascinating, for it tellingly illustrates Sraffa's philosophy (which I believe Krishna shared) that economic theory may only be based on concepts that in principle may be found in reality and measured.[2]

In later years Krishna filled in the historical background to Sraffa's 1960 book in her 1976 Dutt lectures, published in 1978 as *Classical Political*

Economy and Rise to Dominance of Supply and Demand Theories (1978a). As she tells us in the preface, 'In preparing these lectures ... [she had] drawn liberally upon the writings of Piero Sraffa and on the innumerable and stimulating discussions [they had had] over a period'. In the lectures we see explicitly set out the conceptual bases of classical political economy and Marxism, and of its modern revival through Sraffa's work and, equally importantly, the conceptual basis of neoclassical economics – in all its forms. These include an account of the subjective theory of value and of the marginal productivity theory of distribution and its accompanying concept of capital. Krishna wisely included them all under the umbrella term of 'supply and demand theories', for it allowed her to set out the restrictions that had to be placed on the shapes and slopes of the supply and demand curves in order that they produced results that conformed to the conceptual basis of the theory, that price was an index of scarcity and utility, a (the?) central determinant of value.

Sraffa's book was subtitled, *Prelude to a Critique of Economic Theory*. By this he meant neoclassical theory – or so he told me when I asked him, and despite others' attempts to argue that he also had some aspects of Marx's theoretical structure, the labour theory of value no less, firmly in his sights.

In Krishna's view the critique had at least two strands. The first one was concerned with method: by making the concept of the surplus the core of the theory, the place in which, given the value of one distributive variable, the value of the other distributive variable, and the values of the set of relative prices (of production) could be determined, Sraffa also singled out those aspects of the economic system for which generalized propositions could be made. These were to be sharply distinguished in theory from the other aspects where the analysis operated on different planes, usually less abstract, more concrete, historically, institutionally, and *situation-specific*. This method was to be contrasted with the single-dimension, single-level approach of neoclassical economists, in which all the relevant endogenous variables of the economic system (as they saw them) were simultaneously determined by the interaction of the factors underlying supply and demand functions. Not only did these functions all need to be reduced to measurement in terms of utility, about which concept Sraffa was extraordinarily scathing, but they also had to be constrained so as to give, as we have seen, stable equilibrium values that accorded with the concept of price as an index of scarcity – here we move onto the second aspect of her critique. In particular, it was the inability to find within the framework a unit in which capital could be measured independently of distribution and prices, together with the impossibility of ensuring that, when capital was measured in price terms, a well-behaved demand curve for capital could be devised, which constituted the central critique of the supply and demand theory of distribution. Sraffa himself made this critique several times in *Production of Commodities* (see, for example, pp. 38, 70–72, and Part III) and also in his reply to Harrod's review of his book (Sraffa, 1962).

Krishna saw the force of all this and wove it into the arguments of both her 1963 article and the Dutt lectures. She also forcefully rebutted the charge that neither Joan Robinson nor Sraffa could understand the nature of mutual determination, so that they had swallowed the out-of-date and discredited 'arguing in a circle' fallacy. This was a canard, for, as Krishna made crystal clear, the correct argument related to properly identifying which variables could be regarded as exogenous or determining, and which as endogenous or (often mutually) determined in that part of the economic system that was being analysed. The incoherence in the supply and demand approach arose from the logical necessity for 'capital' to be both exogenous and endogenous at the same time – hence Sraffa's rebuke to Harrod (1962, p. 479), which I am sure Krishna would have endorsed, 'what is the good of a quantity of capital ... which, since it depends on the rate of interest cannot be used for its traditional purpose ... to determine the rate of interest[?]'. Unless 'capital' could be measured *before* the analysis began, as it were, no operational sense could be given to the statement, r is high or low partly because the economy concerned has a 'little' or a 'lot' of 'capital' relative to its supplies of labour.

Another aspect of the critique, whereby Sraffa always referred to the rate of profits, a usage that Krishna followed, was that it was the overall, economy-wide, rate of profits that had to be explained because it was what the classical competitive process was always tending to bring about. Hence we have the stress in Krishna's arguments on the concept of centres of gravitation, of which prices of production are a particular example, and of which prices the overall uniform rate of profits is a crucial component.

I mentioned above that the economic theory that Sraffa had in mind to criticize was neoclassical theory; again, Krishna makes clear in the Dutt lectures that Sraffa's positive constructions were designed either to finish unfinished business or to make coherent what was still incoherent in certain key but limited parts of the whole of Marx's system. Though what is in Sraffa's papers has not yet been allowed into the public domain – this was certainly not Krishna's doing or fault, as I argue below – she did tell me that there were many papers there that made it abundantly clear that Sraffa re-garded Marx as the supreme economist and saw his own role as no more than the modest but essential one set out above.

These discussions of theory and method in the development of the subject were not solely the task of scholarly correctness, putting theories into their historical context, making coherent what was previously incoherent, or at best implicit. Krishna was a working, teaching, researching economist vitally interested in explanation and policy, especially in the developing countries, most of all, of course, in India. The surplus approach was for her, therefore, not only an organizing concept for understanding the major developments in economic theory and the organizing device for analysing major debates, but also the working framework for her applied papers and books and for policy proposals. Thus, after Joan Robinson arranged for her to come to Clare Hall in 1967, following the publication of her review article – Krishna 'was most taken by surprise when [she] received complimentary letters from Joan Robinson, Maurice Dobb, Ronald Meek ... and from Piero Sraffa himself' (Bharadwaj, 1992, p. 40) – she wrote for the Department of Applied Economics (DAE) a fine monograph on Indian agriculture (1974). The work was in fact completed in 1968 and in it she fitted her arguments and results into the emerging surplus approach framework. The liberation of her thinking from the restrictions of the demand and supply equilibrium framework allowed her to combine historical, institutional and sociological insights with her earlier expertise on production interdependence and the nature of production processes. She writes: 'In this work ... the idea of interlinked markets and their consequence for the exploitative processes was offered for the first time' (1974, p. 43).

In an article in the *Manchester School* (1979) she deployed the same approach to an analysis of the macroeconomic processes associated with development, or its lack, in India in the 1960s and 1970s. She was critical of some aspects of the application of Arthur Lewis's model to developments in India in the 1960s. She thought it was too simple a framework for the Indian situation and that several of his predictions about the rise of the marketable surplus in agriculture and its use in industry, together with the sweeping prediction about the movement of the terms of trade between agriculture and industry, were not borne out by events. Sociological and institutional diversity in both sectors, oligopolistic behaviour in industry and inflationary pressures spearheaded by the movements in agricultural prices were all combined by Krishna so that a much more complex story emerged, one which, however, could be classified and analysed within the framework she imposed on it. She proposed 'a differentiated production and exchange system in agriculture, adopting a wider differentiation of commodity sectors and introducing a wider integration of income classes' (1992, p. 44). Much of this later work was done after she went to Delhi, in 1971, to Jawaharlal Nehru University where, 'with the help of some other economists, the university offered [her] the opportunity to launch a programme in postgraduate studies for the newly constituted Centre for Economic Studies and Planning' (1992, p. 43).

Jayati Ghosh (15 March 1993) writes that 'in recent years [Krishna's] interest was moving more towards problems of accumulation and distorted development. [She gave several seminar papers and public lectures on the topic] and she had just taken on a big research project on "Changes in the

Rural Labour Process" to be done with assistance from fieldwork in [three] different parts of rural India ... her illness and death prevented her from really going ahead with it. Many of these pieces have been collected ... and are being published by Sage Publications in New Delhi.'

III

My first contact with Krishna was reading 'Value through Exogenous Distribution'. I read it with admiration after Vincent Massaro and I had written our review article (1964) of Sraffa's book during overlapping periods of leave at Cambridge in 1963–4. When Neil Laing and I were putting together a book of readings on *Capital and Growth* (1971), Krishna's paper was, of course, in the subset of 'musts' of the selection. I met Krishna in person – we had already started to correspond – in January 1971 when I came to Cambridge for six weeks to put the finishing touches to the manuscript of *Some Cambridge Controversies* (Harcourt, 1972) and Krishna was working in the DAE on her monograph. Thus began a deep and valued friendship. She was most helpful and supportive about my book (and cheered me up after Joan Robinson and I had a fearful row about tactics in fighting a common enemy; I had advocated using the moderate tactics I always used in the anti-war movement in Australia while Joan, as ever, was a hard-line militant). I read the manuscript of Krishna's monograph. In the following years we met often, memorably for Joan (Harcourt) and me in India in 1979, often in Cambridge, and most years in the 1980s at the International Summer School in Trieste. We regularly exchanged papers, I published some of her articles in *Australian Economic Papers* and I near as dammit resigned from the editorship of the series, Aspects of Political Economy, with Polity Press when, as a result of what I can only term misinformed and ignorant advice, the main editors would not allow me to include in the series a selection of Krishna's papers on the history of theory. Polity's loss was Unwin Hyman's gain (1989).

We both were close to Joan Robinson and Piero Sraffa and, of 'younger' contemporaries, Amit Bhaduri, Pierangelo Garegnani, Luigi Pasinetti (Pierangelo, Luigi and I were graduate students together in Cambridge in the 1950s), Don Harris, Heinz Kurz, Jan Kregel, Alesandro Roncaglia, Bertram Schefold and the rest of the gang at Trieste. A special place in our affections was reserved for the ever-young Josef Steindl, whom we both first met at Trieste (and who, alas, died in March 1993). Krishna and I had many talks and walks together in Trieste, discussing our subject, our friends and our families. Joan, Wendy and Rebecca Harcourt were especially drawn to Krishna. I remember a wonderful night at our home in Cambridge when Joan, Rebecca, Wendy and Krishna talked long and deep – and happily. Our two feminist daughters found in Krishna a role model of courage, commitment and warmth with which to complement the one they already had in their mother. In her letter of 15 March 1993, Jayati Ghosh emphasized Krishna's 'particular warmth, affection and support for women students and colleagues'. She writes that 'there were innumerable women students and researchers who found in [Krishna] a great source of inspiration, support and confidence. Unlike many other successful professional women [Krishna] never wavered in her empathy for other women, however modest their achievements.'[3]

The last time I saw Krishna for any length of time was when she came to Trinity in the middle and late 1980s to put some order into Piero Sraffa's papers; Piero had died in September 1983 and Pierangelo Garegnani, his literary executor, asked Krishna to help with this mammoth but vital task. It was a time of great tension for Krishna, for her love of Sraffa himself and her belief in the importance of his contributions obliged her, she thought, to take on this daunting task; yet she also felt keenly the sacrifice of time she would otherwise have spent working in India on pressing Indian problems. This created an insoluble dilemma for her, a sense of ambivalence and doubt as to whether she *had* done the right thing, made the correct choice, and I fear that the psychological trauma all this undoubtedly caused her was a significant factor leading to her final illness. Certainly, I had never before seen her so agitated and unhappy, working – effectively as ever – and as long hours as ever, but without the usual resilience and *joie de vivre* that went with her sense of purpose and drive. It was desperately worrisome for her friends to see her health deteriorating under the strain; we could offer support but not really relieve her of the essential burden and pressure. I was glad to learn the other day (January 1993) that the papers are in order and catalogued, although not yet opened, for this is another vindication of Krishna's devotion and work – but at what a cost.

I mentioned that we were both close friends of Joan Robinson. For Krishna that friendship ran into difficulties in the discussions between Piero Sraffa's non-British and British friends, especially those of the latter in Cambridge, as to whether, when Piero's health and memory deteriorated in his last years, he should return to Italy, or stay in Trinity and, ultimately, nursing homes in Cambridge. Krishna understood very well indeed the subtle nuances of and differences between British and non-British cultures and perceptions. She felt that Sraffa should have returned to his roots, to be with his Italian friends and pupils and to be looked after in an environment that was familiar and increasingly friendly to him, in contrast to one that again, increasingly, he found alienating and frightening. I think in retrospect that Krishna and Sraffa's non-British friends were right, that his British friends, including Joan, had a blind spot on this, not because of self-interest, but because of a lack of comprehension as to what was involved. This difference of views, deeply felt on both sides, caused Krishna great distress, though, thank goodness, her friendship with Joan was not irreparably impaired by it.[4]

IV

In Krishna's volume of selected papers (1989) are some of her most characteristic articles and views. These include her 1972 *Economica* article on
Marshall's annotations of his copy of Pigou's *Wealth and Welfare*. Sraffa had
given Krishna the volume in order to allow her to write the paper. In it she
emphasizes Marshall's distress at Pigou giving the game away by sharpening
up in analytical terms those parts of Marshall's system that he himself had
deliberately kept vague, or even hidden, in the *Principles* and elsewhere,
hoping that the fudges and hand wavings would not be noticed beneath his
carefully prepared smokescreen. Krishna further exposed his foxiness in her
paper (1978b) on the subversion of classical political economy by Marshall
when he was claiming to fulfil it. There is also her sympathetically critical
tribute to the late Ronald Meek in her review article of his last book, *Smith,
Marx and After* (1977), which was published in *Australian Economic Papers*
in 1980. Part of Krishna's independence and scepticism of neoclassical economics started with her introduction to Keynes and Kalecki by her teachers
when she was an undergraduate at Bombay. Reprinted in this selection is her
balanced account of the long-period versus short-period interpretations of
Keynes' *General Theory* which Krishna wrote for a book edited by Jan
Kregel in 1983. And, most of all, there is her tribute to Piero Sraffa himself,
appropriately initially published in *The Economic and Political Weekly* in
1984, from the pages of which journal their close friendship and professional
relationship began.

The selection is dedicated 'To Piero Sraffa'. The conclusion to the tribute
reads: 'Uncompromising in his convictions but truly modest, solitary but full
of friendly generosity and warmth, Sraffa endeared himself to his close
friends and was a pillar of strength to the younger students who were as much
impressed by him as a person as a scholar. [The deaths of Sraffa and Joan
Robinson in 1983, and of Maurice Dobb in 1976 mark] the close of a
memorable era in Cambridge history … [they] also mark the resurgence of
classical theory and a prelude to new possibilities of exploration in our
science' (1989, p. 332).

Finally, as Bertram Schefold (26 March 1993) reminded me, it is essential
to record Krishna's roles in organizing the conference held in Florence in
August 1985 to celebrate the twenty-fifth anniversary of the publication of
Production of Commodities, and in editing with Bertram the volume of the
conference, *Essays on Piero Sraffa: Critical Perspectives on the Revival of
Classical Theory* (1990, 1992). Bertram writes: 'During the preparations
which lasted for several years, [Krishna] was alone and constantly on the
move, teaching in different places in India, the States and, I think, elsewhere.
… yet she managed to coordinate the whole thing. She also proved very
sober, effective and practical, as well as rigorous and cooperative, when we

had to prepare the conference volume. She thought it was a book of particular importance and hoped that it was going to remain the focus for discussions for many years to come.'

Inevitably, there were difficulties: 'Since [Krishna] was far away, [Bertram] often had to act independently. [He] had often reason to admire her trust and to be grateful for her support. ...[And] when a decision was to be taken jointly, her judgement invariably was firm and fair, and very prompt, too.'

V

I have known several fine scholars who were also admirable people. Within that select band, Krishna Bharadwaj stood out for her intellectual honesty, her basic decency, her courage, her admirable patriotism, her constant support for other women and her deep humanity. In her last years she was in poor health and in her last year she was virtually blind. Jayati Ghosh's perception was that Krishna's last two years in particular were 'desperately unhappy', not least because she was deeply disturbed about economic and political trends in India and developing countries generally. So I was cheered to learn from Sita Narasimhan that, when they last met, Krishna was at the top of her form, full of ideas, bubbling with happiness and at peace in her personal relationships. It is desperately sad for her friends that Krishna is dead. But it is some consolation that she did not have to linger on, unable effectively to do what she did so well – work unsparingly for improvement in the conditions of others.

Notes

I would like to thank Ruchira Chatterji, Jayati Ghosh, Harald Hagemann, Joan Harcourt, Rebecca Harcourt, Wendy Harcourt, Donald Harris, Prue Kerr, Heinz Kurz, Michael Landesmann, Peter Nolan, Luigi Pasinetti, Catherine Price, Claudio Sardoni, Bertram Schefold, Ajit Singh and Ian Steedman for the comments on a draft of this memoir.

1. In a letter dated 15 March 1993, Jayati Ghosh wrote to me of Krishna's 'deep and abiding involvement with Hindustani classical music'. 'Krishna,' writes Jayati, 'was an extremely talented singer who almost turned professional ... she retained great love for and interest in music until the end of her life.'

2. Thus Sraffa (4 June 1962) wrote to Newman: 'Have you not overlooked my Appendix B?... It seems to say exactly the same thing as you say ... True, it says it in humdrum economic language ... no doubt less elegant than mathematics.... it has the advantage of making plain the economic circumstances which may give rise to a negative price for a non-basic,... which you find "obscure".... it makes it obvious how rare (if any) such cases must be in the real world. If, e.g., the ratio of net product to means of production (R) in a basic *system* is 25%, it will be pretty hard to find a *single* commodity (whether basic or not) which requires the using up of more than *four* units of itself in order to produce *five* units of it in a year. I certainly failed to discover any faintly realistic example of this ... and had to invent those "beans"' (Sraffa, 1960, pp. 425–6). Newman (8 June 1962) offered to 'come half-way to meet [Sraffa's] criticisms'. Sraffa replied (19 June 1962): 'I am, of course, delighted, and grateful that you can come half-way to meet me on the subject of non-basics, and I only regret to be unable to move the other half: I cannot yield an inch on this point!' (p. 427). He reiterated his argument succinctly: 'The immense majority of non-

basics are not used in production, not even in their own production: so they do not even form individual systems. Some (mainly animals and plants) are used each in its own reproduction, and form individual systems. A few may be linked with one or two others, because of mixing, or cross-breeding, or if the length of gestation brings out the egg–hen dichotomy. And that is all' (p. 428).

3.   Wendy Harcourt reminded me that Krishna died on International Women's Day.
4.   Inevitably, I have given a simplified account of an intensely complex situation in which a whole spectrum of different views was present. I was very much a spectator, though I did visit Sraffa in Hope, one of the nursing homes he was in, and I had a long conversation with Krishna about all these events on one of our walks at Trieste in the 1980s.

References

Bharadwaj, Krishna (1960), 'Techniques of Transportation Planning, with Special Reference to Railways', unpublished PhD dissertation, University of Bombay.

Bharadwaj, Krishna (1963), 'Value through Exogenous Distribution', *Economic Weekly*, **15**, pp. 1450–54; reprinted in Harcourt and Laing (1971).

Bharadwaj, Krishna (1970), 'On the Maximum Number of Switches between Two Production Systems', *Schweizerische Zeitschrift für Volkswirtschaft und Statistik*, December, 4, (106), 409, pp. 1–29; reprinted in Bharadwaj (1989).

Bharadwaj, Krishna (1972), 'Marshall on Pigou's *Wealth and Welfare*', *Economica*, **39**, pp. 32–46; reprinted in Bharadwaj, (1989).

Bharadwaj, Krishna (1974), *Production Conditions in Indian Agriculture as Reflected in the Farm Management Studies*, Cambridge: Cambridge University Press.

Bharadwaj, Krishna (1978a), *Classical Political Economy and Rise to Dominance of Supply and Demand Theories*, New Delhi: Orient Longman.

Bharadwaj, Krishna (1978b), 'The Subversion of Classical Analysis: Alfred Marshall's Early Writing on Value', *Cambridge Journal of Economics*, **2**, pp. 253–71; reprinted in Bharadwaj (1989).

Bharadwaj, Krishna (1979), 'Towards a Macroeconomic Framework for a Developing Economy: The Indian Case', *Manchester School of Economic and Social Studies*, **47**, pp. 270–302.

Bharadwaj, Krishna (1980), 'On Certain Theoretical Issues in Classical Political Economy', *Australian Economic Papers*, **19**, pp. 349–63; reprinted in Bharadwaj (1989).

Bharadwaj, Krishna (1983), 'On Effective Demand: Certain Recent Critiques', in J.A. Kregel (ed.), *Distribution Effective Demand and International Economic Relations*, London: Macmillan, 1983; reprinted in Bharadwaj (1989).

Bharadwaj, Krishna (1984), 'Piero Sraffa: The Man and the Scholar – A Tribute', *Economic and Political Weekly*, **19**, pp. 1236–50; reprinted in Bharadwaj (1989).

Bharadwaj, Krishna (1989), *Themes in Value and Distribution. Classical Theory Reappraised*, London: Unwin Hyman.

Bharadwaj, Krishna (1992), 'Krishna Bharadwaj (born 1935)', in Phillip Arestis and Malcolm Sawyer (eds), *A Biographical Dictionary of Dissenting Economists*, Aldershot: Edward Elgar, pp. 36–45.

Bharadwaj, Krishna and Bertram Schefold (eds), (1990), *Essays on Piero Sraffa: Critical Perspectives on the Revival of Classical Theory*, London: Unwin Hyman, reprinted by Routledge (1992).

Harcourt, G.C. (1972), *Some Cambridge Controversies in the Theory of Capital*, Cambridge: Cambridge University Press.

Harcourt, G.C. and N.F. Laing (eds) (1971), *Capital and Growth. Selected Readings*, Harmondsworth: Penguin.

Harcourt, G.C. and Vincent G. Massaro (1964), 'Mr Sraffa's *Production of Commodities*', *Economic Record*, **40**, pp. 442–54.

Meek, Ronald L. (1977), *Smith, Marx and After. Ten Essays in the Development of Economic Thought*, London: Chapman and Hall.

Newman, P.K. (1962), 'Production of Commodities by Means of Commodities', *Schweizerische Zeitschrift für Volkswirtschaft und Statistik*, March, **SZ 98**, pp. 58–75.

Sraffa, Piero (1960), *Production of Commodities by Means of Commodities. Prelude to a Critique of Economic Theory*, Cambridge: Cambridge University Press.
Sraffa, Piero (1962), 'Production of Commodities: A Comment', *Economic Journal*, **72**, pp. 477–9.

13 Josef Steindl, 14 April 1912 – 7 March 1993: a tribute*

I

The eminent Austrian-born economist, Josef Steindl, died in Vienna on 7 March 1993, at the age of 80. Though trained initially in the liberal Austrian tradition by Richard Strigl, a pupil of Eugen Böhm-Bawerk, 'a kind man and a good teacher who taught [Steindl] everything he was soon to disbelieve', Steindl (1990, p. 241), Steindl succinctly described his own economics as 'the product of England and Kalecki'. By 'England', Steindl meant predominantly Marshall and Keynes, together with Keynes's immediate followers, Richard Kahn, Nicholas Kaldor and Joan Robinson. It was Gerhard Tintner's organization of a seminar at the Institut für Konjunkturforschung (now the Austrian Institute for Economic Research (WIFO)) to discuss *The General Theory* as soon as it was published that brought about Steindl's 'resulting process of reorientation [from his acceptance of Strigl's liberal views, a process as] painful, slow and difficult for [him] as for most economists' (Steindl, 1990, p. 242).[1] Painful but permanent: one of the most perceptive, reflective papers on Keynes's relevance for the modern world is Steindl's 1983 essay, 'J.M. Keynes: Society and the Economist' (now republished in Steindl, 1990, pp. 276–392). Not only did Steindl provide a brilliant account of how and why Keynes's theoretical and policy views developed from his interaction with the events he was living through, he also brought out acutely the reasons for the defeat of 'Keynesian' policies from the 1970s on. But, like Keynes, he ended on an optimistic note, arguing that, if Keynes was defeated, it was by power, not logic. He asked:

> Was [Keynes] then, was the Clearing Union and the Buffer Stock Scheme, utopian? Yes, and it looks even more so today. Yet ... utopians are the greater realists. We are today faced with the same questions which confronted Keynes in the years 1939–41 in his thinking on international relations. We have practically not got any further in the meantime. If we want to start anew, we have to start where Keynes left off. (Steindl, 1990, p. 300).

Steindl first met Kalecki in Oxford in 1940 at the Oxford Institute of Statistics where Kalecki was its 'inspiration and [Steindl's] guru. [Kalecki] had, independently of Keynes and before him, created economics anew,

* First published in *Journal of Post Keynesian Economics*, summer 1994, **16**, (4), pp. 627–42.

unburdened by the traditions of the subject and inspired by the department scheme of Marx, unaware until the publication of the *General Theory* in 1936 that the same kind of revolution was taking place in Cambridge. Kalecki had a penetrating mind and a passionate interest in what was going on in the world. He continuously absorbed, analysed and discussed the daily flow of events ... and his judgement almost always proved right' (Steindl, 1990, p. 245).

The traits that Steindl so admired in Kalecki and his work are to be found, expressed in Steindl's own unique manner, in him and his work too. Indeed, his own work resembles Kalecki's in style, substance and depth more than that of any other economist of his generation. For me, one of the truly great pluses of the International Summer School at Trieste in the 1980s was the chance to meet Josef Steindl in person and to hear him lecture to the students. Of all the people who were there, you could be certain that he would give a lecture that was highly relevant and topical, presented in a lucid, economically analytical form, with absolutely no frills. Moreover, his lectures were on political economy in the best sense; he identified the villains and heroes (and the innocent victims – and did not pussyfoot around when saying so. There would be a sense of righteous anger when injustice, or even escapable foolishness, was exposed, and proper contempt when hypocrisy or silly–clever sophistication was criticized:

> Economists have tried to throw out all relevant material from the field of economics as if it were stones, and to leave in nothing but the principle of rationality. But this principle is empty as long as you do not know what people expect, nor how their manifold wishes, fears and doubts continue to produce a one-valued decision. To reduce them to a maximum of utility or profit is just begging the question, an infertile kind of a-priorism. (Steindl, 1990, p. 248)

Though the purposes of the lectures were always serious ones, there would be an overlay of wry humour, definitely his own, yet with overtones of which I feel sure Kalecki would have approved.

II

Josef Steindl was born in Vienna on 14 April 1912 and became an economist because his preference for becoming a biologist 'would have taken too much time'. Steindl had an apolitical upbringing 'and no links to left-wing movements'. Nevertheless, he absorbed well his first teacher's maxim that the discussion of policy depended first upon understanding how economies work. He hated 'the anti-rationalist, romantic nationalist trends' that were prominent in the university when he was a student, just as he hated the fascist militaristic movements of the 1930s. He told us that he 'could not fail to be impressed by the surrounding unemployment and misery, the more since it affected also [his] own position'. Concern with unemployment 'remained with [him for the rest of his life] very important'.

Steindl worked from 1935 to 1938 at the WIFO, the research institute started by Ludwig von Mises, in whose 'view economics consisted of tautologies [so making] it irrefutable'. Ironically, WIFO 'was devoted mainly to empirical research' [Steindl, 1990, p. 241). After the German occupation of Austria, Steindl lost his job because of his hostility to the regime. Through the offices of Friedrich Hayek and other Austrian liberals abroad – including von Mises and Gottfried Haberler – Steindl cane to the United Kingdom, first to a research lecturing post at Balliol (1938–41), then as a research worker at the Oxford Institute of Statistics, one of the remarkable group of European exiles from fascism then on its staff. 'My years at Oxford were mainly spent at the Oxford Institute of Statistics which was largely a congregation of European emigrants (Thomas Balogh, Fritz Burchardt, Michal Kalecki, Kurt Mandelbaum-Martin, E.F. Schumacher) with a minority of British scholars (J.L. Nicholson, G.D.N. Worswick and the director, A.L. Bowley)' (Steindl, 1990, p. 245).

In 1950, Steindl returned to Austria. Evidently, for ideological reasons,[2] he could not get a job at the University of Vienna, so he returned to his job at WIFO, retiring in 1978, but remaining actively associated as a consultant with the institute until his death. May 1992 saw a splendid conference under WIFO's auspices to celebrate Steindl's 80th birthday. (The proceedings are published in a special issue of the *Review of Political Economy*, edited by Alois Guger.) In 1970, he was made an Honorary Professor of the University of Vienna and in 1974–5 he was a Visiting Professor at Stanford University in California. In the 1980s, as I mentioned above, Steindl was a regular lecturer at the International Summer School held at Trieste in August. This allowed younger scholars from all over the world to get to know him personally. At Trieste, Steindl formed particularly close friendships with Amit Bhaduri, with whom he collaborated on several papers when Bhaduri spent some time in Vienna, and with the late Krishna Bharadwaj and Jan Kregel.

Steindl had had bouts of ill health during the 1980s and early 1990s. He was in hospital at the turn of the year 1992, and, though he returned to his home in Vienna on 12 January 1993, Alois Guger (17 March 1993) tells us that he 'never really recovered his health'. He was 'mentally alert till his death and not in great pain [but] in a rather depressed mood'. He died on Sunday, 7 March 1993.

III

Steindl published two books that are now recognized as classics in the literature: *Small and Big Business: Economic Problems of the Size of Firms* (1945) and *Maturity and Stagnation in American Capitalism* (1952, 1976).[3] His third big book, *Random Processes and the Growth of Firms. A Study of the Pareto Law* (1965), was, amongst many other things, an important influence on the development of the classic study in Cambridge by Ajit Singh and Geoffrey Whittington (1968) of the growth and profitability of firms. Of his 1965 book, Steindl wrote in the preface:

This book has been written by an economist and its purpose is firmly directed towards economists, yet its approach will be unfamiliar to most economists. It deals with a kind of 'equilibrium' exemplified by the size-distribution of firms and its statistical law ... the law of Pareto; this equilibrium, however, is not the one to which economists are accustomed, but is the 'steady state' of statistical mechanics which results from the balance of actions of a great number of small particles. In economics ... the particles are people, and since there are never as many people as there are particles in a mere cubic millimetre of gas, the macro-laws of economics which relate to aggregates of people instead of to aggregates of particles will never be remotely as accurate as those of statistical mechanics. The more reason, therefore, [Steindl argued] for a stochastic approach in economics, where even the behaviour of aggregates is hard to approximate by a deterministic model. This is why [Steindl] attempted to indicate a way of treating economic problems in terms of stochastic processes. [He had] tried to talk economics in a new language, but those who [were] familiar with the subject of stochastic processes [would] not be surprised to find that [he had] not gone much beyond the elements of grammar. Non-stationary stochastic processes become rather complicated if more than one dimension is introduced, but in economics this is exactly what must be done in order to obtain interesting results.

There is a delicate problem lurking somewhere in the obscure confines between economic theory and statistical application, and which nobody has, so far, seriously touched upon. It appears in the puzzled comments often made on the fact that income elasticities (to give an example) are different according to whether they are computed from time-series or from cross-section data. But why should there be any relation between the two – or what kind of relation should this be? In statistical mechanics there is a similar problem, that of the relation between phase averages and time averages. Gibbs maintained that the two are equal, ... only many decades later, when the mathematical tools had become available, was the theorem proved by von Neumann, Birkhoff and Khintchine. But in statistical mechanics the processes are stationary, whereas in economics they are not: nothing like the Gibbs theorem can be expected to hold in economics. In fact, ... the parameters of cross-section data are influenced by the growth of the system and [Steindl could not] help questioning the usual interpretation, and to a certain extent even the usefulness, of cross-section data. The suggestions [made] in this connection ... are of general interest to economists. Neither time-series nor cross-section data contain sufficient information for the economist to draw general conclusions; the only firm basis is the repeated observation of a constant sample (of firms, households, etc.) over a series of years. The data we need, in other words, must enable us to estimate directly the transition probabilities and the way in which they depend upon various factors. (Steindl, 1965, pp. 5–6)

In Chapter 1 of the same work he wrote that

random processes have invaded economics only recently ... no less remarkable than the long neglect of Pareto and other skew distributions in economics. Questioning and curiosity are usually aroused by the observation of regular patterns.... There are few regular patterns in economics, and the distribution laws are outstanding among these.... For a very long time the Pareto Law has lumbered the economic scene like an erratic block on the landscape – unconnected with anything else in the field.... This justifies an old epigram of Professor Kalecki in his characteristic vein (quoted without permission): 'Economics consists of theoretical laws which nobody has verified and of empirical laws which nobody can explain.' (Steindl, 1965, p. 18)

Steindl added that he had 'taken the satire to heart'.

In 1990, Macmillan published a volume of his essays of the past 40 years, *Economic Papers, 1941–88*. These essays were not only substantial contributions in their own right but also will continue to provide illumination and inspiration for extension by others.[4]

IV

Steindl's work was marked by austere clarity, precise analysis, careful, thorough, intelligent use of data, and a feel for the role of institutions, and of historical, political and sociological factors. Most of all, he could sense and set out the overall, systemic irrationalities of what was on the face of it sensible or at least necessary behaviour by the individuals and/or groups that made up the body economic and politic.

Steindl and his work are splendid role models for many reasons. First, he was a political economist who *insisted* that the *raison d' être* of economics – political economy, that is! – is the application of its principles to the explanation of the malfunctioning of the body politic and economic and the provision of policies with which to tackle the causes of malfunctioning. In 1984, he asked:

What might be done to overcome the sterility of today's economics? The first condition, [he said], is that we go back to the great tradition of the classics, Kalecki and Keynes whose work was rooted in the economic policy problems of their time, and derived its relevance from them. They asked what should be done and how. Economic policy is the main inspiration of economic theory. (Steindl, 1990, p. 251)

Such policies have to be politically and socially realistic to be effective – he despised mechanical crank handlers who ground out instrument for targets while ignoring the political and social realities of the situations to which they were meant to apply. Yet, strange as it may seem, an increasing number of modern economists get angry if Steindl's justification for our discipline – it is mine, too – is made explicit. They really do think that intellectual curiosity – the desire and ability to jump intellectual hurdles – is sufficient reason for our existence. What poppycock! Of course, I applaud intellectual curiosity – would that more of our present-day students had it! – and I admire analytical ability in general. But they are not enough for a social science (certainly not for a branch of moral philosophy) and they would not have been thought so by our founding mothers and fathers.

Because Josef Steindl was a social scientist, he was very conscious of time and place, of situation-specific models. He had no time for grand, all-embracing, universal systems, independent of time and place. Instead, he let the world tell him what was happening, so avoiding what was, until very recently anyway, the mainstream blinkered and question-begging view – there *must* be an equilibrium out there (or several) and it (they) must be (locally or globally) stable. Second, he deplored the Balkanization of our subject into specialist subsets because this lost, often irretrievably, insights and under-standing: 'Instead of evolving towards fundamental multidisciplinary combi-nations of various fields in the social sciences, so urgently needed by the nature of our problems, economics has gone the diametrically opposite way ... has split up into parts which are becoming alienated from each other ... [specialization] leads to fragmentation with all its drawbacks' (Steindl, 1990, pp. 244–5). Like Kalecki – and he like Marx – Josef Steindl always had at the back of his head the complete system of interrelationships for the issues in hand and he systematically filled in the details on each part before fitting them all together. Again, like Marx, Kalecki and Keynes, the simple but profound insight that the whole may be more than the sum of the parts, that the macroeconomic foundations of microeconomics are as important as the microeconomic foundations themselves, informed his approach. The ability starkly to reveal the major factors at work, to produce robust results, both analytically and empirically, was a noted characteristic of his work.

Third, Steindl *was* a good mathematician, so that any mathematics that he used was always his servant, never his master. Having no reason to show off – indeed, it was not in his nature to do so – and because he was in complete control of his chosen tools, what mathematics he did use was chosen because it was appropriate for the economic issues being discussed, not, as is so often the case, and to the great detriment of the discipline, the other way around. Steindl commented wryly on this deplorable aspect of modern developments:

> [A]t a certain period I also had great optimism with regard to the possibilities of mathematics. Kalecki warned me of that, and he also warned me of the computer: he suggested that both were ideally suited as a scientific cloak to cover the lack of economic substance. Whatever the potentialities of mathematics, with regard to the use which was actually made of it he was dead right. [Its role in] economics has been a most unfortunate one. Instead of being a tool ... it has developed a life of its own. Rather than looking for methods to suit [their] economic problems,

[students ask their teachers] to set [them] problems which suit the formal problems [they have] learned. (Steindl, 1990, p. 246)

As a not altogether irrelevant digression, I want briefly to follow up a suggestion by Claudio Sardoni, namely a comparison of the views of Richard Goodwin and Josef Steindl (as set out in Sebastiani, 1989, pp. 249–51, 309–13) on the significance of Kalecki's work on the cycle and the trend and its extensions by both of these authors. Goodwin does not wish to have a role for random shocks in a theory of cyclical growth for his aim, like those of Marx and Kalecki, is 'to explain how and why capitalism [is], by its very nature, bound to oscillate. [Goodwin is] convinced that Kalecki was basically sound in his approach' (Goodwin, 1989, pp. 249–50); he is also convinced that Kalecki never quite sorted out all his puzzles. The solutions came long after his death when, because 'Kalecki's theory requires essentially finite differences *and* non-linearity, it precisely fits potentially into the group of chaotic models, the so-called strange attractors' (Goodwin, 1989, p. 251).

Steindl is more pragmatic: 'the shocks are there in any case.... You have to take them into account in any case [and] it is most important to keep a theory of the cycle flexible ... capable of accommodating all the exogenous influences ... that a simple endogenous model cannot possibly take into account' (Steindl, 1989, p. 312). Steindl himself had 'occasionally made the suggestion that ... shocks could be used to explain ... the cycle ... [and] the trend if it is assumed that they are asymmetric and that their action is predominantly stimulating' (Steindl, 1989, p. 311). There then follows a typically masterful piece of exposition:

> The action of the shocks might be explained in a non-mathematical way as follows. The cycle works like a pendulum. There is Newton's equation of the pendulum, and that will have a damped solution – that is, the movement comes to a rest if you don't do anything. Now if you imagine the pendulum is suspended from a peg which is not quite fixed but which is moved randomly, then the movement of the pendulum will be kept alive. But if these random movements of the peg have a preferred direction, then in this way you could also explain that a the cycle would not only be kept going, but to the cyclical movement would be added a trend, because the level round which the cycle moves will itself be gradually shifted. (Steindl, 1989, p. 311)

Steindl recommends the use of simulations to proceed, not because simulations can help 'you to determine which values of parameters are "right", [or] which models are "good", but because they can ... help you to eliminate combinations of assumptions and ranges of parametic values which are utterly implausible' (1989, pp. 310–11). Such a procedure might also help us to choose between Goodwin's and Steindl's approaches – or to keep on with both of them.

I now return to my main theme. Steindl believed in good, old-fashioned empirical work: understand the meaning, strength and limitations of the data, do not use fancy techniques for their own sake, but rather choose those that are appropriate for the nature of the data that are being used. Sometimes this involved the use of sophisticated techniques in order to extract the utmost from the data, sometimes it involved the use of very simple techniques – a scatter diagram and a regression line, or even a well set out table, may be all that is needed to focus on the economic intuition involved. Like Tinbergen, Steindl knew that diminishing returns set in very quickly in the application of our techniques because of the essential nature of the subject matter of our discipline. But again, this time, like Frisch, Steindl never shrank from making use of difficult techniques and analysis if they were thought to be appropriate for tackling an issue, or an aspect of the issue in hand.

Steindl had a most real sense of relevance and a tremendous seriousness of purpose, to which he remained true all his life. Because he was acutely aware of the terrible economic problems that still plague us (had more notice of his advice been taken in the past, they would have been considerably less), he had strict standards concerning what we should and should not work on in our discipline. Thus, when Steindl came to discuss Sraffa's contributions at the conference in Florence in August 1985 to celebrate the publication of *Production of Commodities* 25 years before, he chose to write on 'Measurement and Aggregation'. Because 'Sraffa's book is concerned with measurement, concepts, aggregation', Steindl thought that 'macroeconomists should be interested in this side of Sraffa, since measurement and aggregation must ultimately be of concern to them…[Even though] the success of macroeconomics is based on the decision to sweep the problem of aggregation [in the sense of the fiction that ill-defined aggregated *do* have meaning in economic theory] under the carpet [yet] sooner or later…the neglected problems may become relevant' (Steindl, 1990, pp. 253–4).

Steindl therefore used Sraffa's concept of the Standard commodity and some of his other insights about the nature of distribution in a capitalist economy to attempt conceptually to solve the vital but thorny problem of the measurement of productivity over time. He put the central question honestly and without fuss:

Has it any meaning to compare the reproductive potential of two economies with different technology and different [S]tandard commodity?… it has, both for the comparison of one economy over time, and for the comparison of entirely different economies … as much meaning as the comparison of net reproduction rates for men or for animals [was Josef still a frustrated biologist?]. Most economists do not hesitate to compare growth rates in India and in Europe, although they know … that it is not the same things which grow here and there. (Steindl, 1990, p. 270)

The final inference that he drew from his extension of Sraffa's work I find, after (almost) a lifetime of thinking about accumulation and distribution theory in classical and Post-Keynesian theory, extremely appealing:

> A slightly more complicated approach is suggested by Sraffa's idea of the split wage ..., consisting of a price of labour power ... based on the cost of subsistence, and of a share in the surplus ... this suggests that both ... the classical and the Cambridge [theories] are relevant ... one determines a hard rock bottom for the real wage ... defended very strongly and ... recognized by the employers themselves. The share of wages in the surplus ... is determined by the growth requirements of capital which determine the rate of [profits], leaving the remainder of the surplus to wages. (Steindl, 1990, p. 274)

V

In this section we discuss Steindl's two key works and then show how up-to-date he always was by taking two recent examples of his ability to anticipate new developments from his 1990 volume of selected essays.

In *Small and Big Business* (1945) Steindl explained the simultaneous presence of small and big firms in industries by the access that small firms have to niche markets for their products and the segregated markets for their labour. Big firms are able to exploit scales of production and of investment that are denied to their smaller rivals, not least by financial limitations, and that allow the big ones permanently to receive monopoly rents. In *Maturity and Stagnation* (1952, 1976) he set out the deep-seated sources of systemic stagnation in advanced oligopolistic industrial societies – especially, of course, the United States – which derived from the strategic need for individual oligopolists to create excess capacity. The outcome is a long-term tendency for overall investment spending cumulatively to decline. The years of the golden age of capitalism, which overlapped the book's publication, masked these forces which now are only too obviously re-emerging. In the introduction to the second edition, published in 1976, Steindl (1976, p. xvi) gave a masterly, succinct account of the emergence of these masked forces, of 'why the cheerful extroverted era of growth has ... come to an end', as well as clarifying and modifying some of his views and arguments of the first edition.[5]

I cannot resist quoting the perceptive closing sentences of his postscript to the introduction, which were written in June 1976 and in which the coming of monetarism, what his former colleague at Oxford, the late Thomas Balogh, so aptly called 'the incomes policy of Karl Marx', is described in telling detail:

> For some time the political and psychological basis of the postwar boom has been sapped by such developments as these: public spending in the United States as a ratio of GNP decreased under Nixon (when for demographic reasons it ought to have increased!); the competition in technology, Research and Development, and

education unleashed by Sputnik has flagged; the development in these fields has been dominated instead by the internal reaction against intellectuals and youth after the student unrest of 1968; the cooperation between the capitalist powers has broken down – witness their political incapacity to resolve the endemic international currency problem; the internal stresses of groups contending for shares in the national income have shown themselves as inflationary; instead of placating the masses by a steady increase in living standards, the aim has become to dampen their spirits by unemployment, which hits hardest at those who are considered to be the most unruly elements. The arguments against full employment have got the upper hand in the councils of the powers, and thus we witness stagnation not as an incomprehensible fate, as in the 1930s, but stagnation as a policy. (Steindl, 1976, pp. xvi–xvii)

In recent years Steindl was one of the first to ask what are the consequences for the system of personal saving becoming more and more institutionalized in pension funds, and to discern the destabilizing effects for the world economy of the increasing dominance of industrial capital by finance capital in the advanced economies. In two of his papers in the section on 'Saving and Economic Policy' (Steindl, 1990, pp. 181–238), he brings out the subtle differences in the effects on activity of private and corporate saving, respectively. The first is always and unequivocally a leakage, a drag on activity that needs to be offset by investment or other (short-term) autonomous injections of spending. The second, because it *may* be combined with a simultaneous decision to raise investment expenditure, may not prove to be such a drag. How great the expansionary effect is depends in part on whether the increased saving is at the expense of dividends, at least in the short term, or is brought about by decisions to exploit any unused monopoly power by raising margins and so prices in order to try to increase the flow of retained profits. Much of Steindl's best work contained analysis in depth of both the micro *and* macro implications of these sorts of decisions. Here, as always, Steindl was true to himself: 'The division into macro and microeconomics has not been good for students. In one course they are taught the trees and in another the wood, but what has one to do with the other?' (Steindl, 1990, p. 244).

In one of his last papers he combined his statistical skills with his understanding of the nature of dominant speculative processes on stock markets, to produce an analysis worthy of Keynes's famous account of the phenomena in the 1930s. He modestly said at the end of the paper that his 'brief note has made use, without quotation, of elements which are well known from the writings of creative economists like Keynes or Schumpeter'. He added: 'My point is that those elements would fit in very well with the type of stochastic approach which aims at objective and social concepts, instead of a psychological and subjective treatment of expectation and uncertainty ... ultimately an analysis along these lines will lead to a new understanding not only of speculative markets but perhaps of the market as such, which has been identified all too long with a cliché' (Steindl, 1990, p. 375).

Steindl has allied himself in this note with the critique of D.H. Robertson, Kaldor and (J.R.) Hicks which Richard Kahn and Joan Robinson made in the 1950s and 1960s, to wit, that in a macroeconomic analysis of markets where expectations are important and stocks dominate flows, it is necessary to have more than one 'representative agent' present. The uneasy rest states in these markets are only achieved by the setting of prices that balance at the margin the differing opinions as to the levels and/or rates of change of prices of the operators in the markets. Moreover, not even the uneasy balances will be achieved unless there is 'a generally accepted idea of a normal price level to which prices will ultimately tend to return' (Steindl, 1990, p. 371). As examples of such norms, Steindl referred to the notion of purchasing power parity in foreign exchange markets and to Keynes's conventional level of the rate of interest in the market for financial assets. He then pointed out that it is the disappearance of such norms – I would add to his list the disappearance in the labour markets of the advanced industrialized countries in the 1970s of generally agreed notions of what are reasonable and fair rates of increase of money wages – that is one of the causes of the great instability in these markets. 'The undermining of concepts of normalcy in certain markets has been accompanied by great instability, so that it does not contradict but rather tends to confirm the rule that generally accepted ideas of a standard of normalcy are necessary in order to maintain more or less stable markets' (Steindl, 1990, p. 371).

Of course, I cheered these comments to the echo. One of the most profound lessons I learnt from Nicky Kaldor and Joan Robinson I recently formulated in terms of a wolf pack analogy, see Harcourt (1992), Chapter 1 above. That Josef Steindl's intuition backed this up, and that he developed a framework in which to think about and tackle these problems, is not the least of his incisive contributions to modern economics.

Steindl said in the preface to his 1990 collection of papers that he had 'made no attempt to refer to the literature which [had] become available since the papers were written. Since all [his] ideas [ran] somewhat counter to the mainstream of economic thinking of the last decades this omission may perhaps be felt less acutely than it otherwise would [have been]' (p. viii). In fact, it is refreshing to read his papers which are uncluttered with spurious scholarship, are lucid, clear and honest, always as critical of himself in previous incarnations as of others now, completely unshowy and always to the point and positive.

VI

In my paper (Harcourt 1994) at the WIFO conference in May 1992 honouring Josef's 80th birthday, I set out what Josef meant to me. I included among my mentors, Dobb, Kalecki, Keynes, Joan Robinson and Sraffa, and I named as the paper that the most influenced me as an undergraduate, 'Price Theory and Oligopoly' (1947), a classic written by Josef's great friend and colleague of many years, Kurt Rothschild. Naturally, with this set of mentors, I had to discover Josef's work. I was immediately enthralled by it and I have remained an enthusiastic fan ever since.

I first met Josef himself at Udine in 1980 at the preparatory conference for the first International Summer School at Trieste in 1981. I have already discussed his lectures at these schools (see section I above). My lasting memories of him there are, first, as one of the courageous band of swimmers who risked stings from the jellyfish of the Adriatic in the interest of keeping fit (and perhaps sane, given the strenuous and demanding programme that the organizers set us). Second, I have an abiding memory of him listening and now and then talking to kindred souls, his face lit up by his wry but gentle smile, at the sumptuous and leisurely mealtimes that also enabled us to see through what the organizers had imposed on us.

Josef Steindl was an unassuming, rather solitary person who hated careerism and ruthless ambition. I am sure that is one of the main reasons why Josef and Krishna Bharadwaj became such close friends. In his work, let me repeat, he explicitly identified heroes, villains and victims – and said so. Like his mentor Kalecki, he had a deliciously dry sense of humour, able to deliver telling asides in a few words. He wanted his discipline to wipe out unemployment and poverty, so that others could, *if they wished*, have the opportunity to do what he himself loved so much to do – walk in the mountains, listen to music and enjoy the company of close friends who shared his decent humane values – with a smile.

Notes

In writing this tribute the author has drawn freely on Nina Shapiro's essay on Josef Steindl in the Arestis and Sawyer volume (1992), his paper at the WIFO conference in honour of Josef Steindl's 80th birthday, held in Vienna in May 1992, the obituary of Steindl which he wrote for *The Independent*, 27 March 1993, and the notes on Steindl's life which Alois Guger very kindly sent him. He would also like to thank John King, Alessandro Roncaglia, Claudio Sardoni and Roberto Scazzieri for their comments on a draft of the tribute, and Kurt Rothschild for allowing him to quote from his letter to John King.

1. Kurt Rothschild (8 April 1993, letter to John King) recounts a strange tale concerning Steindl and Tintner: 'A strange event occurred [after Steindl's death]. Since there were no relatives alive a young friend of Steindl from the Institute of Economic Research looked after all the things to be done and had also to arrange the burial of the urn in the very big central Viennese cemetery. He left it to the office of the cemetery to choose a free place among the hundreds of graves. When we finally attended the burial we noticed that Steindl's

urn was placed – by pure chance – immediately next to the grave of Gerhar[d] Tintner who had been a very close friend of Steindl since prewar days when they were both young researchers in the Austrian Institute of Business Cycle Research.'

2. John King (7 June 1993) tells me that this may be the surface reason and that the real reason was a general prejudice against bright 'returnees' such as Rothschild and Steindl himself. When the Austrian higher education system was reformed in the late 1960s, I suspect that Steindl felt it was too late to make another move.

3. John King (7 June 1993) thinks that *Maturity and Stagnation* was Steindl's masterpiece for which *Small and Big Business* was 'a sort of dry run', and that his 'technical stuff was more of a sideline'. I do not disagree with this assessment but I thought it worthwhile, in this very technical age, to draw attention to Steindl's innovative contributions.

4. About half of the essays written by Steindl after 1980 and reprinted in Steindl (1990) were published in the *Banca Nazionale del Lavoro Quarterly Review*. His own splendid 'Reflections', on which I have drawn heavily for this tribute, were first published there in 1984. The article was written in response to a request from Alessandro Roncaglia for an essay by Josef in the journal's 'recollections and reflections' series.

5. John King (7 June 1993) would have me emphasize *Maturity and Stagnation* more, and especially its influence on left thinking, including the contribution of the two Pauls, Baran and Sweezy. Again, I concur.

References

Arestis, P. and M. Sawyer (eds) (1992), *A Biographical Dictionary of Dissenting Economists*, Aldershot: Edward Elgar.

Goodwin, R.M. (1989), 'Kalecki's Economic Dynamics: A Personal View', in M. Sebastiani (ed.), *Kalecki's Relevance Today*, Basingstoke: Macmillan, pp. 249–51.

Harcourt, G.C. (1992), 'Markets, Madness and a Middle Way', The Second Donald Horne Address, Melbourne, Monash University.

Harcourt, G.C. (1994), 'What Josef Steindl Means to My Generation', *Review of Political Economy*, **6**, pp. 459–63.

Rothschild, K.W. (1947), 'Price Theory and Oligopoly', *Economic Journal*, **57**, pp. 299–320.

Sebastiani, M. (ed.) (1989), *Kalecki's Relevance Today*, Basingstoke: Macmillan.

Shapiro, N. (1992), 'Josef Steindl (born 1912)', in P. Arestis and M. Sawyer (eds), *A Biographical Dictionary of Dissenting Economists*, pp. 549–55.

Singh, A. and G. Whittington (in collaboration with H.T. Burley) (1968), *Growth, Profitability and Valuation*, Cambridge: Cambridge University Press.

Steindl, J. (1945), *Small and Big Business: Economic Problems of the Size of Firms*, Oxford: Basil Blackwell.

Steindl, J. (1952), *Maturity and Stagnation in American Capitalism*, Oxford: Basil Blackwell: 2nd edn, 1976.

Steindl, J. (1965), *Random Processes and the Growth of Firms: A Study of the Pareto Law*, London: Griffin.

Steindl, J. (1989), 'Reflections on Kalecki's Dynamics', in M. Sebastiani (ed.), *Kalecki's Relevance Today*, pp. 309–13.

Steindl, J. (1990), *Economic Papers, 1941–88*, Basingstoke: Macmillan.

14 Ruth Cohen, 10 November 1906 – 27 July 1991*

Ruth Cohen, the economist, was Principal of Newnham College, Cambridge, from 1954 to 1972 and Labour City Councillor for the Newnham Ward of Cambridge in 1973–87.

She was a militant agnostic but practised all the civic virtues of the large middle-class Jewish family from which she came. She read economics at Newnham, graduating in 1929 with a respectable first. One of her teachers was Richard Kahn, an inspiring mentor who kindled her enthusiasm for the subject. She won the Adam Smith Prize in 1930 and went as Commonwealth Fund Fellow to Stanford and Cornell universities for two years, in 1930–32. Returning to the United Kingdom she worked for several years in Oxford as a research officer at the Agricultural Economics Research Institute. She wrote the *History of Milk Prices* (1936) and *The Economics of Agriculture* (1939), the latter for the Cambridge Economic Handbook series. It is a sturdy, down-to-earth book which has served generations of students well.

Ruth Cohen was elected to a fellowship at Newnham just before the Second World War. During the war she worked at the Ministry of Food (1939–42) and then at the Board of Trade (1942–5). She helped to design the scheme whereby there was milk for all in schools, a splendid initiative which survived until scrapped in the 1970s by Mrs Thatcher, when Minister of Education and Science: two acts which highlight the difference between Ruth Cohen's generous nature, ever mindful of the position of others less privileged and well-off than herself, and the mean-spirited attitudes of more recent times.

In 1945, she resumed her Newnham fellowship and was appointed to a university lectureship in the Faculty of Economics and Politics at Cambridge. Lecturing was definitely *not* her forte, and though she continued spasmodically to publish, especially on mergers, in collaboration with her former pupil Lesley Cook, the administrative aspects of the university life became more and more to her liking. So to be elected Principal of Newnham in 1954 proved to be a happy example of the principle of comparative advantage.

Sustained by the effortless confidence of the British upper-middle classes (and, in her case, unaffected by the thoughtless anti-semitism of that same social grouping), she was a direct, formidable and extraordinarily energetic

* First published in *The Independent*, Wednesday 31 July, 1991.

185

Principal, always well prepared and far-sighted, if not always able gracefully to delegate or put up with people less intelligent and quick than herself. Her manner was direct, unstuffy and unselfconscious, as, for many years, she chain-smoked through meetings and beat all-comers for speed at eating at High Table. Pupils and colleagues initially may have been intimidated; yet usually this soon turned to affection. Her friendships were legion, not only in committee rooms but also on vigorous long walks.

Ruth Cohen retired as Principal in 1972 and after a year in France returned to direct her energies into local politics in Cambridge. She took great pains on behalf of her constituents, she was a tireless campaigner and canvasser, as well as the scourge of the would-be profligate in her role as Chair of the Finance Committee. In her later years she became almost completely lame; though naturally frustrated, she refused to curb her activities and her electrically powered chariot became a familiar – and dangerous – sight in Cambridge.

She maintained her abiding interest in political, faculty, college and sporting events. She loved a good gossip, except over the Wimbledon fortnight, when her friends knew better than to interrupt her expert absorption of the dramas unfolding on the television screen.

Ruth Cohen's economics combined pragmatic common sense with critical acumen, and it was always directed to practicable policies. Ironically, her name is more likely to live on in the theoretical literature. The term, 'The Ruth Cohen Curiosum', was given by another close friend and colleague, Joan Robinson, to a theoretical result which destroys the simple conceptual basis of price as an index of scarcity in the demand-and-supply approach to the theory of distribution.

Characteristically, Ruth Cohen left her body to the School of Anatomy.

15 A.K. Dasgupta, 1903–1992*

Professor Amiya Kumar Dasgupta, the eminent Indian economist, died in his 89th year on 14 January 1992 at Santiniketan. AK, as he was always known, was born on 16 July 1903 in a rural part of what is now Bangladesh. Ashok Mitra tells us that he came from a sect which gave him passion for and pleasure in logical propositions, which attributes flourished when he started to read economics at the University of Dacca in 1922. After graduating he became a lecturer at the university. He spent two years at the LSE in the mid-1930s, a period when Robbins, Hayek and Rosenstein-Rodan were major influences, together with some brilliant 'youngsters' – Hicks, Kaldor, Abba Lerner, Shackle and also Kalecki, who was in London at the time. Dasgupta held a number of teaching and research posts in India after he left Dacca, with much hesitation, at the end of the Second World War. He was for many years Professor of Economics at Banaras Hindu University. He spent three years at the IMF in Washington, returning to India in the 1960s, first to Banaras and then to Delhi. He also played an important part in official policy making. But he did not like metropolitan life; so it is good that, at the very end of his life, he returned to his roots in rural India.

Dasgupta was Commonwealth Visiting Professor at Cambridge (1963–4). President of the Indian Economic Association (1960), an Honorary Professor of Jawaharlal Nehru University (1976) and an Honorary Fellow of the LSE (1978). He published a number of books and many articles. He wrote mainly on economic theory, on the history of economic theory and policy, and on planning and development, always including the international dimensions. His mentors were the classical political economists, Marx, Wicksell, Marshall (especially), Keynes, Kalecki and Robbins. Of other contemporaries, Hicks, Kaldor and Joan Robinson were the most prominent, together with a life-long friend from his student days, Sachin Chaudhuri, founder of the influential *Economic Weekly*, which contains many of Dasgupta's papers. His writings were noted for their proper scholarship, lucidity, independence of mind and analytical rigour. His approach is summed up in the title of his book, *Epochs of Economic Theory* (1985). He argued that each time and place must have their own relevant theory for their own issues; predecessors may be learnt from and general ideas may be passed onto successors but, overwhelmingly, we must create our own approaches and appropriate apparatus.

* First published in The *Guardian*, Tuesday 21 January, 1992.

Dasgupta was a truly remarkable teacher, not only face to face with pupils, but also through correspondence. He responded to requests with encouragement and incisive criticism (which left no bruises). His enthusiasm, kindness, simple patriotism, acute understanding of issues and analytical ability left a direct mark on many of India's foremost economists and on countless others who knew him or his work. Dasgupta's son, Partha, and Amartya Sen, to whom *Epochs* is dedicated, regarded him as the major influence and inspiration of their lives. The volume of essays which Ashok Mitra edited for Dasgupta's 70th birthday contains contributions by distinguished economists from all over the world, a true index of Dasgupta's benign influence.

AK and his wife, Shanti, were married for 57 years. They gave generous hospitality to countless visiting economists. The Dasguptas had an extraordinarily happy family life. They were lovingly proud of their children, their children's spouses and their grandchildren, who responded with love and admiration for a truly modern sage and his essential companion.

16 Professor Sir (Edward) Austin (Gossage) Robinson, 20 November 1897–1 June 1993*

To the discerning, Austin Robinson was the unsung hero of Cambridge economics. Through selfless service, often as secretary, sometimes as chairman of the Faculty Board of Economics and Politics, before and after the Second World War, Austin Robinson, more than anyone else, enabled the various opposing factions of the faculty to coexist, and its intellectual life thereby to thrive. He was the guiding spirit behind the creation in the 1960s of the building which now bears his name; it was christened so at his 90th birthday party in the faculty coffee room, at which he gave a typically eloquent account of his supervisions by C.R. Fay, who was 'full of enthusiasms and excitements [but] completely innocent of any real understanding of Marshallian economics' (Robinson, 1992, p. 206), and by Gerald Shove and Dennis Robertson. Most of all, he contributed, unobtrusively but profoundly, to the various revolutions in economic thinking that occurred in Cambridge and the profession generally. He himself thought that the 1930s was the most 'creative period' in which to be an economist. For it was then, he argued, that the 'revolution' in value theory, welfare economics, employment theory and the quantification of economics occurred (Robinson, 1992, p. 209).

Both in the 1930s, when he had two spells working on Africa, including a visit to what was then Northern Rhodesia, and during the Second World War, when he held posts in the Cabinet Office, the Ministry of Production and the Board of Trade, Austin proved himself to be an extremely able civil servant. He combined hard work with attention to detail and a clear understanding of what the problems were and what their feasible solutions could be. He made important contributions to manpower planning and to an understanding of the structural changes that would need to be made in order that the United Kingdom could export enough to cover its imports after the war. Had he wished, he could have become a permanent civil servant. But despite Sir Stafford Cripps's efforts to secure this, winkling him away from Cambridge on two occasions – a year in London helping to draft the *Economic Survey for 1948* and the *Economic Survey for 1948–52*, six months in Paris with the Organization for European Economic Cooperation (OEEC) ensuring that the Marshall Plan could go through – he decided to return to academic life. He

* This essay was written as the first draft of the 'Appreciation' of Austin which Alan Hughes, Ajit Singh and I wrote for the *Cambridge Journal of Economics*, **17**, 1993, pp. 365–8. It also draws on the obituary of Austin which I wrote for *The Independent*, Saturday 5 June 1993.

had no family life for seven years and he 'knew [he] was not tough enough to carry on indefinitely under the pressure that [he] had worked during the [war] years' (Robinson, 1992, p. 218).

He certainly fooled us all; even allowing for his long life, the breadth and depth of his subsequent, indeed *all* his contributions are remarkable. He was assistant editor and then joint editor of the *Economic Journal* for 36 years and secretary of the Royal Economic Society for 25 years; treasurer of the International Economic Association for nine years and its president for three years. Many of the volumes of the latter's conferences were edited or jointly edited by Austin. He was associated with the National Institute for Economic and Social Research. John Howell remind us (*The Independent*, 17 June 1993) that Austin 'did much to foster British interest in policies to improve incomes and welfare in poor countries and in 1960 he was a prime mover in the establishment of the Overseas Development Institute where he remained an active member of its governing body'. He carried a full lecturing load at Cambridge. In the 1920s and 1930s, when he became a fellow, first of Corpus Christi and then of Sidney Sussex, he had many supervision pupils, as well as two years (1926–8) tutoring the young Maharajah of Gwalior when, soon after they married, Austin and Joan Robinson went to India.

Austin Robinson was the 'son of an impecunious parson'. Scholarships took him to Marlborough and then Christ's to read classics. But first (this was 1916) there was active service in the Royal Naval Air Service followed by testing and delivering new flying boats. This period was to remain an extremely significant episode in his life, about which he was writing in the months before he died. After the war he came up to Cambridge, not an orthodox pacifist yet a member of that generation of returned service people 'naive' [perhaps but] sincere' who were determined to see that war was never again used to settle differences between nations. Though he obtained a first in classics after 15 months, his wartime experiences, together with Keynes's lectures on what was to become *The Economic Consequences of the Peace* – 'a revelation' – determined him to become an economist. He wanted to understand how economies function or malfunction and what could be done about this. All his writings reflect this noble motivation.

He wrote two books in the 1930s, *The Structure of Competitive Industry* (1931) and *Monopoly* (1941); both were in the Cambridge Economic Handbook Series and both are now regarded as classics. (Dennis Robertson asked him to write the second one and the first grew out of his preparations.) With his first book, Austin, in effect, resurrected the theory of the firm in Cambridge. It is a book firmly rooted in the realities of industrial life, and it reflects his view that economic efficiency is not just a matter of technically correct choices of production techniques. Management skills, labour relations and competitive behaviour are all emphasized as important determinants of industrial performance and the optimum size of firms. Naturally, he and his 1931 book were important influences on Joan Robinson when she wrote *The Economics of Imperfect Competition* (1933), Austin's 'very bright' pupil, Charles Gifford, introduced Joan and Richard Kahn to that book's central concept which Austin himself named 'marginal revenue'. Joan Robinson also reported that an 'ingenious' scheme to make monopolists behave 'was first suggested by Mr Robinson in an answer written in an examination' (Joan Robinson, 1933, p. 163, n. 1). In the first chapter of *Monopoly*, having set out the purpose of the book – 'to consider what we mean by monopoly, the conditions in which monopolies can be created and ... continue to exist, the forms that they take, their virtues and vices ... and the attitude to them of the law and ... public opinion' – Austin added two sentences which succinctly capture his approach to economics: '[the book] is intended to be ... a tin-opener to open the tin of knowledge. But there is nothing in the world so useless as a tin-opener, unless it is a tin without a tin-opener' (Robinson, 1941, p. 1).

Austin Robinson was a member of the Cambridge 'circus' which, he argued, was an important irritant which helped Keynes to make his major pearl, *The General Theory* (1936) as he moved on from *A Treatise on Money* (1930). He was Keynes's close and trusted colleague for many years. His devoted and arduous role in editing (with Elizabeth Johnson and, then, Donald Moggridge) the 30 volumes of Keynes's *Collected Writings* has ensured that Keynes's own legacy to future generations is secure. A serious limitation of the subsequent development of Keynesian thought at Cambridge after Keynes's death in 1946 was that Austin's stress on the need to understand, empirically and theoretically, the behaviour of firms, industries and regions as well as the *overall* workings of the economy did not receive anywhere near enough attention.

Austin set out his misgivings and reservations in his 1966 Marshall Lectures, *Economic Planning in the United Kingdom: Some Lessons* (Robinson, 1967). There was a question which he 're-iterated through [the lectures]: Is macro-economics enough?' (p. 46). He clearly thought it was not. Although an avowed Keynesian, Austin firmly believed that it was not enough to simply get the broad macroeconomic aggregates right, stand back and then expect free markets to do the rest. Anyone reading his 1966 Marshall lectures would be left in no doubt of his belief in the virtues of industrial policy and supply-side economics: although not supply-side economics of the kind practised, much to his dismay, in the United Kingdom in recent years!

Early in the Lectures, he stressed (and illuminated from his own experiences) that it may be essential in wartime that 'very rapid, very dramatic' structural changes are made. Moreover, this could not be done 'solely by macro-economic measures', it was necessary also to watch 'all the time the adequacy of the micro-economic changes [and] to have statistics adequate to your purpose' (p. 12). Looking back to these lessons and achievements over 20 years on, he lamented the abandonment of microeconomic attempts 'to balance the economy and ... steer its structural changes' in peacetime (p. 43). Nevertheless, he believed 'that macro-economic planning [had] brought such benefits to the human race' that it would be unthinkable to surrender it. 'The completely unplanned world is not a world of perfect macro-economics *plus* all the results of perfect competition. It is a world without macro-economics, a world of trade cycles and two million unemployed' (pp. 44–5) – a qualitatively correct and far-sighted judgement, alas coupled with quantitative optimism that has not in fact been fulfilled 27 years on. Austin added another challenging reflection on 'the one common feature' of the microeconomic measures that were practised in fact: 'It is, in some sense, regarded as fair to help the failing, but unfair to help the vigorous and successful' (p. 46). He himself had conscious manpower planning in mind, but he has enunciated here a general principle which has been almost completely lost from sight since he wrote.

Partly because of his early Indian experience and his work on Africa, a considerable proportion of his published work was concerned with the practicalities of economic development. Moreover, over the years, he was an adviser, especially on energy policies, to many developing countries. Ever the pragmatic interventionist, he had no time for the niceties of pure theory or the misleading philosophy that maintains that only freely competitive markets can bring about socially desirable outcomes in either developing or developed economies. His 'fierce arguments' in supervisions with Fay taught Austin, first to identify the problem, then to combine theory and empirical understanding in order to frame down-to-earth policy suggestions which, in turn, were as careful to take in political constraints as they were to exploit a deep understanding of the economic processes themselves. His work on the *Economic Survey* in the late 1940s led him always to insist that policies for the long term cannot be isolated from those for the short term. 'If you attempt to do so, all the decisions required by long-term considerations will have been wrongly taken on the basis of short-term considerations' (Robinson, 1967, p. 4). Sir Alec Cairncross's chapter on 'Austin the Economist' in his biography of Austin Robinson (Cairncross, 1993) should be required reading for anyone aspiring to be what his subject was *par excellence*, an applied political economist. In Austin's view, 'no economist is more dangerous than the pure theorist without practical experience and instinctive understanding of the real world that he is attempting to analyse, seeking precision in a world of imprecision, in a world he does not understand' (Robinson, 1992, p. 221). For him the point of being an economist was to improve the state of the world.

To the end of his life, though ultimately physically frail, Austin remained mentally vigorous and alert. During a recent scare about French cheeses, Austin was asked at lunch in Sidney Sussex by a fellow in his late eighties whether they should eat them. Austin said: 'It is only dangerous for pregnant women and old people – and we do not belong to either category.' Some of his best papers (and trenchant referee reports for the *Cambridge Journal of Economics*) were written in his late eighties and early nineties, especially his fascinating autobiographical essay, 'My Apprenticeship as an Economist' (Szenberg, 1992, pp. 203–21). His 1947 obituary article on Keynes in the *Economic Journal* is an excellent example of his approach: lucid and balanced, subtle, perceptive and affectionate, its judgements will stand the test of time and its prose is worthy of Keynes's own. Perhaps the judgement which is most apt for today's world is the following: 'It was ... a great step forward in economic thought when Keynes insisted that we should have a *general* theory – a theory that was valid not only with full (or near-full) employment, but also with unemployment – and that we should know quite clearly which of the propositions of economics were universally valid, and which were valid only in conditions in which it might be true that an increase of one activity was possible *only* at the expense of another activity' (Robinson, 1947, p. 44). Austin believed that 'in the Cambridge thought of [his] time ... no single forward step [had] been so important [, that it had] gone right to the heart of the method of estimation of the opportunity costs of doing anything. Before, [they believed] the paradox that it might be profitable to a society to allow resources which might have produced something to stand idle. [They] came to see why that paradox was, in fact, untrue' (ibid., pp. 44–5). Would to God that our present 'leaders' and their 'advisers' had such clear sight!

Austin Robinson was a polite and courteous person, certainly a workaholic yet proud and mindful of his family and friends as well as of his country, college and faculty. He could be stubborn and imperious, but his kindly concern for particular individuals and his devotion to the underprivileged of all manner of societies aptly fulfilled his early hope that while 'not a crusading Christian ... he [would retain] the essentials of ... Christianity' (Robinson, 1992, p. 207).

References

Cairncross, Alec (1993), *Austin Robinson. The Life of an Economic Advisor*, Basingstoke: Macmillan.

Keynes, J.M. (1919), *The Economic Consequences of the Peace*, London: Macmillan; *CW*, Vol. II (1971).

Keynes, J.M. (1930), *A Treatise on Money*, 2 vols, London: Macmillan; *CW*, Vols V and VI (1971).

Keynes, J.M. (1936), *The General Theory of Employment, Interest and Money*, London: Macmillan; *CW*, Vol. VII (1973).

Robinson, Austin (1931), *The Structure of Competitive Industry*, London: Cambridge University Press.

Robinson, Austin (1941), *Monopoly*, London: Cambridge University Press.

Robinson, Austin (1947), 'John Maynard Keynes 1883–1946', *Economic Journal*, **LVII**, March, pp. 1–68.

Robinson, Austin (1967), *Economic Planning in the United Kingdom: Some Lessons*, Cambridge: Cambridge University Press.

Robinson, Austin (1992), 'My Apprenticeship as an Economist', in Szenberg (1992), pp. 203–21.

Robinson, Joan (1933), *The Economics of Imperfect Competition*, London: Macmillan.

Szenberg, Michael (ed.) (1992), *Eminent Economists. Their Life Philosophies*, Cambridge: Cambridge University Press.

PART IV

GENERAL ESSAYS

17 'Tommy' Balogh's last stand*[1]

As unemployment in the world capitalist system approaches the worst levels since the 1930s, inflation rates stay stubbornly high, the system of international payments and capital flows becomes increasingly fragile, the rate of increase of world trade shrinks and interest rates soar, disillusionment with the economic policies of governments and the theories which underlie them is emerging at an accelerating pace. A new book, *The Irrelevance of Conventional Economics* (Weidenfeld & Nicholson, 1982) written by Harold Wilson's former economic adviser, Thomas Balogh, contains a lucid, absorbing account of the principal objections to those theories and policies. It also contains highly individual and sometimes idiosyncratic additions of Balogh's own, including what he thinks needs to be done.

Balogh strips away the jargon and squiggles which characterize most discussions of modern economic theory and policy and goes straight for the conceptual issues involved. His credentials for this task are probably unique – he has been a financier, a banker, an Oxford don, a director of the British National Oil Corporation and a minister of state – and he was born in Hungary. His arguments deserve to have a considerable impact. This may be lessened by his engaging but Quixotic habit of hitting his potential allies as hard as his enemies. For example, recently there have emerged some effective theoretical arguments which serve to undermine the system of thought to which Balogh most objects, but Balogh rejects the critique because it uses the same techniques and framework as the theories it attacks.

The short list of Balogh's heroes of modern economics does not get into double figures. It includes John Kenneth Galbraith, Nicholas Kaldor, Joan Robinson and Balogh's collaborator of many years, Paul Streeten, all unfashionable figures within the profession itself but, to the humane and the discerning, admirable and enlightened.

Balogh's villains hail from Chicago – Friedman and the monetarists, including the most up-to-date variety, the 'rational expectations', 'New Classical macroeconomics' school. He blames them for pushing economic theory back to its pre-Keynesian irrelevancies, and for persuading governments and their advisers to adopt tragically wrong-headed policies based on their not always complete or correct understanding of the theories. Balogh is not an uncritical admirer of Keynesianism either, at least of Keynesianism in the

* First published as 'The Irrelevance of Conventional Economics: A review article' in *Social Alternatives*, **3**, No. 2, March, 1983, pp. 61–2.

form in which it got into the textbooks and the policies of the Treasuries in the postwar period. Keynes himself receives some of his harsher barbs, especially for having disagreed with Balogh about international trade and capital movements.

Balogh particularly dislikes the yearnings of the premier social science to be thought of as 'scientific', to produce a determinate, universalist system in which are embedded harmonious laws and outcomes – a self-correcting, shockproof system provided governments apply a few simple and well understood rules, for example, that the money supply increases at a particular rate. Orthodoxy argues that the natural resting place of the system is a fully employed one where people (agents as they are called in modern theory) are all to be found in their preferred positions. (We have to take as given their initial endowment of resources.) The theory supposes that our world may be viewed 'as if' it were made up of people who have no discretion over the prices that they charge for their products or their services; that is, that economic and political powers are diffused equally between all, and no one person, or group, has any substantial power – an idealized, not to say vulgarized version of the powerful benefits of competition in Smith's *Wealth of Nations*. All required information is provided through prices over which only market forces have any influence. Provided only that we all follow our own self-interest, we are led by an invisible hand to create a solution which is also socially optimal. There are a few provisos about the arbitrariness of the initial endowments (which end up as important influences on the distribution of income and wealth) and the divergences of private costs and benefits from their social counterparts (which come under the heading of externalities).

Superimposed on this real system of production and exchange (in the orthodox view) is a monetary system which does not affect its workings in any permanent way, but does serve to determine the general level of prices, and therefore the money prices in which the relative prices of the system are expressed. Both nationally and internationally, the orthodox theorists see a long-run equilibrium of the forces of demand and supply, adjusting appropriately when tastes and technology change. Change comes best from the initiative and enterprise of dynamic businessmen, who flourish best in a system where institutions guarantee that it works in reality 'as if' it were the harmonious theoretical system sketched above.

Balogh points out that the neoclassical Keynesians (Joan Robinson called them 'bastard Keynesians') accepted this story – with two modifications. First, they did not accept that the system *as a whole* would tend to settle at a full employment position without the help of 'fine-tuning' – fiscal and monetary measures designed to produce an overall level of spending that was consistent with full employment. Secondly, because of their yearning for determinate solutions and established laws, they believed that they had found a trade-off relationship between unemployment and inflation – the Phillips curve – which would allow societies consciously to choose their own menu of overall levels of activity and rates of price increases. When the empirical estimates on which this was based broke down in the 1970s (Balogh doubts that it ever existed) and stagflation emerged, governments and their citizens were so disillusioned that the enemy was able to pounce, providing deceptively simple diagnoses and solutions – reduce government spending, cut taxes, keep the rate of increase of the money supply steady (and low), deregulate wherever possible and let the system work out its own solutions. The private sector became sacrosanct. The public-sector bureaucracies and the unions became the devils of the piece, all enemies of free people and the competitive process.

Balogh sees this as an ideological rationalization of more sinister purposes. He does not believe in grand overall designs and systems, suitable for all times and places, or in harmonious self-regulating systems of a determinate nature. His key word is 'indeterminate'; he is a 'horses for courses' man. Systems are open; it is necessary to understand their past history, their political and other institutions, their sociological groupings, before suitable models can be conceptualized for their problems and suitable policies be designed to tackle them. Processes are more likely to be cumulative than self-correcting. Moreover, a model in which power is assumed to be widely diffused is unable to illuminate the processes at work in systems where power is concentrated. For example, full employment upset the distribution of power between capital and labour – domestic servants became hard to get and shop assistants ceased to be servile; it 'entailed grave social and economic drawbacks for the propertied and managerial classes' (Balogh, 1982, p. 52).

Monetarist policies, especially the inflation-first strategy, are explained by their proponents as pushing unemployment momentarily above its so-called 'natural rate' so that the self-regulating forces of the economic system may allow it smoothly to find its way back to its natural equilibrium in a changed, more healthy climate of lowered expectations about inflation. In reality, their objective is to shift the balance of power back to capital (including, in the Australian case, international capital) and away from labour. Prolonged depression and rising unemployment are to cow the workers into accepting wage cuts or, at least, cuts in the rate at which money wages increase. As Balogh says (ibid. pp. 177–8) 'monetarism is the incomes policy of Karl Marx .... By deliberately setting out to base the viability of the capitalist system on the maintenance of a large 'industrial reserve army', monetarists may validate Marx's analysis'.

Balogh does not minimize the dangers of inflation (he writes as cogently about its disrupting social effects as did Keynes in the *Tract*) but he does savage the packages of the Thatchers, Frasers and Reagans of this world as cruel and ineffective: ineffective because they are based on models which fail to illuminate the processes at work in a world characterized by oligopolistic industries and strong unions, by price making rather than price taking, by multinational corporations and oil cartels, by rich industrialized nations and poor undeveloped ones – that is to say, the world in which we actually live. It is a world, moreover, in which, historically, actual movements have tended to be cumulative rather than stabilizing or, at best, cyclical. He argues that economic and political factors are indissolubly mixed, that ' "Science" has to give way to history and politics, a truly shocking prospect!' (p. 204). He believes that consensus policies and political education are the only sure ways to tackle problems such as stagflation. He fears that the disruptive spin-offs of the policies of recent years – embittered, despairing and angry youth and unemployed, destroyed industries, the sustained shock to the 'animal spirits' of the investing and managerial classes – may have come close to destroying those vestiges of good will which would allow progressive governments to try again.

Full employment is a necessary prerequisite. Balogh pays a grand tribute to the 20 or so years of the long boom when, by and large, we had it, together with unprecedented rates of growth and capital accumulation in the capitalist world. The psychological significance of full employment is that it makes people feel wanted and needed members of a dynamically advancing society: 'Human dignity and satisfaction are incompatible with unemployment, even if the fear of penury has been completely eliminated by the social services – which it has not' (p. 151).

But full employment by itself is not enough. It has to be coupled with consensus policies on incomes – 'free collective bargaining [is] the incomes policy of the jungle' – and a more equitable distribution of wealth, internally and, ultimately, externally.

Balogh believes in comprehensive economic planning, including controls and protection, not as a dogma or as a buzz-word, but as a commonsense response to national and international problems. He knows that checks and balances have to be provided for bureaucrats as well as for industrialists and powerful unions in the private sector. What worries him most is that the destabilizing effects of Thatcherism and Reaganism (to which we should add Fraserism in Australia) may already have made it too late for democratic socialism to try again or, possibly, to try for a first time.

Note
1.   I am indebted to Hugh Stretton for his comments on a draft of this review essay.

18 On mathematics and economics*

I

I am delighted to be the opening bat for John Cornwell's second Jesus symposium, 'Mathematics: what should non-mathematicians know?' Some months ago John asked me who amongst the economists would be a suitable person to give this lecture. I ran through a *Who's Who* of the great and the good in modern economics: Ken Arrow, Paul Samuelson, Bob Solow, Leo Hurwicz and Gerard Debreu in the United States, Frank Hahn, Jim Mirrlees, Partha Dasgupta and Bob Rowthorn in the United Kingdom. I then reverted to childish behaviour (which I had hoped I had put behind me) by suggesting that I be considered for the slot.

Why did I behave so egotistically, since, though there are squiggles galore in my early papers, by no stretch of the imagination could I ever be considered a mathematical economist? Indeed, after the seminar I gave at Monash just before I returned to Cambridge in 1982, when I asked how my paper was received, one of the participants 'softened' the blow by saying 'You must remember, Geoff, half of them think you are a sociologist'. And Amitava Dutt in a most generous review in the *Manchester School* (Dutt, 1993), of a selection of my essays from the last 30 years, Sardoni (1992), wrote: 'While the [formal] models of the first part of the selection] are fascinating ... they might have received more of the attention they deserve had they been more technically elegant' (Dutt, 1993, p. 212).

Yet I do not think it was egotism *alone*, that ever-present desire for the limelight, so much so that I am depriving you of good drinking time by talking after dinner, that led me to ask whether I could do it. The primary reason was that, though I am an awful mathematician, as an undergraduate I desperately wanted to acquire some mathematics because I wanted, most of all, to be a theoretical economist and so needed to take mathematical economics in my fourth year at Melbourne University. (I had taken its appropriate complement, History of Economic Thought, in the third year.) Even in the early 1950s this required considerable knowledge of at least elementary mathematics, no doubt kids' stuff now but daunting even then – for me.

I was an awful mathematician partly because I had a bright twin brother who was a good mathematician. We were upped two grades at our primary school so that we were one and half years younger than the average age in

* Originally given at the Science and Human Dimension Conference on 'Mathematics: what should non-mathematicians know?', Jesus College, Cambridge, 3–5 September 1993.

our form, a disaster for me as far as maths and foreign languages were concerned. John helped me with my homework for the first and I copied his homework for the second. This left me with a lack of confidence in my mathematical (and other) activities which I have never been able completely to throw off. But, with the help of a very great teacher at Melbourne, Keith Frearson, who had a first in maths *and* in economics from the University of Western Australia, and by hard work, I did manage to acquire a smattering of maths, enough to understand R.G.D. Allen's excellent 1938 text, *Mathematical Analysis for Economists*. Moreover, because I was such a duffer, I could recognize the stumbling-blocks which caused me trouble. So when, in later years, I gave the 'maths for idiots' course (in Adelaide and Cambridge) with me as idiot, LCD, I think I was a good teacher just because I had to think about how to make explicit what the difficulties were and how they could be overcome, partly by using simple examples and analogies. Good and/or original and natural mathematicians may have never recognized what the stumbling-blocks were because to them they were not, so they did not exist. Certainly, when in my third year at Melbourne, I went to the first-year lectures on pure maths, I found the lectures (by an excellent mathematician) incomprehensible – too much was assumed, too much 'background' was taken for granted, too many steps in arguments were left out. I gave up in despair after one term and, with Keith's help, worked through Allen instead.

It is true that, if you look through the selection of my essays, you will see that the use of maths in them peaks at about 1968 (significant year of the French riots) and that now, going against the trend, as you move towards the present day, you will find that the essays become just English (Oz variety). Nevertheless, I have always been careful to make explicit that I am not a techniques Luddite and that I welcome the *proper* use of mathematics (and econometrics) by others. So I think I am well placed to praise, not to bury maths in economics, just because of my limitations and difficulties; whereas the others I mentioned to John Cornwell may either have been blissfully unaware of the problems or may regard them as reasons for excluding persons such as me from the economics profession itself. (On reflection, the latter remark is grossly unfair to most of those I named – but not to their unthinking and less wise clones.)

II

But why as a fledgling economist did I feel that I needed to know maths, especially the differential calculus and also (though I never did get on top of it – no facility with foreign languages striking again) linear algebra? Two things stand out in my mind. The first was when Keith Frearson pointed out to me that the profit-maximizing position of a firm could be put much more elegantly and succinctly once you understood the first- and second-order conditions for a maximum (or a minimum). Here he was giving a particular example of one of the two major generalizing principles which Paul Samuelson argued in his 1948 *Foundations of Economic Analysis* ran through the whole of economic theory (as he understood it) – maximizing or minimizing under constraints. Indeed, once *the* economic problem was defined, as it has been at least since Jevons in the 1860s, as doing the best you can with what you have, it was inevitable that this aspect of the calculus would be used.

The other event was when I realized, as I was reading Kenneth Boulding's fine text, *Economic Analysis* (1948a), that the *formal* structures of consumer demand theory and of production theory were identical. Whether you were climbing the hill of pleasure, striving to reach the top, that is, Bliss (and avoid going past it to Vomit Point) or were doing production theory, looking at the production surface with its smooth, convex-to-the-origin, isoquants (and trying to avoid going so far round them as to be on their uneconomic stretches), the same *mathematics* was involved. This gave me great pleasure then (though for the life of me, I cannot remember why now – this is not completely true!).

There is no doubt that even this simple mathematics made economic theory elegant, precise, simple and explicit. It was also seductive, for it led some to argue, at least implicitly, that, unless economic theory could *always* be stated thus, it was not good theory, or even theory at all. This is an illustration of the principal theme of my lecture, that, though mathematics is always a good servant, it is, even more, a bad master. I want to illustrate this with some simple examples. But first let me take a brief excursion through the views of some of the masters of economics, almost all of whom either have been trained as mathematicians, or have trained themselves to be so – just as others have been physicists or have taken physicists as their role models. (One of the favourite sayings, though, of my mentor, Joan Robinson, was to the effect that, as she had never learnt mathematics, she had had to think.)

III

In Cambridge we must of course start with Alfred Marshall, the founder of the economics tripos as we know it today. He was second wrangler in 1865 and became Professor of Political Economy in 1885. He always had a guilty conscience about doing maths (which he loved) because his unspeakable father had tried to make him read classics so that he could become a missionary, peddling his father's brand of gloom to the benighted. He even stopped the young Alfred playing chess and solving chess problems

Alfred Marshall's most famous comment on the use of mathematics in economics is in his letter to Arthur Bowley of 27 February 1906. After admitting that he now had 'very indistinct memories of what he used to think on the subject' and that he had forgotten 'how to integrate a good many things', he went on:

> But I know I had a growing feeling in the later years of my work at the subject that a good mathematical theorem dealing with economic hypotheses was very unlikely to be good economics: and I went more and more on the rules – (1) Use mathematics as a shorthand language, rather than as an engine of inquiry. (2) Keep to them till you have done. (3) Translate into English. (4) Then illustrate by examples that are important in real life. (5) Burn the mathematics. (6) If you can't succeed in 4, burn 3. This last I did often. (Pigou, (quoted in 1925, p. 427)

Even earlier (3 March 1901), he had written to Bowley:

> In my view every economic fact, whether or not it is of such a nature as to be expressed in numbers, stands in relation as cause and effect to many other facts: and since it *never* happens that all of them can be expressed in numbers, the application of exact mathematical methods to those which can is nearly always a waste of time, while in the majority of cases it is positively misleading;... the world would have been further on its way forward, if the work had never been done at all ... [Only] when the mathematical method is used ... to train sound instinctive habits ... [does it seem] to me generally helpful. (Ibid. p. 422)

In these comments to Bowley, which arise partly from a discussion of the use of mathematics in theoretical work, partly from its use, together with statistical methods, in applied work, Marshall reveals one of the causes of his disquiet about the use of mathematics in economics generally. Marshall's greatest original gift to the economics profession was the use of supply and demand functions, and especially the curves corresponding to them, in static analysis. They were his intellectual pride and joy but, like all Englishman (at least of his day), scared to have pleasure without pain, he was loath to allow them to be taken too far in economic analysis. Anticipating modern developments in the application of evolutionary ideas in economic analysis, and the understanding of such processes in the firm, the industry and the economy alike, he warned us (typically in an appendix, his famous appendix H to the *Principles*) that his long-period supply curves were not reversible functions, as was implicit in the use of static theory and the accompanying analogy of a pendulum.

Yet long-period supply, and demand curves, especially to be found in Book V of the *Principles*, where they were used to explain the formation of long-period prices and quantities, were its core. He was therefore aware of the weaknesses in the analysis. They were not to be found in the mathematics as such. If the conditions underlying the construction of the curves were satisfied, in particular the mutual independence of the demand functions from the supply functions and the ability of the system to select the intersection of the curves, which was itself the solution of the set of simultaneous equations of the system, one relating demand quantities to price (and other variables), the other, supply quantities to price (and other variables); if the other variables affecting demand and supply could be regarded as constants, at least for the time being; and if the curves had the 'right' shape, *then* an equilibrium could be proved to exist *and* it could be shown, by then physical analogies, to be locally and globally stable. (Even in Marshall's day the dynamics by which the position was reached were pretty complicated and limiting.) But, as I said, though he loved this analytical system, he was very aware of its limitations in applications to the real world. Moreover, he would claim that going beyond it would tax our strength beyond endurance – a confession, I have always thought, that, though he had the high intelligence to *see* the problems, he was not always willing explicitly to admit that he did not have the techniques to provide the answers. Joan Robinson did not call him an old fox for naught.

Keynes was Marshall's pupil in many, many ways. He has left us lots of comments on the role of mathematics in economics as well as descriptions of the characteristics which you need to have to be a good economist, 'An easy subject, at which very few excel!' (Keynes, 1933; *CW, X*, 1972, p. 173), adding in effect that, while Marshall had nearly all of them, they were not present in the right proportions, that is to say, in Keynes's own:

> The master-economist must possess a rare *combination* of gifts. He must reach a high standard in several different directions and must combine talents not often found together. He must be mathematician, historian, statesman, philosopher – in some degree. He must understand symbols and speak in words. He must contemplate the particular in terms of the general, and touch abstract and concrete in the same flight of thought. He must study the present in the light of the past for the purposes of the future. No part of man's nature or his institutions must lie entirely outside his regard. He must be purposeful and disinterested in a simultaneous mood; as aloof and incorruptible as an artist, yet sometimes as near the earth as a politician. (*CW, X*, 1972, pp. 173–4)

Keynes, too, was trained as a mathematician but he was not as distinguished a mathematician as Marshall – twelfth wrangler in 1905. Moreover, as I have documented elsewhere (Sardoni, 1992, pp. 235–49, Harcourt, 1994), he was much more of a philosopher and his philosophical understanding was much more important for his subsequent contributions as a great economist. For our purposes let me first remind you of his views on the nature of economic theory. He argued that, in a discipline such as economics, there is a whole spectrum of languages, running continuously from intuition and poetry to mathematics and formal logic, taking in lawyer-like arguments on the way. *All* these languages *may* be relevant at appropriate steps in arguments and for particular issues, or aspects of issues, in economics. There is therefore a place for mathematics and *The General Theory* is smattered with it, at a pretty rudimentary level, it is true, with much of it subsequently shown to be incorrect (Keynes was 52 when *The General Theory* was published).

In a number of places he has explained why he thought the use of mathematics was limited. First, there is the well-known quote from *The General Theory* itself:

> It is a great fault of symbolic pseudo-mathematical methods of formalising a system of economic analysis ... that they expressly assume strict independence between the factors involved and lose all their cogency and authority if this hypothesis is disallowed; whereas, in ordinary discourse, where we are not blindly manipulating but know all the time what we are doing and what the words mean, we can keep 'at the back of our heads' the necessary reserves and qualifications and the adjustments which we shall have to make later on, in a way in which we cannot keep complicated partial differentials 'at the back' of several pages of algebra which assume that they all vanish. Too large a proportion of recent 'mathematical' economics are mere concoctions, as imprecise as the initial assumptions they rest on, which allow the author to lose sight of the complexities and interdependencies of the real world in a maze of pretentious and unhelpful symbols. (Keynes, 1936; *CW, VII*, 1973, pp. 297–8)

Secondly, there is his comment on Edgeworth and mathematical psychics.

> Mathematical Psychics has not, as a science or study, fulfilled its early promise ... When the young Edgeworth chose it, he may have looked to find secrets as wonderful as those which the physicists have found since those days. But this has not happened. The atomic hypothesis which has worked so splendidly in physics breaks down in psychics. We are faced at every turn with the problems of organic unity, of discreteness, of discontinuity – the whole is not equal to the sum of the parts, comparisons of quantity fail us, small changes produce large effects, the assumptions of a uniform and homogeneous continuum are not satisfied. (Keynes, 1933; *CW, X*, 1972, p. 262).

(I understand from Brian Pippard that Keynes was even too optimistic about mathematics as a servant of physics.)

Even so, we have Keynes's admiration for Jevons *vis à vis* Marshall: having called Jevons's *Theory of Political Economy* (1871) 'The first modern book on economics', he added that Jevons 'chiselled in stone where Marshall knits in wool' (*CW, X*, 1972, p. 131). (Though earlier he had said: 'Jevons saw the kettle boil and cried out with the delighted voice of a child; Marshall too had seen the kettle boil and sat down silently to build an engine' (ibid., p. 185).

Keynes's confining mathematics to its proper place in economics was based on philosophical arguments that some of the essential concepts remained vague in the sense of the arguments of Wittgenstein, by their nature not reducible to the basic constructs of mathematics and logic. George Shackle's favourite example was Keynes's use of the word 'sentiment', a multidimensional concept which affected crucial behaviour in the economic system. Sentiment was diffused through the entire workings of the system, yet it could not be 'put in' a theory by saying: Let S=sentiment (S for saving got there first). Again, Keynes told his old pal, Gerald Shove, to lift his game when Shove complained that he could not make the analysis of expectations in his theory 'precise'. Keynes said: 'As soon as one is dealing with the influence of expectations and of transitory experience, one is, in the nature of things, outside the realm of the formally exact' (*CW, XIV*, 1973, p. 2). Keynes argued that much of economic analysis consisted of telling a plausible story, of 'being vaguely right [rather] than precisely wrong' (Shove, 1942, p. 323).[2,3]

We now move forward to the modern age, starting, of course, with Paul Samuelson and his *Foundations of Economic Analysis* (1948). He quotes J. Willard Gibbs, *Mathematics is a Language*, on the title page. He tells us that his 'own interest in mathematics has been secondary and subsequent to [his] interest in economics'. Fair enough. Then, in the Introduction, he puts the boots into the literary economist: 'The laborious literary working over of essentially simple mathematical concepts such as is characteristic of much of modern economic theory is not only unrewarding from the standpoint of advancing the science, but involves as well mental gymnastics of a peculiarly depraved type' (Samuelson, 1948, p. 6). He argues that he is going to enfold the whole of what has passed for economic theory before him within two all-embracing principles, maximizing (or minimizing) under constraints and what he calls the *Correspondence Principle* between comparative statics and dynamics, whereby what he also calls 'definite *operationally meaningful* theorems can be derived from so simple a hypothesis … that the system [as a whole] is in "stable" equilibrium or motion' (ibid. p. 5). And off he goes in one of the trinity of books which inspired and instructed my generation (including me). The others were *The General Theory* and *Value and Capital* (1939). The latter was written by J.R. Hicks. The mathematics, as was always his custom, was put in the appendices while the text was written in such beautifully lucid prose that, as my great friend, the late Eric Russell, used to say, the confusions were made clear.

A deep and far-sighted review of the *Foundations* (one which nevertheless brought about a permanent rift between author and reviewer) was by the late Kenneth Boulding (1948b, 1971). His wise remarks still make sense today and I quote some of them now. First, by the use of homely examples, he showed that he understood – well – Samuelson's two guiding principles and their applications. He then put them properly in their place (in both senses of the phrase). First, he pointed out that mathematics can be a limited, one-dimensional mode of thought, unsuitable for dealing with complex structures (echoing here Shackle's assessment of Keynes's mode of theorizing, what John Coates calls 'ordinary language economics'). 'It makes very little sense to say "let *Hamlet* equal *H* and *Macbeth* equal *M*"' (Boulding, 1948b, 1971, p. 236). It may be, he adds, 'an understatement to say that mathematics is a language, for, while it is probably true that all mathematical expressions can be translated into "literary" language ... it is not true that all "literary" expressions can be translated into mathematics ... [Boulding knew] of no mathematical expression for the literary form, "I love you"' (ibid., pp. 236–7). Mathematics 'is a way of talking about certain things but not all things' (ibid., p. 237).

Boulding clearly foresaw in 1948 the danger that our ability to communicate, both within the boundaries of our trade and outside, to policy makers and ordinary citizens, is greatly reduced by an over-reliance on mathematical arguments. He admonished those '"literary" economists who, from wilful egotism ... refused to acquire that modicum of mathematical training which yields clearly increasing returns'. But he then speculated that 'the greatest danger [may now be] from the other side. The mathematicians themselves set up standards of generality and elegance in their expositions which are a bar to understanding' (ibid., p. 247). Why? Because of the very nature of mathematics and its application to economics, its strength *and* its weakness. The strength derives from the fact that by abstracting from 'the internal structure of variables certain basic relationships may be seen more clearly and inconsistencies exposed'. The weakness arises 'because mathematical treatment distracts attention from the actual complexity of the internal structure of the variables concerned and hence is likely to lead to error where this structure is important' (ibid., p. 237). Boulding also warned – how right he has turned out to be – that, 'if economics becomes a preserve of the higher mathematicians, it will lose its essentially humanistic and empirical quality' (ibid., p. 247).

Boulding's wisdom contrasts with the, sometimes startling, claims of the mathematical economists. Let us start with Gerard Debreu, the 1983 Nobel Prize winner, whose work, it must be said, has inspired generations of his students at Berkeley, where he holds a joint chair in economics and mathematics. In his Nobel Lecture, by a rather free reading of both Adam Smith and Leon Walras, Debreu itemizes four major problems which every economic system has to solve: the efficiency of resource allocation, the decentralization of decisions, the incentives of decision makers and the treatment of information. All of these and more have been

> the subject of an axiomatic analysis in which primitive concepts are chosen, assumptions concerning them are formulated, and conclusions are derived from those assumptions by means of mathematical reasoning disconnected from any

intended interpretation of the primitive concepts. The benefits ... have been numerous. Making the assumptions of a theory entirely explicit permits a sounder judgement about the extent to which it applies to a particular situation. Axiomatization may also give ready answers to new questions when a novel interpretation of primitive concepts is discovered.... Axiomatization, by insisting on mathematical rigor, has repeatedly led economists to a deeper understanding of the problems they were studying, and to the use of mathematical techniques that fitted those problems better. It has established secure bases from which exploration could start in new directions ... Rigor undoubtedly fulfils an intellectual need of many contemporary economic theorists, who therefore seek it for its own sake, but it is also an attribute of a theory that is an effective thinking tool. Two other major attributes of an effective theory are simplicity and generality.... Simplicity makes a theory usable by a greater number of research workers. Generality makes it applicable to a broad class of problems.

The axiomatization of economic theory has helped its practitioners by making available to them the superbly efficient language of mathematics. It has permitted them to communicate with each other, and to think, with a great economy of means. At the same time, the dialogue between economists and mathematicians has become more intense. (Debreu, 1984, pp. 274–5)

Thirty years earlier, another Nobel Prize Laureate, the late Tjalling Koopmans, who received the prize in 1975 and who was initially a physicist, also exhibited calm confidence as well as (seeming) down-to-earth common sense:

The appropriateness of mathematical reasoning in economics is not dependent upon how firmly or shakily the premises are established. Let us assume for the sake of argument that the attempt to establish or at least to explore their implications is worthwhile, that is, economics itself is worthwhile. In that case the justification for mathematical economics depends merely on whether the logical link between the basic premises economists have been led to make and many of their observable and otherwise interesting implications are more efficiently established by mathematical or by verbal reasoning. (Koopmans, 1954, p. 378)

In his best known book, *Three Essays on the State of Economic Science* (Koopmans 1957) itself an inspiration to a generation of theoretical and applied economists alike, he told us:

that the mathematical method when correctly applied forces the investigator to give a complete statement of assuredly noncontradictory assumptions has generally been conceded as far as the relations of the assumptions to the reasoning is [sic] concerned. To this may be added that the absence of any natural meaning of mathematical symbols, other than the meaning given to them by postulate or by definition, prevents the associations clinging to words from intruding upon the reasoning process. (Koopmans, 1957, pp. 172–3)

In a wide-ranging essay, Philip Mirowski (1986) criticizes these views, pointing out that mathematics imposes limits on what can be thought because of the models of which the mathematics were originally inseparable parts. He urges economists, therefore, always to look for 'a mathematics grounded in economic theory, rather than vice versa' (p. 235), putting forward Marx (in the early chapters of Volume I of *Capital*) as an early and illustrious example of what he has in mind.[4]

Jim Mirrlees, whose influence and example have had a dominant effect on Oxford economics (and elsewhere) since he went there as a very young professor in the late 1960s, expresses very clearly his attitudes to ways, other than the mathematical, of doing economics. Here he is reviewing (Mirrlees [1978] Malinvaud's book on unemployment, the theory of, reconsidered (Malinvaud, 1977).

> If macroeconomics means analysis based on simple relationships among aggregate economic variables, then it seems to be dying. In recent years economists have been trying to handle unemployment and inflation, monetary and fiscal policy, with the same explicitness of assumptions, attention to detail, and rigour that has long characterised microeconomics. The task is actually quite a hard one. The models are necessarily more recalcitrant than the standard model of competitive equilibrium; a great variety of factors and considerations must be borne in mind; and a long and powerful tradition of somewhat casual and speculative argument has to be resisted. Maybe it is not surprising that economists avoided doing the hard work for forty years. As Malinvaud says, the task is just beginning. (Mirrlees, 1978, pp. 15–17

Even so, he nearly gives the game away by undermining his praise of Malinvaud's performance: 'Those who know Malinvaud will expect the arguments to be presented with rigour, precision, and clarity. They will not be disappointed' (ibid., p. 154). For he suggests that Malinvaud's special examples may have produced results which are not robust, a worry I have about many of the contributions of modern mathematical economics, and of which the wiser practitioners who are not overawed by their own techniques have frequently warned us.

But the paper which really takes the cake for, I must admit, its endearing optimism as well as its confident assertions and predictions, is by Graciela Chichilinsky. It is entitled "On the Mathematical Foundations of Political Economy". It was originally given as the Political Economy Lecture at Harvard in March 1990 and published in, of all places, *Contributions to Political Economy* (1990). In the section on 'Markets and Democracy', we are told that 'the connection between [the two] is not at all clearly understood ... [It] has indeed been analysed by literary means, but it has not been logically or mathematically analysed in the context of a well-defined model ...[,] the foundation which is needed. Since both the theory of markets and ... of social choice have been mathematically formalised ... not an impossible task ... we need a logical foundation and a mathematical edifice to build upon these areas which are the daily concern of many people across the world' (Chichilinsky, 1990, p. 27). 'Political economy must build an abstract and general mathematical thinking. It is the *only* way to assure clarity, a strong foundation and the desired advance in areas which are of great importance for intellectuals and for those whose lives depend upon it' (ibid., p. 39, emphasis added). Eat your hearts out, Adam Smith, Karl Marx, and John Maynard Keynes!

It is instructive at this point to contrast the views of two great political economists, Richard Goodwin and Josef Steindl (who died earlier this year), on the use of mathematics in economics. Goodwin was greatly influenced by the French mathematician, Philippe le Corbeiller, whose work on the theory of oscillations was crucial for Goodwin's thinking about the nature of the cyclical processes at work in capitalist economies, as were the techniques Goodwin acquired when he lectured on physics at Harvard during the Second World War. This experience alerted him to how much more complex economic and social structures are than physical or astronomical ones, so that from then on he has been sceptical of our ability ever completely to master our subject matter. Nevertheless, Goodwin praised Michal Kalecki (a fledgling engineer before he became an economist) for trying, in the spirit of Marx, to model the process of cyclical growth as an endogenous process, instead of as a damped process revived by random shocks *à la* Frisch (see Goodwin, 1989). Goodwin's own most fundamental insight was that the separation of trend and cycle in economic (and econometric) analysis was unjustified, that what we observe is a process of cyclical growth which can be 'explained', at least in an illustrative way, by drawing on modern mathematical work on bifurcation and chaos theory. Kalecki had never quite sorted out the puzzles within his basic approach because the solutions came long after his death (he died in 1970), when his theory could be fitted 'into the group of chaotic models, the so-called strange attractors' (Goodwin, 1989, p. 251).

Steindl thought that, as random shocks would always be with us, we might as well work out the implications of their impact on the system in a pragmatic manner. Steindl had regarded Kalecki as his 'guru' from the time they worked together at Oxford in the 1940s. He tells us (Steindl, 1984, 1990) that he once 'had great optimism with regard to the possibilities of mathematics. Kalecki warned [him] of that ... and of the computer ... both were ideally suited as a scientific cloak to cover the lack of economic substance. [Steindl feels Kalecki] was dead right ... instead of being a tool ... it has developed a life of its own. Rather than looking for methods to suit [their] economic problems [(Steindl's own admirable procedures), students ask their teachers] to set [them] problems which suit the formal problems [they have] learned' (ibid., p. 246).

Frank Hahn, in a number of places, has made a careful defence of the use of mathematics in economic theory and of economic theory itself as he understands it (see Hahn, 1985, pp. 10–28). He praises this conception of economic theory because 'it is one of the highways to understanding ... has already provided a good deal of it'. He adds that it should also be praised for 'its honesty and modesty and ... for the occasional excitement and beauty which it provides' (ibid., p. 28). Above all, it deserves praise because a serious theorist could never be 'enslaved by the slogans and shibboleths of practical men and women', so that, 'if we were all theorists, it just might be a better world' (ibid.).

Hahn feels that, if you are to use mathematics effectively in theory, you are forced to define precisely the problems investigated and the conditions which have to be fulfilled in order that the results, again precise, may be applicable. In doing so you fine up what were previously vague conjectures and find explicitly and precisely the conditions under which they may be realized. In doing so you may find very good reasons why the conditions are unlikely to be met in the real world the theory is meant to illuminate. In reviewing Kenneth Arrow's six volumes of *Collected Papers*, Hahn (1986) attributes Arrow's many fundamental contributions to his ability to write down precisely what the questions are and therefore *exactly* what the answers are. Arrow's 'strength has been that he has only concerned himself with establishing what it is that can be claimed as true if certain assumptions are made; and nothing more' (Hahn, 1986, p. 833). Referring to his interpretation of Adam Smith's argument (conjecture?) than an economy of many greedy people interacting through markets would not only be 'compatible with a coherent disposition of economic resources but would also be in some sense beneficial', Hahn argues that 'Arrow and Debreu ... demonstrated ... the logical possibility of the truth of Smith's claims. They had *not* offered a description of any actual economy. [Arrow more than anyone saw] that what was needed for the logical demonstration would not do for the world' (ibid., emphasis added). Fine, impressive and admirable, provided that we do not commit the non sequitur of supposing that truth only comes in the guise of a mathematical model.

Finally, we have the measured wisdom of Richard Stone, whose applied work was invariably fruit and light-bearing and never the source of heated controversy; he was perhaps the greatest of the English gentlemen to grace our discipline. Here are his views on the use of mathematics in the social sciences.

> Except in a few obstinate pockets of resistance, the use of mathematics in the social sciences is now generally accepted. The reason is not to be found in the outcome of any high-flown philosophical battle but in a number of simple facts. In the first place, many branches of the social sciences are obviously, one might almost say aggressively, quantitative; demography and economics are clear examples of this. In the second place, while theories about the complex systems which

are the subject matter of the social sciences can be expressed verbally, their analysis and comparison are greatly helped by formulating them mathematically. In the third place, the application of such theories must remain very general unless the terms in their relationships can be quantified. In the fourth place, mathematics provides a means of obtaining insight even into subjects whose concepts are rather vague and where precise information is hard to come by. Finally, in the social sciences we are interested not only in a description of what happens and of how the different parts of the social system are related, but also in the rational processes that lie behind effective as opposed to ineffective decisions; to a large extent these processes too can be formulated and analysed mathematically, so that our decisions may eventually come to rest a little more on knowledge and a little less on guesswork than they do at present. (Stone, 1966, p. 1)

He was perhaps a little too sanguine about those 'obstinate pockets of resistance'.

IV

So where does this leave us? Clearly, to take a weighted average of such divergent views would be a cop out. I want to close, therefore, by using two simple examples to show why I think mathematics can be a good servant but, even more, a bad master; and to suggest that this will become increasingly important in the future. In arriving at the latter conclusion I have been much influenced by a recent article by Geoff Hodgson (1993) on the nature of evolutionary processes in economic theory past and present. Just contemplating these processes and their accompanying difficulties immediately suggests to the reader how fiendishly difficult it is to capture them within a mathematical system. For we are dealing with qualitative as well as quantitative changes in variables and parameters, as well as in their relationships one to another – relationships which we cannot expect to be stable; nor can we expect to be able to predict how they will change.

My first example comes from the modern approach to Marxist economics; it is concerned with preciseness, rigour and the proper specification of a model of an economic process. One of Marx's most profound insights was that the origin and size of profits and the rate of profits in a capitalist economy were to be found in the class structure of such an economy whereby one class had access to finance and so control over the physical means of production (and the conditions of production as well), while the other class through an historical process had only its labour services ('power') to sell. As a result, in a competitive situation, business people as a class have both the power and, individually, the incentive to make their wage-earners work longer and with greater intensity than would be necessary for the latter to produce with the existing techniques and means of production (themselves, the result of accumulation in the past), their wage goods alone. This additional or surplus labour was the source of surplus value in the sphere of production. It, in turn, is reflected in the component of profit in the prices of commodities produced and the rate of profits received on capital, as well as in the commodities produced in surplus over and above the wage goods themselves.

In the late 1970s, Ian Steedman in a justly famous book, *Marx after Sraffa* (1977) (to which I gave a light-hearted review, 'Can Marx survive Cambridge?', Harcourt, 1982, pp. 199–204), claimed to have shown that this plausible economic intuition could be overthrown if we took account of an important empirical phenomena, joint production, the *analysis* of which had been applied to an outstanding feature of an industrialized capitalist economy – the production, pricing and use of durable capital goods. Technically, a joint production process is one in which labour and means of production are combined to produce, not marijuana joints, I hasten to add, but more than one final product. (The classic examples are wool and mutton and wheat and chaff; in the case of durable capital goods they are treated as one period older goods jointly produced with the final product(s) that is (are) to be sold.)

Now a problem with joint production is that you cannot directly attribute to any one of the jointly produced commodities the amount of labour (say) responsible for its production. How then would we do this, at least by imputation, and so be in a position rigorously to show that the necessary labour associated with wage goods production in a joint production system was *always* less than the actual labour used for the total production in the system (so that surplus labour and value were positive), provided only that we observed in the same system positive profits and a positive rate of profits in the prices and on the capitals, respectively, in its sphere of distribution and exchange? What Steedman showed was that, when you used equalities indirectly to estimate these various amounts of labour in a system which has positive profits and rate of profits, it was possible to have negative surplus labour; that is, the amount of labour estimated to be associated with the wage goods *alone exceeded* the actual amount of labour associated with the wage goods *and* the commodities in the actual physical net product of the joint production system. Since it takes only one counter-example to disprove a theorem, what had become known in the literature as the fundamental Marxian theorem seemed to have been overthrown.

But wait, there must be something wrong: Marx's sturdy intuition surely should have survived not only the existence of an obvious fact of life – joint production – but also its specification in a mathematical model? Exactly, and it was soon shown that, with correct specification, that is, using inequalities and linear programming techniques, it *was* possible rigorously to prove that a positive rate of profits was always to be found associated with positive surplus labour, as was obvious anyway from common sense and observation. After all, if the actual system was producing more commodities than the wage goods alone, it is inconceivable that *more* labour working with the same techniques of production and capital goods would be needed to produce the latter.

My second example is a topical one in the light of the recent debates on Maastricht and the Social Chapter. It concerns how we model the labour market in a mathematical form.[5] Uncritical free marketeers regard the demand and supply of labour as analytically akin to the demand and supply of peanuts (possibly because they are such peanuts themselves). This allows them to use simple supply and demand functions where it is legitimate to suppose that the demand and supply functions may be taken as independent of one another – man does not live by peanuts alone – and that we are dealing with homogeneous quantities, peanuts just as much as labour services. Hence it may be argued that there is a tendency for the actual price and quantity of peanuts to be indicated by the intersection of two curves, itself, as we have seen, the solution of a set of simultaneous equations.

But suppose that the productivity of labour –its quantity and quality – is affected by the wage that labour receives and that the demand for such labour services is derived from employers' perceptions of what this productivity is. Then there is not a unique relationship between the quantity of labour services offered and the productivity associated with them, for the latter in turn will be affected by the real wage (which is a proxy for the conditions of employment) expected to be received. There would be, therefore, a whole family of such relationships, each defined by its own expected real wage. Similarly, it is hard, nay, impossible, to define a supply function, for associated with each possible expected real wage will be a different *quality* of labour services on offer. Instead of having a nice neat unique intersection of a supply and a demand curve and a plausible (well, not *that* plausible) story about how such an intersection will be achieved by market forces, so that we may postulate a 'correspondence' between it and what we observe in the 'real world', we have at best multiple equilibria with no obvious reasons to prefer one to another either as a description or as a desirable outcome of policy. At worst, we have an incoherent analysis, mathematics – at least this mathematics – having failed to be the appropriate tool with which to think about these important problems.

And this is the rub. Now that, more and more, we are coming to realize that qualitative as well as quantitative change is the essence of economic processes, it is not clear that traditional mathematical techniques are the appropriate ones to capture this, even in an illustrative manner. Of course, we must continue to try to do so but we must remember that there are other, often more appropriate, languages to be used in economics as well. Keynes sensed, many years ago, that the philosophers had so refined their formal logic that they had cut the umbilical cord that connected their self-contained and consistent systems with the world they were trying to illuminate. Today, we are in danger of doing this too in economics, because of an overemphasis on the use of mathematics, more to the exclusion or at least the playing down of other, more traditional, forms of analysis in economics.

Let me end with a quote from perhaps the greatest mathematician of them all, John von Neumann[6]

> As a mathematical discipline travels far from its empirical source, or still more, if it is only a second or third generation only indirectly inspired by ideas coming from reality, it is beset with very grave dangers. It becomes more and more purely aestheticising, more and more purely *l'art pour l'art*.... There is a grave danger that the subject will develop along the line of least resistance, that the stream, so far from its course, will separate into a multitude of insignificant branches, and that the discipline will become a disorganised mass of detail and complexities. In other words, at a great distance from its empirical source, or after much 'abstract' inbreeding, a mathematical subject in danger of degeneration. (Dore *et al.*, 1989, p. xiv)

That sums it up: a good servant but oh-so-bad a master.

Notes

1. I thank but in no way implicate Prue Kerr, Trevor Stegman and Michael White for their comments on a draft of this paper.
2. In writing this paragraph, I have been much helped by reading Wylie Bradford's 1993 MPhil essay, 'Words and Deeds: Keynes's "Spectrum of Appropriate Languages" and the Formulation of Macroeconomic Theory and Policy'.
3. Trevor Stegman pointed out to me that 'mathematics loves symmetry – it is hard to write functions where the sign of the derivative is dependent on the direction of the change in the independent variable. But economic behaviour is rarely symmetric. ([He] thinks it is the false reliance on symmetry in relationships that has led policy makers to make such a mess of monetary policy, for example.)'
4. I am indebted to Michael White for reminding me of Mirowski's argument.
5. I am much indebted to Roy Jones for helping me to see the significance of the modern work on labour markets which underlies the example in the text.
6. I am indebted to Paul Lewis for bringing this quote to my attention. After I wrote this section, Michio Morishima's new book, *Capital and Credit. A New Formulation of General Equilibrium Theory* (1992) was sent to me for review. He, too, had noted von Neumann's remarks and had commented: '[General Equilibrium Theory] economists ... have sunk into excessive mental aestheticism. If this bad habit is not corrected [his new book is itself a most healthy corrective] ... the twenty-first century will see the degeneration of their subject' (pp. 196–7).

References

Allen R.G.D. (1938), *Mathematical Analysis for Economists*, London: Macmillan.

Boulding, K.E. (1948a), *Economic Analysis*, rev. edn, New York: Harper.

Boulding, K.E. (1948b), 'Samuelson's *Foundations*: The Role of Mathematics in Economics', *Journal of Political Economy*, **LVI**, June, pp. 187–99. Reprinted in Boulding, Kenneth E. (1971), *Collected Papers, Volume One*, edited by Fred R. Glane, Boulder, Colorada: Colorado Associated University Press, pp. 233–47.

Bradford, Wylie (1993), 'Words and Deeds: Keynes's "Spectrum of Appropriate Languages" and the Formulation of Macroeconomic Theory and Policy', mimeo, Cambridge.

Chichilinsky, Graciela (1990), 'On the Mathematical Foundations of Political Economy', *Contributions to Political Economy*, **9**, pp. 25–41.

Debreu, G. (1984), 'Economic Theory in the Mathematical Mode', *American Economic Review*, **74**, (3), pp. 267–78.

Dore, M.H.L., S. Chakravarty and R.M. Goodwin (eds) (1989), *John von Newmann and Modern Economics*, Oxford: Clarendon Press.

Dutt, Amitava Krishna (1993), 'Review of Claudio Sardoni (ed.), *On Political Economists and Modern Political Economy. Selected Essays of G.C. Harcourt*, London: Routledge', *Manchester School of Economic and Social Studies*, **LXI**, (2), pp. 212–13,

Goodwin, R.M. (1989), 'Kalecki's Economic Dynamics: A Personal View', in Mario Sebastiani (ed.), *Kalecki's Relevance Today*, Basingstoke: Macmillan, pp. 249–51.

Hahn, F.H. (1985), *Money, Growth and Stability*, Oxford: Basil Blackwell, pp. 10–28.

Hahn, F.H. (1986), 'Living with Uncertainty in Economics', *Times Literary Supplement*, August, pp. 833–4.

Harcourt, G.C. (1982), *The Social Science Imperialists. Selected Essays*, edited by Prue Kerr, London: Routledge & Kegan Paul.

Harcourt, G.C. (1994), 'John Maynard Keynes 1883–1946', in R.V. Mason (ed.), *Cambridge Minds*, Cambridge: Cambridge University Press, pp. 72–85.

Hicks, J.R. (1939), *Value and Capital*, Oxford: Clarendon Press.

Hodgson, Geoffrey M. (1993), 'Theories of Economic Evolution: A Preliminary Taxonomy', *Manchester School of Economic and Social Studies*, **LXI**, (2), pp. 125–43.

Jevons, W.S. (1871), *The Theory of Political Economy*, London: Macmillan.

Keynes, J.M. (1933), *Essays in Biography*, London: Macmillan, *CW*, X (1972).

Keynes, J.M. (1936), *The General Theory of Employment, Interest and Money*, London: Macmillan: *CW*, VII, (1973).

Keynes, J.M. (1973), *The General Theory and After. Part II Defence and Development*, edited by Donald Moggridge, *CW*, XIV.

Koopmans, Tjalling (1954), 'On the Use of Mathematics in Economics', *Review of Economics and Statistics*, **36**, pp. 377–9.

Koopmans, Tjalling (1957), *Three Essays on the State of Economic Science*, New York: McGraw-Hill.

Malinvaud, Edmond (1977), *The Theory of Unemployment Reconsidered*, Oxford: Basil Blackwell.

Mirowski, Philip (ed.) (1986), *The Reconstruction of Economic Theory*, Boston/Dordrecht/Lancaster: Kluwer-Nijhoff Publishing.

Mirrlees, James A. (1978), 'Review of Malinvaud (1977)', *Economic Journal*, **88**, March, pp. 157–9.

Morishima, Michio (1992), *Capital and Credit. A New Formulation of General Equilibrium Theory*, Cambridge: Cambridge University Press.

Pigou, A.C. (ed.) (1925), *Memorials of Alfred Marshall*, London: Macmillan.

Samuelson, Paul (1948), *Foundations of Economic Analysis*, Cambridge, Mass.: Harvard University Press.

Shove, G.F. (1942), 'The Place of Marshall's *Principles* in the Development of Economic Theory', *Economic Journal*, **52**, pp. 294–329.

Sardoni, Claudio (ed.) (1992), *On Political Economy and Modern Political Economists. Selected Essays of G.C. Harcourt*, London: Routledge.

Steedman, Ian (1977), *Marx after Sraffa*, London: New Left Books.

Steindl, Josef (1989), 'Reflections on Kalecki's Dynamics', in Sebastiani, *Kalecki's Relevance Today*, Basingstoke: Macmillan, pp. 309–13.

Steindl, Josef (1990), *Economic Papers, 1941–88*, Basingstoke: Macmillan.

Stone, Richard (1966), *Mathematics in the Social Sciences and Other Essays*, London: Chapman & Hall.

19 John Maynard Keynes, 1883–1946*[1]

The obituarist of *The Times* of London wrote on 22 April 1946: 'Lord Keynes, the great economist, died at Tilton, Firle, Sussex, yesterday from a heart attack. By his death, the country has lost a very great Englishman.' This is a faultless judgement: Keynes was a 'great economist', arguably the greatest of the twentieth century, and he was, indisputably, 'a very great Englishman'. In order to have a proper perspective on his life, his economics and his contributions generally, these attributes have always to be remembered. Keynes was a proper patriot. He was as aware of the faults of his fellow citizens as he was of their virtues; but he always attempted to devise policies and to design institutions which would enable them, if they so wished, to be able to live better, while at the same time fitting his and their society into an international order in which there could be desirable outcomes for all. Even more important, we should remember that Keynes's own life was an example of a person who was wrestling unceasingly but increasingly optimistically with the Moorean problem: is it possible both to *be* good and to *do* good? In the end Keynes literally killed himself for his country and for the wider international community. His heroic efforts and his death are the ingredients of a Greek tragedy, not least because it was the Americans and not Keynes and the British who triumphed at Bretton Woods concerning the details, and especially the orders of magnitude established for the new international institutions. The new international order thus set up contained within it the seeds of its own destruction.

In this chapter, though, I concentrate on the developments which led to Keynes's greatest intellectual achievement, the writing of *The General Theory of Employment, Interest and Money* (1936).

II

To understand Keynes's economics, it is vital to remember that, though he read mathematics as an undergraduate at King's, he seems to have spent as much time on philosophy. He was in fact an outstanding and original philosopher in his own right. (Keynes himself always regarded economics as a branch of moral philosophy and, as Andrea Maneschi has reminded me, Adam Smith was Professor of *Moral Philosophy* in Glasgow and always viewed political economy as a branch of philosophy.)

* First published in R.V. Mason (ed.) *Cambridge Minds*, Cambridge: Cambridge University Press, 1994, pp. 72–85.

Keynes's philosophical understanding brought to his economics at least three vital characteristics, the neglect of which literally makes it impossible correctly to interpret his books or articles and especially the arguments of his *magnum opus*. Economists who have neglected this aspect of Keynes's thought have been pushed, still puzzling, into acknowledging it when they themselves have worked on the issues and problems which Keynes addressed. A candid admission of this was made by Frank Hahn in 1982 when, in his admirable crusade against the disastrous effects on theory and policy of the new classical macroeconomics, he said that he found himself at times able only to provide 'arguments that are merely plausible rather than clinching' (Hahn, 1982, p. xi).

Keynes's first major research project, as we would say now, was on philosophical issues; published in 1921 as *A Treatise on Probability*, it was originally written as his fellowship dissertation for King's in the first decade of the century. Though he was to respond to criticisms of it, especially by Frank Ramsey, it nevertheless continued to provide the base for all his subsequent intellectual work.

How did it affect his economics? First, there is the argument that in a discipline such as economics, there is a whole spectrum of languages, moving continuously from intuition and poetry to mathematics and formal logic, taking in lawyer-like arguments on the way. *All* these languages *may* be relevant at appropriate steps in arguments and for particular issues, or aspects of issues, in economics. *The General Theory* has puzzled many modern economists just because they are unaware of, or unwilling to accept that economic *theory* may be done in this manner. Even as shrewd and as deep a thinker as Keynes's colleague and friend in King's, Gerald Shove, fell into this trap. When he first read *The General Theory* he wrote to Keynes that he had been trying to bring expectations, and the influence of current and immediate past experience on them, into the analysis of the industry and firm, but that he could not make the analysis 'precise'. Keynes in effect told him that he need not do so. 'As soon as one is dealing with the influence of expectations and of transitory experience, one is, in the nature of things, outside the realm of the formally exact' (*CW*, 1973b, p. 2). As we said above, on the path between intuition and formal logic, we come to lawyer-like arguments, the sorts of balances of probabilities and the use of evidence which Keynes himself captured in the term 'weight' and which is the essence of those plausible but non-clinching arguments experienced by Hahn. As Richard Kahn has told us, Keynes became increasingly more comfortable (indeed, was probably always so) with this part of the languages spectrum. He much preferred to write for a wider public audience (even if his essays were often 'the croakings of a Cassandra' ahead of his time and taken notice of too late, as has happened again to another Cassandra of the Fens, Wynne Godley), than to write formal economic theory, especially of the kind which now dominates the economic journals.

Secondly, there is Keynes's realization that, again in a discipline such as economics, the whole *may* be more than the sum of the parts, a realization which he came to long before he wrote *The General Theory* but in which it played a crucial role. My favourite quote which illustrates this point comes from his biographical essay on Edgeworth. Keynes is discussing 'The application of mathematical method to the measurement of economic value': 'We are faced at every turn with the problems of organic unity, of discreteness, of discontinuity – the whole is not equal to the sum of the parts, comparisons of quantity fail us, small changes produce large effects, the assumptions of a uniform and homogeneous continuum are not satisfied' (*CW*, X, 1972, p. 262).

Thirdly, Keynes thought of probability as a form of objective belief and of uncertainty as an absence of probabilistic knowledge – 'We simply do not know' (*CW*, 1973b, p. 114). This distinction and understanding permeated the whole of Keynes's economic reasoning, especially in relation to the formation of expectations, decisions concerning investment expenditure and the formation of portfolios, including the holding of money. In this Keynes was both drawing on and deepening greatly the tradition in which he was brought up and which he himself taught, Cambridge economics as dominated by Afred Marshall. Marshall had a wide and detailed knowledge of 'mankind in the ordinary business of life' and he framed his own principles of economics so as to illuminate the behaviour of sensible people doing the best they could – as business people, as consumers, as workers – in environments characterized by uncertainty. This led Shove to apply to Marshall Wildon Carr's dictum that 'it is better to be vaguely right than precisely wrong' (Shove, 1942, p. 323) – a dictum which is even more applicable to Keynes.

Next, to stress the obvious, Keynes as well as being an intellectual was a deeply practical person, well versed in the ways of the world, soon wanting his philosophy and his economics to be applicable to practical issues of explanation and policy, and right behaviour. Robert Skidelsky has charted this development in his first two volumes (1983, 1992), showing how Keynes's friendships and experiences in the First World War brought this particular member of Bloomsbury from being a superbly clever (but perhaps too flippant, too brilliant) all-rounder to becoming a deeply serious and committed political economist. Keynes was outraged by the behaviour of the politicians at Versailles and determined to speak up for decent, humane values, not only because to do so was morally correct but also because it was intelligent, *Realpolitik* as well.

Keynes's system of thought started from observations on, and intuitions and conjectures concerning, reality as such. The *Treatise on Probability* abounds in homely examples which are then generalized in propositions which are vital links in his arguments. Though he was not a great mathematician in any formal sense, he did have that characteristic of the greatest mathematicians of intuitively knowing the answer and stating a conclusion, long before the steps in the argument needed to reach them were stated, a priceless gift for someone as interested in policy as in theory and explanation. Because of these traits, it was no accident that he soon became and remained primarily a monetary economist. He was fascinated by the properties of money, what caused it to arise and then become a vital institution of what he was eventually to call a monetary production economy, how it operated in society and how dispassionate, intelligent people, by taking thought, could tame it so as to make it a good servant instead of a bad master. (He did *not* have in mind independent central bankers.) It is true that the first serious work in economics that he read was by Jevons and that Marshall as his teacher encouraged him to read all of volume I of the *Principles*. But his interest in value (and distribution) theory was only a means to the end of constructing an appropriate structure of thought through which to understand the monetary aspects of the system. Real long-period theory, 'the real business of the *Principles*', Kahn (1989, p. xxiii) called it, left Keynes cold, a subject suitable only for undergraduates – or the dead. Keynes especially loved making up policies for the short term, though he tried always to be conscious of the ensuing implications of them for the medium to the longer term. From the *Tract on Monetary Reform* (1923) on, he directed his theoretical apparatus towards making understanding of the short period, and policies appropriate to it, central objects of study in their own right.

Let me enter a further slight caveat at this point. Both in *The Economic Consequences of the Peace* (1919) and right at the end of his life in his speech to the House of Lords, he did emphasize the longer term. Having in mind those longer-term persistent and dominant forces at work in healthy, competitive societies, Keynes said: 'Here is an attempt to use what we have learnt from modern experience and modern analysis, not to defeat, but to implement the wisdom of Adam Smith' (*CW*, 1980, p. 445). But explicitly, in both sources, there is a presumption that the *appropriate* short-term policies have been designed and implemented.

In his first example there is his justly famous description (*CW*, II, 1971, pp. 11–13) of how the European economy functioned before the First World War. Here the importance of institutions and of tacit understandings between classes combined with mutual knowledge of the rules of the game are brilliantly evoked. Keynes also admits that there may be forced acceptance of all this by one class and he gives a dire warning concerning the 'unstable psychological' base on which the whole edifice is placed. In the second example, with his appeal to our founder, Keynes keenly appreciated the stress by Smith on interrelationships between regions and nations, on cumulative processes which, if benign, could bring harmony and well-being, but also discord and increasing misery if inappropriate institutions and behaviour were allowed to dominate.

III

At first Keynes was inhibited in his endeavour to make the short period and accompanying appropriate policies centre stage because of the structure of the ideal *Principles* which Marshall had imposed on the profession as Keynes understood it. Volume I was to be on real things, relative quantities and relative prices, primarily long period and normal, Volume II on money and the absolute or general price level, and never the twain should meet. True, in the *Tract*, while Keynes pays lip-service to this, he nevertheless concentrates on the short-period consequences of changes in the velocity of circulation for the twin but opposite processes of inflation and deflation, such as had plagued the economies of Europe after the war. He was cheeking his old teacher in the passage in which his best known quote, '*In the long run* we are all dead', appears, for he adds: 'Economists set themselves too easy, too useless a task if in tempestuous seasons they can only tell us that when the storm is long past the ocean is flat again' (*CW*, IV, 1971, p. 65), a reference to the analogy of storm and sea beloved by Marshall himself.

Nevertheless the *analysis* was still strictly Marshallian. Moreover, Marshall's shadow was to continue to overlie *A Treatise on Money* (1930), the publication of which Keynes hoped would establish him as *the* outstanding monetary economist. That it might not do so Keynes himself realized, so that he wrote to his mother when the book was finished, that 'Artistically it is a failure' (*CW*, 1973a, p. 176).

It is important to understand the nature of this 'failure' and the details of the way Keynes liberated himself from the hold which Marshall had on his thinking. In the process we should note, as well as Keynes's own critical and creative genius, the crucial role played by his favourite and most devoted disciple, Richard Kahn, and the group of brilliant young people who were Keynes's colleagues and/or pupils – and friends. In Cambridge itself there was the 'circus' in which in addition to Kahn there were Piero Sraffa, Austin and Joan Robinson – Austin has just been taken from us in his 96th year – and James Meade, still happily with us in his 87th year and then 'learning his trade' by having a year in Cambridge before starting teaching at Hertford in Oxford. (An index of how fast economics was advancing is that ten years or so earlier Harrod only needed six months!) Then we must mention Keynes's alter ego of many years, Dennis Robertson, and Roy Harrod, Ralph Hawtrey and Gerald Shove.

The hold which Marshall had reduces to two interrelated propositions – Say's Law and its corollary, the Quantity Theory of Money (of which Kahn in particular had always been sceptical as a *causal* explanation of the general price level). I mention this not only because of its biographical and historical interest but also because of the grip which this former approach has taken again on modern theory and policy making. From this development stems in considerable part the misery of those who have been condemned to poverty, unemployment and insecurity because of the often man-made malfunctioning of our economies over the past two decades.

Marshall used partial equilibrium analysis in Volume I to examine the workings of individual industries in the short period in order to build up to the long period and show how in competitive conditions there was a tendency for markets to clear, for prices to settle at levels where voluntary demands and supplies matched. This model was as applicable to the market for labour as it was for the market for peanuts. Nevertheless, he had a general equilibrium model – a model of all markets of the system taken together – hidden (as ever) in an appendix where, he argued (as Walras had before him), the same result went through for the system as a whole. It follows that the question, 'what determines employment and output as a whole?', while clearly of practical significance, for Marshall knew much about the trade cycle, was neither an interesting nor a necessary *theoretical* question. Hence Say's Law that, as a tendency, total supplies create total demands so that undesired unemployment and a general glut of commodities were not a long-term possibility was established as a deduction in Volume I without the need, *analytically*, to mention the role of money or financial institutions at all.

Moreover, when accumulation was discussed it was in terms of the market for saving and investment which was equilibrated by its own particular price, the natural rate of interest, a *real* not a monetary phenomenon. Its role was to equilibrate the desire to spread consumption out of income over the lifetimes of the individuals in society with the incentive of business people now to use postponed consumption and available resources in productive investment in the best known techniques of production in order to convert them into streams of consumption in the future, in the process deciding the *composition* but not the size of the Say's Law level of overall employment and output.

In the ideal Volume II this Say's Law level was carried over in order to determine, with the help of V, the velocity of circulation (which was historically and institutionally given) and M, the quantity of money (which was the provenance of the monetary authority), the overall level of prices, P – the (in)famous Quantity Theory of Money, which in fact is a theory of the general price level. This provided the long-period background for a discussion of why economies might fluctuate around such positions – the trade cycle and all that – and how institutions could be designed to allow economies to recover as quickly as possible from shocks and return to these positions, or move as smoothly as possible to new positions if the fundamental determinants of the Say's Law positions – tastes, techniques and resources – had changed.

IV

When Keynes was writing *A Treatise on Money*, even though he was getting more and more interested in cycles and prolonged lapses from full employment, he nevertheless told us that he felt constrained from following out too far the intricate theory of short-period production because it was not an acceptable way to proceed in a treatise on money. He still thought he was providing a more usable version of the Quantity Theory of Money and that his 'fundamental equations', which 'explained' the price levels of available (consumption) goods and unavailable (investment) goods, as well as the overall price level, were just another way of writing down the Quantity Theory. Indeed they were, especially in the long-period position, but they also drew attention to another theory of price formation in which wage costs were a key element, an innovation which was to have lasting consequences.

In the *Treatise on Money* it was still true that real things rule and monetary things have to adjust to them. For example, if the economy was malfunctioning this meant that the banking system had set money rates of interest which were inconsistent with the underlying natural rate and that the malfunctioning would continue until the banking system came to its senses.

However, Keynes was too impatient to be completely true to himself; after all, unemployment in the United Kingdom in the 1920s had never been less than one million people. He therefore analysed short-period production and employment problems in, for example, his famous banana plantation parable. In the parable there is no endogenous process which can stop a cumulative process once it has started. Keynes tells the story of a thrift gospeller who comes to 'help' the people of this economy where investment is setting up plantations and consumption is harvesting bananas. The thrift campaigner tells the inhabitants to save more. As a result, on the *Treatise on Money* equations, there is a cumulative downturn in prices, employment and production until the inhabitants either starve to death or decide to change their investment behaviour or scrap their new-found habits with regard to thrift.

Peter Clarke (1988) has told us the fascinating story of the interrelationship between Keynes's evidence and arguments before the Macmillan Committee and the writing and rewriting of the proofs of his book as he responded to the debate. We need also to note the important intervention by Keynes and Hubert Henderson in the election at the end of the 1920s when they wrote *Can Lloyd George do it?*, a reference not to the obvious answer which history was to provide but to the case for using expenditure on public works to lower unemployment. In both places Keynes was taking on the so-called 'Treasury View' (which still more than lingers on today) that public works could not cure unemployment because there is only so much saving around for society's investment, so that what goes into the public sector must be at the expense of the private sector.

Keynes used the apparatus of his book in these debates. Wherever there was a difference between saving and investment (on the definitions of the *Treatise on Money*) cumulative processes occurred, principally with respect to movements of prices but also, as we have seen, with regard to output and employment as well. But he did not have a convincing answer as to where the saving would come from, nor a coherent answer as to how the process would stop, until Richard Kahn, using Keynes's theoretical apparatus and aided by 'Mr Meade's relation', provided them in his famous 1931 *Economic Journal* article on the multiplier. Kahn and Meade provided the endogenous process whereby activity and employment would change, following a change in investment expenditure, until voluntarily saving was again equal to the new level of investment, even on the *Treatise on Money* definitions. Investment led and saving followed, a tremendously liberating move which allowed Keynes to go from his 1930 book to *The General Theory*. For Kahn's article and Meade's demonstration that, as income changed so, too, did saving until it too had reached the new level of investment, gave an explicit answer to the Treasury View that there was only a certain amount of saving to go round.

Actually Keynes rather blew it as a debater because he revealed prematurely his answer in the exchanges. The Treasury witnesses were therefore able to counter by saying that this was not their argument after all. Rather, they were arguing that the public sector is so inefficient that it should not be allowed to invest because private people would do so much more efficiently and profitably. (This has a certain modern ring to it.)

Keynes now began to realize that Say's Law did not hold and therefore that the Quantity Theory was not an explanation of prices. He started to rebuild his system of thought, with money there right from the start. He argued that the Marshallian dichotomy between the real and then the money was wrong, that we had to have a theory of a monetary production economy in which money had several roles to play: as a medium of exchange, as a unit of account and as a store of value, *all at the start of the story*.

What other changes occurred? Keynes liked to make things stark so that the fundamental strands of the argument could be seen in very simple outlines before he put in the modifications. As we have seen, in the earlier book, the natural rate of interest equilibrated real saving and investment and the money rate of interest had to be consistent with this. By the time Keynes came to *The General Theory* he had turned all this around by 180 degrees. He argued that the money rate of interest, determined by the demand for money, including liquidity preference (which reflected its store of value role) and the supply of money, ruled the roost. His version of the natural rate of interest, which had now become the expected rates of profit on potential investments (he called them marginal efficiencies of capital), had to measure up to the money rate of interest. This is the subject principally of Chapters 11 to 17 of *The General Theory* and of the papers Keynes published in 1937 in reply to his critics.

Another major change was to build up the theory of consumption and saving for the economy as a whole – the propensity to consume and to save schedules – and the theory of investment, on which we have already touched. Together they constituted the theory of aggregate demand in the form of an aggregate demand function, a concept which goes back at least to Malthus – the first Cambridge economist, Keynes called him – but which Keynes considered had been lost to sight following Ricardo's (alleged) trouncing of Malthus in the debate on general gluts after the Napoleonic wars. Finally, there was Chapter 21 on the general theory of prices in which he said we should bring again to the fore those 'homely but intelligible' concepts of short-period elasticities of supply and marginal costs. Here Keynes was Marshallian, adapting Marshall's great gift to the profession (and parrots) of supply and demand curves, to obtain an *overall* short-period Marshallian supply curve as the basis of the aggregate supply function. The point of intersection of the aggregate demand and aggregate supply functions was christened by Keynes the *point of effective demand*. He argued that it could be associated with considerably high and sustained levels of unemployment, involuntary unemployment in the sense that wage-earners wished to work yet it was not profitable for them to be employed. Moreover, there were no actions that they could take, either individually or collectively, which would make it profitable for them to be employed.

The base on which total demand was built was the desire to accumulate by business people. 'Accumulate, accumulate, that is Moses and the prophets!' was a theme common to both Marx and Keynes. The desire itself depended primarily on their expectations of *future* sales and profits in relation to the cost and availability of finance, and the prices of capital goods. Moreover, there was nothing in the signals of the system which would ensure that the combined outcome of these interacting forces would be such to ensure, *even on average*, that investment would be at the level which could absorb the saving that the community would make if the workforce and the capacity of existing capital goods both were fully employed. And for all the sophisticated advances in theory that have been made since then, this basic insight still holds concerning the operation of industrialized economies, the activities of which are predominantly determined by the decisions of private business people.

V

When *The General Theory* was published in early 1936, Keynes only had ten years more to live, two of which were (relatively) washed out by his severe heart attack in 1937. Yet in those years he was to leave us more major contributions. First, in replying to his critics he showed that, while investment was not constrained by saving (except if the economy were to be fully employed), it could be constrained by lack of finance, primarily from the banking system and ultimately from the stock exchange and the other financial institutions which are designed to gather up and allocate or reallocate new and past savings, both domestic and from abroad.

Secondly, while naturally the policy emphasis and analysis initially concerned unemployment and recession, when war came in 1939 he showed how his system could equally well tackle the problems of shortages and inflationary pressures. He identified an inflationary gap – demands in real terms which outstrip even the full employment supplies of the system, such as happens (alas, usually only) when there is full mobilization for a war effort. This aggregate excess demand would show its effects in tendencies for prices to rise and/or for queues to form and it would be a *cumulative* inflationary process *unless* steps were taken to reduce demands in real terms in order to match them with available supplies. Here again the significance of his use of the word 'general' in the title of the book and his warning that we should be on our guard against the fallacy of composition – what may be true for an individual taken in isolation may not be so for all individuals taken together – come to the fore. Moreover, had Keynes's aggregate supply and demand analysis gone into the textbooks, understanding and analysing the postwar stagflation episodes would have been so much easier and better informed.

And, finally, there were his valiant efforts to help to design institutions and new rules of the game for the postwar world so that unemployment would never again be a scourge and the benefits of the international division of labour through free trade and flow of capital funds could do their thing in raising world living standards. This is what Bretton Woods tried to establish through the creation of the IMF and the World Bank. Keynes himself returned to his long-sustained interest in the functioning of the international order, something which he had temporarily suppressed in order to set out the crucial new ingredients of how the economic system worked. Donald Moggridge in his official biography of Keynes (1992) has given us, in his superb historical chapters on the two world wars, the details of Keynes's contributions. Here I wish only to emphasize that Keynes's sense of the need to have or to design appropriate institutions for implementation of effective policy was never more in evidence. His last major act was to try to persuade his compatriots and their government to accept the harsh conditions of the American loan. There all his greatest qualities came together – his high intelligence, his persuasive eloquence, his proper patriotism, his fine sense of orders of magnitude and interrelated processes of nevertheless different time spans, his realization of what was possible as opposed to what may have been ideal. Exhausted by his efforts, Keynes died on Easter Morning 1946.

VI

Let me close by quoting Austin Robinson's reflections on the death of Keynes.

> His death left a gap everywhere [in the Treasury, the world of academic econom-
> ics, his college and university, the world of ballet and the arts, and], not least, in
> his own family. But perhaps some day we may learn to say that it was right that
> he, like others whom the gods love, should die young. At sixty-two he was in the
> plenitude of his powers. That brilliant mind was still at its best – rapier sharp,
> leaping always with intuitive rapidity far ahead of the rest of us. The memory that
> will remain is of that mind at its perfection. (Robinson, 1947, p. 66)

In this chapter I have concentrated on Keynes's greatest intellectual achievement. But it is only the tip of an iceberg in the story of a man who not only
did good but who was also, despite many unattractive features (which his
biographers report, it must be said, with some glee) truly good himself.

Note

1.   In addition to the references at the end of the essay, I want to record here my indebtedness
     to Rod O'Donnell's seminal work on the relationship between Keynes's philosophy and his
     economics, *Keynes: Philosophy, Economics and Politics*, Basingstoke: Macmillan, 1989,
     and to John Coates's PhD dissertation, 'Ordinary Language Economics. Keynes and the
     Cambridge Philosophers', Cambridge, 1990. My thanks also to Andrea Maneschi for his
     comments on a draft of the essay.

References

Clarke, Peter (1988), *The Keynesian Revolution in the Making 1924–1936*, Oxford: Clarendon
    Press.
Hahn, F.H. (1982), *Money and Inflation*, Oxford: Blackwell.
Kahn, R.F. (1931), 'The relation of home investment to unemployment', *Economic Journal*, **41**,
    pp. 173–98.
Kahn, R.F. (1989), *The Economics of the Short Period*, London: Macmillan.
Keynes, J.M. (1919), *The Economic Consequences of the Peace*, London: Macmillan; *CW*, II
    (1971).
Keynes, J.M. (1921), *A Treatise on Probability*, London: Macmillan; *CW*, VIII (1973).
Keynes, J.M. (1923), *A Tract on Monetary Reform*, London: Macmillan; *CW*, IV (1971).
Keynes, J.M. (1930), *A Treatise on Money*, 2 vols, London: Macmillan; *CW*, V and VI (1971).
Keynes, J.M. (1933), *Essays in Biography*, London: Macmillan; *CW*, X (1972).
Keynes, J.M. (1936), *The General Theory of Employment, Interest and Money*, London:
    Macmillan; *CW*, VII (1973).
Keynes, J.M. (1973a), *The General Theory and After: Part I, Preparation*, *CW*, XIII.
Keynes, J.M. (1973b), *The General Theory and After: Part II, Defence and Development*, *CW*,
    XIV.

Keynes, J.M. (1980), *Activities 1940–1946. Shaping the Post-War World: Employment and Commodities, CW*, XXVII.

Moggridge, D.E. (1992), *Maynard Keynes. An economist's biography*, London/New York: Routledge.

Robinson, Austin (1947), 'John Maynard Keynes 1883–1946', *Economic Journal*, **LVII**, pp. 1–68.

Shove, G.F. (1942), 'The place of Marshall's *Principles* in the development of economic theory', *Economic Journal*, **LII**, pp. 294–329.

Skidelsky, Robert (1983), *John Maynard Keynes. Volume One. Hopes Betrayed, 1883–1920*, London: Macmillan.

Skidelsky, Robert (1992), *John Maynard Keynes. Volume Two. The Economist as Saviour, 1920–1937*, London: Macmillan.

20 What Adam Smith really said*[1]

Adam Smith is frequently invoked as the patron saint of freely competitive markets, often by people who have never read the *Wealth of Nations* (*WN*), published in 1776 and have never heard of the *Theory of Moral Sentiments* (*TMS*), published in 1759.[2] Yet Smith himself regarded *TMS* as complementary to and the equal of *WN*. In the years before his death in 1790 it was *TMS* that he was revising. Smith argued that there existed a natural order of morality; that 'man was endowed with the moral sentiments which [made] society possible' (Joan Robinson, *Collected Economic Papers*, V, 1979, pp. 46–47). The thrust of the argument of *TMS* is the need to design institutions which allow altruism, or 'sympathy', to prevail. Without such institutions, society could not become a coherent coordinated whole, a system of natural liberty, but would disintegrate, politically, socially and economically, in ways not unlike the terrible trends we are witnessing emerging at the moment in certain parts of Eastern Europe, the former so-called 'socialist economies', and in Russia. There a crude version of the (perceived) lessons of *WN* has been implemented without the *necessary* constraints associated with *TMS*.

Smith, ever a realist, recognized the intense drive of self-interest in us all, and he did not waste his time either deploring or admiring it. Rather, he wanted to see how it might be harnessed to good effect in the organization of society and the production of wealth. But he knew it could not be left to dominate completely either the lives of individuals or the behaviour of important groups in society. He felt that an indirect but effective check on it was a down-to-earth application of the golden rule, do unto others as you yourself would be done by (as opposed to its counterpart which seems more to rule today – do others or they will do you or, a variant, *before* they do you). Smith put it thus: 'How selfish soever man may be supposed, there are evidently some principles in his nature, which interest him in the fortune of others, and render their happiness necessary to him, though he desires nothing from it except the pleasure of seeing it' (*TMS*, p. 1). (So the concept of self-interest had more dimensions to it than mere selfishness or greed.) He then postulated the existence of the impartial spectator who took into account, to some extent, the reactions of others to the actions of the person(s) involved. Each individual would temper his or her behaviour by their perception of how it would affect others and how they themselves would feel if the action they contemplated doing was done to them. Hence the need for those institutions

* First published in *Economic Review*, **12**, (2), November, 1994, pp. 24–7.

to allow such altruism to prevail, to some extent. As Robert Heilbroner (1986, p. 58) puts it, 'A socially stable society is a pre-requisite for an economically successful one.'

It should be noted that this social stability was to include a dependable hierarchy. Smith was *not* a democrat and those who look to free market capitalism as the means to obtain and maintain democratic government (or the other way around) get no support from Smith's writings. 'Nature has wisely judged that the distinction of ranks, the place and orders of society, would rest more securely upon the plain and palpable difference of birth and fortune, than upon the invisible and often uncertain difference of wisdom and virtue' (*TMS*, p. 226). So, in Smith's book, Demos is *at best*, third, behind Philosopher Kings (no Queens), second, and rank and wealth, first. Not that I agree with Smith on this for our time, but it is what he wrote and, for his time, he was probably right. Heilbroner adds: 'Men do seek wealth and they do submit willingly to structures of social inequality. If this were [not so], civilized society as we know it would not exist, and ... capitalism could not count on the motives or the cohesion for its existence' (Heilbroner, 1986, p. 62). This is a lesson which Keynes also taught us in *The Economic Conse-quences of the Peace* (1919, *CW*, II, 1971, pp. 11–13), in which he described the fragile conventions combined with the unequal distribution of income and wealth on which the prosperity and stability of pre-First World War Europe were argued to rest.

Only if the conditions outlined in *TMS* were met would it be desirable and effective, Smith tells us, to dismantle the overgrown, overblown bureaucratic regulations and monopolies, and to escape from the corruption of the state bodies, of the mercantilist period and allow the instinct of self-interest, guided by the invisible hand, to operate in an environment of vigorous dynamic competition. I stress 'dynamic', for Smith's work was *not* the forerunner of the static model of resource allocation so beloved of the textbooks. He was rather the proponent of an environment which would encourage growth and promise a distribution of the product between the main classes of society which would, in turn, be favourable to the continuation of this growth. Like all the classical political economists, he did not think that growth could go on for ever. Eventually, through its very success, the fall in the rate of profits which accompanied growth would end the incentive for and the means to achieve the accumulation of capital which was the principal source of growth in output and well-being in the first place. Such a situation was, though, still a long way off:

> In a country fully stocked in proportion to all the business it had to transact, as great quantity of stock [Smith's word for capital] would be employed in every particular branch as the nature and extent of the trade would admit. The competi-

tion, therefore, would be everywhere as great, and consequently the ordinary profit as low as possible.

But perhaps no country has ever yet arrived at this degree of opulence. (*WN*, p. 111)

Despite this modification, Smith took a very dynamic view of economic progress. He first postulated man's 'certain propensity' ... to truck, barter and exchange one thing for another' (*WN*, p. 25) and the operation of the invisible hand which harnessed this inbuilt propensity (as we would say now) to a social process. In *TMS*, Smith argued that God, 'the Author of nature', had instilled in people strong drives, 'passions', to overcome the deficiencies of their reasoning powers to plan desirable outcomes for themselves, let alone the communities to which they belonged. They seek wealth, driven partly by envy and the desire to emulate those who are better off. 'The poor man's son, whom heaven in its anger has visited with ambition, when he begins to look around him, admires the conditions of the rich' (*TMS*, p. 181) – though, too late, he discovers that 'wealth and greatness are mere trinkets of frivolous utility [yet requiring] a labour of a life to raise [them]' (ibid., p. 183). Such efforts in the vain pursuit of money create the extraordinary achievements of capitalism which Marx was to praise in the *Communist Manifesto* and *Capital*. And so onto the *one only* passage on the invisible hand in *WN*: A person 'neither intends to promote the public interest, nor knows how much [he or she] is promoting it. [He or she] is in this case, as in many cases, led by an invisible hand to promote an end which was no part of [his or her] intention' (*WN*, p. 456).

Though Smith pays lip service to the proposition that consumption is the be all and end all of economic activity – 'Consumption is the sole end and purpose of all production' (*WN*, p. 660) – he was far too much of a realist actually to believe himself. (Indeed, by 'consumption', Smith virtually meant 'selling'.) In any event, Smith knew that what drove the system along was the desire for profits, together with a liking by business people for a particular way of life. This was aided by what we now call risk-taking attitudes: 'The chance of gain is by every man more or less overvalued, and the chance of loss is by most men undervalued' (ibid., p. 125). The incidental role of markets in all this – their primary role was to promote growth – was to establish prices, of two sorts: the ephemeral market prices which reflected the immediate state of supply of, and demand for, various commodities; and the much more fundamental natural prices – roughly, those which, if established, would in existing conditions allow landlords to receive the natural rate of rent and encourage business people to produce at levels which satisfied the effectual demand of their purchasers, while at the same time allowing business people to receive the natural rate of profits for their activities after they had paid their workforces their natural rates of wages. The latter were those rates of payment which led people to be content with (perhaps, resigned to) their lot in the various occupations. What they, in turn, depended upon was whether the economy overall was growing, stationary or declining. 'The liberal reward of Labour ..., as it is the necessary effect, so it is the natural symptom of increasing natural wealth' (ibid., p. 91).

Smith argued that in a competitive system, in which economic power was very widely dispersed and with freedom of movement of both capital and labour, people would respond to current differences in rates of profit by moving their capital from activities which were receiving less than the natural rate of profits in general (Smith was not that coherent as to what determined *its* level; it was left to, first, Ricardo and then Marx to try to provide coherent answers) into activities where the rate of profit was greater than the natural rate. Similarly, people would tend to move from occupations where market rates of wages were less than the natural rates for those occupations to those where they were above, often a long-term process requiring training or retraining. By these movements, which Smith argued would take long stretches of time to occur, there was a tendency for market rates to approach their natural rates, what Smith called their centres of gravitation. (It was not always clear whether the processes involved were convergences on or fluctuations around these centres of gravitation.)

The proviso about strong competitive forces and the diffusion of power, the absence of monopolies and cartels, is absolutely vital, as Smith made clear: 'People of the same trade seldom meet together even for merriment and diversion, but the conversation ends in a conspiracy against the public, or in some contrivance to raise prices' (*WN*, p. 145); 'We rarely hear, it has been said, of the combination of masters; though frequently of those of workmen. But whoever imagines, upon this account, that masters rarely combine, is as ignorant of the world as of the subject. Masters are always and everywhere in a sort of tacit, but constant and uniform combination, not to raise the wages of labour above their actual rate. ... the law, besides, authorises or at least does not prohibit their [the masters'] combinations, while it prohibits those of the workmen' (ibid., p. 84). 'When masters combine together in order to reduce the wages of their workmen, they commonly enter into a private bond or agreement, not to give more than a certain wage under a certain penalty. Were the workmen to enter into a contrary combination of the same kind, not to accept a certain wage under a certain penalty, the law would punish them very severely' (ibid., p. 158); 'To widen the market and narrow the competition is always the interest of the dealers ... an order of men, whose interest is never exactly the same with that of the public, who generally have an interest to deceive and even to oppress the public, and who accordingly have, upon many occasions, both deceived and oppressed it' (ibid., p. 267).

Accompanying his analysis of these processes are two of Smith's greatest insights about the nature of a competitive industrialized society: first, the notion that (again as we would say now) rising productivity is associated with the division of labour, 'the necessary, though very slow and gradual consequence of [that] propensity ... to truck, barter and exchange' (*WN*, p. 25). Here the famous example of the pin factory is usually quoted. Secondly, the extent of the division of labour is constrained, 'limited', by the size of the market. Smith recognized the interrelationships of markets – how they expanded together in a cumulatively reinforcing manner, thus opening the way for the division of labour to do its thing through capital accumulation, new inventions and innovations in raising productivity in existing and new industries. (Allyn Young was one of the first modern economists to respell this out explicitly and Nicholas Kaldor, Young's pupil, devoted much of his working life to elaborating this essential theme. But it was 'all in Smith' to begin with.)

As we have noted, Smith approved of the government providing an efficient infrastructure for society and a just and efficient taxation system for society's citizens. Thus 'the sovereign has only three duties to attend to; three duties of great importance, indeed, but plain and intelligible to common understandings: first, the duty of protecting the society from the violence and invasion of other independent societies; secondly, the duty of protecting, as far as possible, every member of the society from the injustice or oppression of every other member of it, or the duty of establishing an exact administration of justice; and, thirdly, the duty of erecting and maintaining certain public works and certain public institutions, which it can never be for the interest of any individual, or small number of individuals, to erect and maintain; because the profit could never repay the expense to any individual or small number of individuals, though it may frequently do much more than repay it to a great society' (*WN*, pp. 687–8). What he did not like was unnecessary regulation to protect established monopolies and limit initiative.

Again, as we have seen, Smith, a wise person, recognized that one of the essential conditions for competitive markets to function in a 'socially desirable' manner was that consumer and producer, employer and employee, should meet as equals – and pretty powerless equals at that – when products and services were exchanged. (This notion has been formalized in modern economic theory in the concept of price-taking as opposed to price-making behaviour; not that Smith reasoned in terms of price taking, it was *not* a component of Smith's vision of competition.) Nor was he under any illusions as to which class was likely to have most power. He would have recognized that one of the aims of the contractionary policies followed by most western governments over the last 15 years or so was to re-establish that power for a particular class. This is an insight which was fully developed earlier on by

Marx and acknowledged by the late Lord Balogh when he described monetarism as 'the incomes policy of Karl Marx' – the attempt to re-establish after the postwar years of full employment a situation euphemistically described as a flexible labour market.

Though Smith recognized the positive aspects of the division of labour, he was under no illusion as to how destructive and alienating freely competitive, industrial production of the sort immortalized by Charlie Chaplin in *Modern Times* could be for those unfortunate workers inescapably involved in it.

> The man whose whole life is spent in performing a few simple operations, of which the effects too are, perhaps, always the same, or very nearly the same, has no occasion to exert his understanding, or to exercise his invention in finding out expedients for removing difficulties which never occur. He naturally loses, therefore, the habit of such exertion, and generally becomes as stupid and ignorant as it is possible for a human creature to become.... In every improved and civilised society this is the state into which the labouring poor, that is, the great body of the people, must necessarily fall, unless government takes some pains to prevent it. (*WN*, p. 782)

So we may see at the back of all Smith's arguments in *WN* the *prior* importance of the restraints on anti-social behaviour in society set out in the arguments of *TMS*.

Smith would also have been scathing about arguments that huge but, at the same time, *just* differences in rewards in society are needed in order to get the best out of people:

> The difference of natural talents in different men is, in reality, much less than we are aware of; and the very different genius which appears to distinguish men of different professions, when grown up to maturity, is not upon many occasions so much the cause, as the effect of the division of labour. The difference between the most dissimilar characters, between a philosopher and a common street porter, for example, seems to arise not so much from nature, as from habit, custom, and education'. (*WN*, pp. 28–9)

If, then, we cannot find in Smith unqualified support for letting the market rip, as it were, can we find in modern theory a justification for the policies of recent years? On balance, no. In fact, modern theory has laid down very stringent conditions which have to be satisfied before it can be claimed, even in theory, that the market outcome is socially desirable.[3]

Of course it must be said – and this is the core of the argument of the serious pro-marketeers – that it is a non sequitur, that is to say, not an automatic logical progression, to go from establishing that there may be market failures, immediately to claiming that therefore government intervention will make things better. It may well be that, in an imperfect world, the market failure outcome is nevertheless the best we can hope for, especially if a huge weight is put on the absolute desirability of individual freedom. This is the philosophical position of that most profound proponent of modern liberal thought, the late Friedrich von Hayek. With this proviso, let us look at the commonsense meaning of some of the conditions which have to be met in order for markets to do their thing.

The first is that actual prices of products should be a true measure both of the social costs of the resources used to create them and of the satisfaction which their use is expected to bring to their purchasers. That is why price takers are needed. Producers can then match their costs to externally given standards which simultaneously signal to purchasers the terms on which they can expect to achieve satisfaction. This requires that prices, most of the time, should be such that what is voluntarily demanded is equal to what is voluntarily supplied. This in turn requires that flows of purchases and flows of supplies in markets should dominate the setting of prices. Inventories or stocks, though important for smooth production and sales, nevertheless need to play a subsidiary role in the determination of actual prices. (Yet there are some important markets, those for financial assets and houses immediately spring to mind, where the existing stocks dominate the new flows.) Moreover, if current prices are not achieving the match between the flows, they must directly or indirectly give out signals which encourage measures to be taken which will quickly achieve such a match, often a very tall order indeed in many important markets.

This brings out the big difference between vigorous free marketeers and the sceptics. The former think of individual markets, or even whole economic systems, as wolf packs running along smoothly. If, perchance, one or more of the wolves get ahead or fall behind, forces come quickly into play which return them to the pack. The latter group argue that if the breakaways get ahead, or fall behind, the forces which come into play are much more likely to allow them to get further and further ahead – or fall further and further behind, at least for long stretches of time. Belief in the efficacy and equity of markets as institutions is fundamentally affected by which scenario is believed to be true of the 'real world', as we economists lovingly like to call that which I am sure many of you feel we have never experienced. It is ironic that Smith's own vision took in the second scenario, while those who most loudly proclaim Smith as their authority are much more likely to have the first as their vision.

It also has to be supposed that prices act solely as rationing devices. That is to say, nothing else may be deduced from the price of a good or service about its qualities other than its relative scarcity or abundance. Modern work suggests that the demand and supply of labour services, and of credit, do not set up prices with this required characteristic.

If demands are dominated not by expected satisfaction but by guesses about what prices may be in the future, so that a large element of speculation is present in the formation of prices, and if supplies are offered not in response to perceived costs but in anticipation of future movement of prices, or of other people's expected anticipations of such movements, then the ensuing prices which are set may bear no systematic or reliable relationship to the real economic factors of the regular economic activity which, it is argued, prices ought to reflect. And all this is independent of whether power is diffused equally on both sides of the market, or whether it is concentrated in the hands of either buyers or sellers, or both.

To sum up: from Adam Smith we learn the need for social institutions and constraints to back up a competitive environment of 'initiative and enterprise'. From modern theory we learn that if we want markets to work well we must beware of situations where stocks dominate flows, speculation dominates enterprise or real economic factors, power is not evenly diffused, prices give out complex signals, and processes are cumulative rather than quickly equilibrating.

Finally, to show that Smith really was on its side after all, let me quote some passages which could have come straight from any one of the present government's manifestos: 'What is prudence in the conduct of every private family, can scarce be folly in that of a great kingdom' (*WN*, p. 457); 'Capitals are increased by parsimony, and diminished by prodigality and misconduct' (ibid., p. 337); 'Parsimony, and not industry, is the immediate cause of the increase of capital' (ibid., p. 337). Smith backed up these propositions with allegiance to what would become Say's Law, an allegiance which was *not* unreasonable for the time at which he wrote: 'What is annually saved is as regularly consumed as what is annually spent, and nearly in the same time, too; but it is consumed by a different set of people' (ibid., pp. 337–8); 'By what a frugal man annually saves, he not only affords maintenance to an additional number of productive hands, for that or the ensuing year, but like the founder of a public workhouse, he establishes as it were a perpetual fund for the maintenance of an equal number in all times to come' (ibid., p. 338).

So what is the moral of all this? Not that Adam Smith was without blemish, nor that modern Smithians are entirely vulgar. Rather, it is that a person's arguments should be examined in their primary sources and judged by the received standards of logic and methods of arguing, and of relevance.

Notes

1. In writing this essay I have been helped by reading the excellent text, *The Essential Adam Smith*, Oxford: Oxford University Press 1986, edited by Robert Heilbroner assisted by Laurence J. Malone. I would also like to thank, but in no way implicate, William Brown, Heinz Kurz, Barry McCormick, Peter Nolan, Prue Kerr, Alessandro Roncaglia, Claudia Sardoni and Trevor Stegman for their comments on a draft of the essay.
2. All page references are to the 1976 Glasgow editions of *TMS* and *WN*: *The Theory of Moral Sentiments*, edited by D.D. Raphael and A.L. Macfie, Oxford: Clarendon Press,

1976; *An Inquiry into the Nature and Causes of the Wealth of Nations*, edited by R.H. Campbell and A.S. Skinner, textual editor W.B. Todd, Oxford: Clarendon Press, 1976.

3. The paragraphs which follow (until the final two) are taken from 'Markets, Madness and a Middle Way' (see Chapter 1) with only a few alterations. I apologize for the repetition, but it would have upset the balance of the arguments of the present chapter to have omitted them.

Name index

Subject index

Economists of the Twentieth Century

Monetarism and Macroeconomic Policy
Thomas Mayer

Studies in Fiscal Federalism
Wallace E. Oates

The World Economy in Perspective
Essays in International Trade and European Integration
Herbert Giersch

Towards a New Economics
Critical Essays on Ecology, Distribution and Other Themes
Kenneth E. Boulding

Studies in Positive and Normative Economics
Martin J. Bailey

The Collected Essays of Richard E. Quandt (2 volumes)
Richard E. Quandt

International Trade Theory and Policy
Selected Essays of W. Max Corden
W. Max Corden

Organization and Technology in Capitalist Development
William Lazonick

Studies in Human Capital
Collected Essays of Jacob Mincer, Volume 1
Jacob Mincer

Studies in Labor Supply
Collected Essays of Jacob Mincer, Volume 2
Jacob Mincer

Macroeconomics and Economic Policy
The Selected Essays of Assar Lindbeck, Volume I
Assar Lindbeck

The Welfare State
The Selected Essays of Assar Lindbeck, Volume II
Assar Lindbeck

Classical Economics, Public Expenditure and Growth
Walter Eltis

Money, Interest Rates and Inflation
Frederic S. Mishkin

The Public Choice Approach to Politics
Dennis C. Mueller

The Liberal Economic Order
Volume I   Essays on International Economics
Volume II Money, Cycles and Related Themes
Gottfried Haberler
Edited by Anthony Y.C. Koo

Economic Growth and Business Cycles
Prices and the Process of Cyclical Development
Paolo Sylos Labini

International Adjustment, Money and Trade
Theory and Measurement for Economic Policy, Volume I
Herbert G. Grubel

International Capital and Service Flows
Theory and Measurement for Economic Policy, Volume II
Herbert G. Grubel

Unintended Effects of Government Policies
Theory and Measurement for Economic Policy, Volume III
Herbert G. Grubel

The Economics of Competitive Enterprise
Selected Essays of P.W.S. Andrews
Edited by Frederic S. Lee and Peter E. Earl

The Repressed Economy
Causes, Consequences, Reform
Deepak Lal

Economic Theory and Market Socialism
Selected Essays of Oskar Lange
Edited by Tadeusz Kowalik

Trade, Development and Political Economy
Selected Essays of Ronald Findlay
Ronald Findlay

General Equilibrium Theory
The Collected Essays of Takashi Negishi, Volume I
Takashi Negishi

The History of Economics
The Collected Essays of Takashi Negishi, Volume II
Takashi Negishi

Studies in Econometric Theory
The Collected Essays of Takeshi Amemiya
Takeshi Amemiya

Exchange Rates and the Monetary System
Selected Essays of Peter B. Kenen
Peter B. Kenen

Econometric Methods and Applications (2 volumes)
G.S. Maddala

National Accounting and Economic Theory
The Collected Papers of Dan Usher, Volume I
Dan Usher

Welfare Economics and Public Finance
The Collected Papers of Dan Usher, Volume II
Dan Usher

Economic Theory and Capitalist Society
The Selected Essays of Shigeto Tsuru, Volume I
Shigeto Tsuru

Methodology, Money and the Firm
The Collected Essays of D.P. O'Brien (2 volumes)
D.P. O'Brien

Economic Theory and Financial Policy
The Selected Essays of Jacques J. Polak (2 volumes)
Jacques J. Polak

Sturdy Econometrics
Edward E. Leamer

The Emergence of Economic Ideas
Essays in the History of Economics
Nathan Rosenberg

Productivity Change, Public Goods and Transaction Costs
Essays at the Boundaries of Microeconomics
Yoram Barzel

Reflections on Economic Development
The Selected Essays of Michael P. Todaro
Michael P. Todaro

The Economic Development of Modern Japan
The Selected Essays of Shigeto Tsuru, Volume II
Shigeto Tsuru

Money, Credit and Policy
Allan H. Meltzer

Macroeconomics and Monetary Theory
The Selected Essays of Meghnad Desai, Volume I
Meghnad Desai

Poverty, Famine and Economic Development
The Selected Essays of Meghnad Desai, Volume II
Meghnad Desai

Explaining the Economic Performance of Nations
Essays in Time and Space
Angus Maddison

Economic Doctrine and Method
Selected Papers of R.W. Clower
Robert W. Clower

Economic Theory and Reality
Selected Essays on their Disparity and Reconciliation
Tibor Scitovsky

Doing Economic Research
Essays on the Applied Methodology of Economics
Thomas Mayer

Institutions and Development Strategies
The Selected Essays of Irma Adelman, Volume I
Irma Adelman

Dynamics and Income Distribution
The Selected Essays of Irma Adelman, Volume II
Irma Adelman

The Economics of Growth and Development
Selected Essays of A.P. Thirlwall
A.P. Thirlwall

Theoretical and Applied Econometrics
The Selected Papers of Phoebus J. Dhrymes
Phoebus J. Dhrymes

Innovation, Technology and the Economy
The Selected Essays of Edwin Mansfield (2 volumes)
Edwin Mansfield

Economic Theory and Policy in Context
The Selected Essays of R.D. Collison Black
R.D. Collison Black

Location Economics
Theoretical Underpinnings and Applications
Melvin L. Greenhut

Spatial Microeconomics
Theoretical Underpinnings and Applications
Melvin L. Greenhut

Capitalism, Socialism and Post-Keynesianism
Selected Essays of G.C. Harcourt
G.C. Harcourt

Time Series Analysis and Macroeconometric Modelling
The Collected Papers of Kenneth F. Wallis
Kenneth F. Wallis

Foundations of Modern Econometrics
The Selected Essays of Ragnar Frisch (2 volumes)
Olav Bjerkholt

Growth, the Environment and the Distribution of Incomes
Essays by a Sceptical Optimist
Wilfred Beckerman